You, I,
and the Others

Paul Weiss

Southern Illinois University Press
CARBONDALE AND EDWARDSVILLE
Feffer & Simons, Inc.
LONDON AND AMSTERDAM

LIBRARY OF CONGRESS CATALOGING IN PUBLICATION DATA

Weiss, Paul, 1901–
    You, I, and the others.

    Includes index.
    1. Personality. I. Title.
BF698.W4   155.2   79-13375
ISBN 0-8093-0923-8

BOOKS *by Paul Weiss*

PRINCIPAL CONTRIBUTIONS *by Paul Weiss*

AMERICAN PHILOSOPHERS AT WORK, *edited by Sidney Hook (1956)*

AMERICAN PHILOSOPHY TODAY AND TOMORROW, *edited by H. M. Kallen and Sidney Hook (1935)*

THE CONCEPT OF ORDER, *edited by Paul Kuntz (1968)*

CONTEMPORARY AMERICAN PHILOSOPHY, *edited by John E. Smith (1970)*

DESIGN AND AESTHETICS OF WOOD, *edited by Eric A. Anderson and George F. Earl (1972)*

DETERMINISM AND FREEDOM, *edited by Sidney Hook (1958)*

THE DIMENSIONS OF JOB, *edited by Nahum N. Glatzer (1969)*

DIMENSIONS OF MIND: A SYMPOSIUM, *edited by Sidney Hook (1960)*

EVOLUTION IN PERSPECTIVE, *edited by G. Schuster and G. Thorson (1971)*

THE FUTURE OF METAPHYSICS, *edited by Robert Wood (1970)*

HUMAN VALUES AND ECONOMIC POLICY: PROCEEDINGS, *edited by Sidney Hook (1967)*

LAW AND PHILOSOPHY, *edited by Sidney Hook (1964)*

MID/TWENTIETH CENTURY AMERICAN PHILOSOPHY, *edited by Peter A. Bertocci (1974)*

MOMENTS OF PERSONAL DISCOVERY, *edited by R. M. MacIver (1952)*

MORAL PRINCIPLES IN ACTION, *edited by R. Anshen (1952)*

PERSPECTIVES ON PEIRCE, *edited by R. Bernstein (1965)*

PHILOSOPHERS ON THEIR WORK, *edited by André Mercier (1979)*

PHILOSOPHICAL ESSAYS FOR A. N. WHITEHEAD, *edited by O. Lee (1936)*

PHILOSOPHICAL INTERROGATIONS, *edited by S. and B. Rome (1964)*

PHILOSOPHY AND HISTORY, *edited by Sidney Hook (1963)*

THE PHILOSOPHY OF BARUCH SPINOZA, *edited by R. Kennington (1979)*

THE RELEVANCE OF WHITEHEAD, *edited by I. Leclerc (1961)*

SCIENCE, PHILOSOPHY, AND RELIGION: PROCEEDINGS *(1941–)*

STUDIES IN THE PHILOSOPHY OF CHARLES SANDERS PEIRCE, *edited by C. P. Wiener and F. H. Young (1952)*

EDITED WORKS *by Paul Weiss*

COLLECTED PAPERS OF CHARLES SANDERS PEIRCE (six volumes), *editor, with Charles Hartshorne (1931–35)*

FOR ROBERT CALHOUN

----

theologian, philosopher, scholar, and friend

Contents

Preface

A SYSTEMATIC, realistic study of man's primary dimensions and roles should be guided by basic principles, as well as by a decent regard for what everyone knows and says. The principles will help keep us from conclusions which are not compatible with what else there is, and should make it possible to explain what otherwise would have to be taken to be irreducible fact. A respect for common practices will discourage arbitrary conceit and willful abstraction. But neither principles nor common ways should be allowed to control completely. With these considerations in mind, I have tried to attend to what all can and should note about men, frequently backing observation with analysis and argument, and drawing consequences which many have failed to note.

Therapy, psychology, sociology, law, and education are some of the enterprises that depend for success on their ability to identify the main dimensions of man, to understand their functioning, and to remove or to compensate for distortions. The distinctions and connections here examined should offer both a base line and a test for such theoretical and practical ventures. A satisfactory approach to man will then be seen to be no simple matter of setting an unconscious in contrast to a consciousness, a private being to a public, or a lived existence to what is scientifically known. It will not justify a complete reliance on ordinary language or experiments.

Each man has a complex private life, continuing into, supporting, and supplementing a public one. Each expresses himself from a private depth, making himself present in a world with other men and other actualities. Each has a self epitomized in an I; each is a person with a limit at a me; each is faced as a you, is one among others, and is encompassed by a common we. One of the main functions of this work is to clarify, justify, and ground these claims.

Washington, D.C.   PAUL WEISS
April 1979

PART ONE

Encountering Persons

CHAPTER 1

You, Public and Sustained

1.1. You are confrontable.

YOU ARE present *for* others. That is why they can attend to you. You are present *to* them, when they attend to you. For others, you are able to be confronted; to others you already are a terminus of a relation which begins at them.

You are never merely for others, since you continue beyond the point where another could confront you. Were you there not apart from everything else, you would not be singular, private, or responsible.

You are relative to others since you are the terminus of relations which originate with them. You may also be the terminus of their distinctive actions or of their specific references. When you terminate their actions, you limit, qualify, or bring these to a close; when you are made a referent of 'you,' you are known. Either way, you are confrontable from a number of positions. Could you be confronted from only one position, you would not even be a terminating point, since a point terminates not only one but innumerable lines. What is at the end of only one line is on that line, never able to bring it to an end.

You are in a world with others. You continue to be there in the absence of any conscious regard by them, for you are still you when unnoticed or forgotten. Fallen into a deep sleep in an isolated chamber, it would still be you who was asleep.

Known or not, you would terminate relations. Known or not, you would be part of a larger group, and might be included in some sweeping reference. You are you when no one says 'you' or is actually attending to you.

You are multiply confrontable because you are present in a world where you can be approached from a number of positions. You are able to be arrived at again if only at another time or as that at which some other could also arrive. Conceivably, you could vanish at the very moment I attend to you, but at that moment you are in fact present for and to others.

Were I to just terminate with what was only then and there available, I would not know something confronted. Indeed, I would not confront anything at all. Instead, I would be something like Berkeley's perceiver to whom God presented perceptual content, as a way of talking to him. What was provided would not be encountered by such a perceiver, but just received and accepted.

A thing and an animal also terminate many relations and can be acted on from many positions. They, too, make themselves be present to and for others. But men do more. When they present themselves they distinguish but do not divorce what they privately are from what they make available. What they do not bring into the open may be privately enjoyed, used to begin self-conscious acts, ground a concern for principles, or provide agencies for rectifying what is amiss. No such distinctions can be made by a thing or an animal.

There is no division in men, any more than there is in animals and things, between what they are privately and what they are as present in a public world. But, unlike animals and things, men distinguish the two. Just how this is done is difficult to understand, but that difficulty does not prevent the distinction from being made and known. It is difficult, also, to know how a child learns its language, but that it learns, it is easy to see.

No one of us is two people, one inside the other. Each is single. A man's privacy is continuous with what he is publicly. The pain he feels is often expressed in his grimaces. The grimaces are the pain made public at the same time that they are distinguished from it. Sometimes the pain is hidden, sometimes it is exaggerated, but it is always both private and expressible in terms others can note. When I attend to you, I attend directly to what is presented from a privacy which remains continuous with it.

You are confronted in public. What I see, others may see as well. Everything I say about you might be checked and confirmed by others, for you are as observable as a stone. But if it is you whom I confront, it is because you are able to be confronted. Not faced by me, or perhaps even by any living being, you are still available.

1.2. You have a dense depth.

There is more to you than what is confrontable, whether by humans or nonhumans, the living or nonliving. Otherwise you would never be other than what was or could be terminated at.

"You are kind," "You are insensitive," "You think," while they publicly speak of a publicly available you, also pass beyond this toward what maintains it on its own terms and in its own way. Confronted, but also as confrontable, you offer a permeable limit to others. When you terminate observation and references you allow others at the same time to move beyond that limit, in depth, further into you. Did you not exist beyond the limit which others can and sometimes do confront, anything that was beyond the limit could conceivably be indifferent to what could be or was confronted. You would be just a surface, unable to act, or at best would provide a spur or a prop for this. Were there, instead, a depth to you, but one not penetrable in any way or to any degree, it would not be known. It would not be known that it was you who was smiling or frowning; there would be just muscles pulled and a face contorted. When you smile or frown, you do more than alter a visible surface; you express yourself, carry out in public what is rooted in, begun at, and sustained at another level.

Though I never get beyond you, I do get beyond what I confront and beyond what is confrontable. When I confront you, and particularly when I confront you in sympathy, hate, fear, or love, I penetrate beyond what is confrontable. I do not merely encounter you at those times; I move into you. On your side, what I reach is continued into a depth I never fully probe. But though I do not confront what is at that depth and is actually maintaining and possessing the you into which I penetrate, that still does not (as we shall see) place it beyond all knowing.

Were your depth as clear as a mountain spring, I might be able to reach the source and possessor of the presented you at the very moment you are encountered. I would come to it, of course, from a direction opposite to that along which it had been exhibited, but I would, on the hypothesis, still be able to reach the very center of it. Since your privacy would have been fully penetrated, it would not be a true privacy. Instead, I find that I am slowed and eventually brought under the subjection of what lies beyond the confronted and even the confrontable, maintained in contradistinction to these, not penetrated by me.

You can be treated brutally, told to move on. But even then you are dealt with as having a dense depth, ineluctably private and unreachable. You are addressed as one who has an unexpressed power to respond and not merely to react, one who is more than a body at that place with such and such features, or even one who is able to exhibit itself in other ways. Brutalized, used as a mere means, you are denied the opportunity to express yourself well, to develop yourself, to function in public with all that you could bring to bear from your depths. Yet, all the while, you remain inviolable, penetrable only to a degree. All know this, because all both pass beyond what they confront and are stopped before they reach your center.

No one, of course, can fully penetrate the privacy of animal or thing. One is, in fact, stopped sooner by these than he is by a man. One always fails to make contact with the dense unity of what is publicly presented by a thing or an animal. In the case of man, one also fails to make contact with content maintained in contradistinction from what is publicly occurring. Privately, animals and things are incipiently public; privately, men have dense distinguished unities with many divisions, engaged in many different acts, many of which are not directed toward the public world.

You continue into a dense depth. Progress into this is soon blocked. Rarely does anyone get very far. There is, though, no particular point at which one must stop, no antecedently fixed limit beyond which a penetrative act cannot go. At one time it is possible to go further than at another. Wherever we stop, we find ourselves thrusting still further, though more blindly, less effectively. On your side, you insistently make yourself present, privately make yourself public, but only in part. Some of your depth awaits a more propitious occasion for expression in public. So far you differ from an animal or thing only in richness, only in degree. But you also maintain your privacy apart from all expression, and can use some of it to attend to conditions and final realities governing what is public.

What I finally come to acknowledge is at a point of equilibrium between my most penetrative insistence and an insistence by you from a counter direction. That counter insistence begins beyond the you that is publicly available, and is met at a point far short of you in your full privacy.

1.3. What is confronted neither speaks nor acts.

As continuous with what you are in depth, you are not just public but publicized. As wholly public, all surface, apart from what you are in depth, you are just a qualified portion of a space, time, and causal process. No one speaks to you as a man who is merely public or publicized. You are spoken to as one able to express himself in public from a private depth. And it is from your privacy that you reply. As public or publicized, you have nothing to say and say nothing. To be sure, something of what is said to you and what you say can be located in a common space, time, or causal process; but were there nothing more, you would be spoken at, not spoken to. You would react but not reply.

Speech is directed toward one who can listen and perhaps speak. Both the listening and the speaking begin beyond the point where another's penetration can reach. This is not another surface, still to be uncovered. It is not some item like a tongue, teeth, larynx, or brain, which another set of observations, a surgeon's knife, or some machine might make available. It is more than an event, taking place over a stretch of time. It has an identity and a power of its own.

Speech has a source. It is directed. It has a terminus. Beginning beyond the reach of the deepest penetration possible, it precludes an identification with what another reaches. In turn, it is addressed to what is not nor ever will be made wholly public. If it is answered, it is by one who is able to accept what is heard, and can initiate speech of his own, relevant to what had been accepted. The denial that there is a second you beyond what can be reached from a public position does not require one to deny that what you say and do is begun privately.

The claim that no one can speak is perverse or paradoxical. Men publicize themselves in many ways, and one of these at times is by making assertions, claims, demands, commands, and the like. They publicize themselves in other ways as well, by their gestures and looks, movements and silences. What is common to all these is an origin in a dense depth. Reference is being made to that origin when it is said that someone speaks sincerely. The publicly manifested speech is then tacitly taken to be continuous with what can also express itself in other ways.

Your speech passes through your public you. From this it

acquires a public starting point. Your public you can then be said to speak, but only derivatively, mediating what you are expressing. Of course, what you mean to say will not be known by others except so far as it is in accord with some established public rules, conventions, and practices. But they will not have something to know unless you make it available, by putting it before them, by presenting it to them.

Every time one attends to you, addresses you, speaks to you, or listens to you, you are dealt with as having an un-reached depth. If men and things are to be understood in common terms, things, too, would therefore have to be recognized to have privacies where they originate what they present to others. The step down to things is no steeper than the step up to men. But there is a difference between things and men, and between them and animals, and between animals and men, even though they are equally real and may be copresent. Things present themselves but penetrate to nothing and allow for only a minimal penetration into themselves. Animals present themselves, can be penetrated somewhat, and are themselves able to penetrate a few for short distances. Men penetrate and are penetrable to a degree the others are not. They also distinguish what they present from what they experience, from what they intend, and from what they know. Things have energy in reserve; animals have experiences and memories as well; men, in addition, distinguish their privacies from whatever they make available, even without knowing that they do. Men, animals, and things differ in kind because of what they can do with their privacies. Men maintain their privacies in contradistinction to what they make public; animals, though they privately undergo pains and pleasures, cannot contrast what is private with what is public; things, in contradistinction from both, cannot distinguish or contrast the private and public at all.

Man is a dancer not to be identified with a dance. Nor is he a dance in slow time; if he were, he would not even provide an occasion for, and surely could not intend to dance or create one.

1.4. Discourse transforms language.

A language joins an accepted set of signs with common, steady ways for combining them. It provides a structure for an entire community, sharing in its history while undergoing a history of its own. There are other structures no less basic and occasionally as extensive—art, religion, economics, mythology, morality, and various standards of what is to be believed, claimed, and known. Each provides grounds for the others. Each can be readily taken to offer a primary way for explaining the functioning and nature of society and men. There was a time when religion was thought to be the most basic; now economics has that role for Marxists; the others also have had their advocates. A well-rounded culture allows each to function in independence of the others, and yet to subtend the rest and be affected by them. There is warrant for an emphasis on one of them rather than on the others just so far as it makes possible a readier and clearer grasp of what we are trying to understand.

A common view is that language is a distinctive kind of tool, like a hammer or a paint brush, which men use with more or less skill. Reporters and poets, on such a view, differ from other men in the dexterity and control with which they use the common means. What is needed to produce good works of craftsmanship and art are then recognized, but the distinctive natures of reports and poems ignored.

One learns to use the language of a community. This requires more than adjustments to grammatical units, structures, and practices. By incorporating the words and grammar of a common language in expressive acts, discourse vitalizes and thereby alters it. Language is transformed in discourse into something new, somewhat as carpentry and painting change lumber and pigment into chair and scene. The parts of a language become parts of a discourse when they are transformed into units dynamically related—sometimes in different ways—by speaker and listener. Each unit has three aspects: It is its user in a limited, verbalized, available form; it is integral to his expressive or receptive acts, able to be used as a symptom of what is being expressed or accepted; and it functions as a means for referring to something. The first allows you to have a public role; the second exposes you, thereby enabling those interested in you—lover, enemy, biographer, therapist—to be alert to cues and clues; the third exhibits you making use of language in a discourse about something.

Children and foreigners must be taught the established ways. For them, language has a prescriptive character insisted on by the established members of the community in somewhat the way that a carpenter insists that his apprentice use this rather than that saw and in such and such a manner. Not until the apprentice has met the demands of his master does he really use the saw. Until then he is engaged in learning how to use it. The distinction between the learning and the using becomes too sharp if it is allowed to override the fact that the carpenter is also learning, and that the apprentice does saw. The carpenter, though, is not learning how to make his sawing measure up to some prescription, while the apprentice has not yet made his sawing entirely integral to an effort to make something. Not until child and foreigner speak as the communicative members of a community do, will they properly discourse by using the language as raw material transformed by and in expressive and acceptive acts.

A cry of pain usually arouses an emotional response in another. Sometimes it awakens sympathy or some way of penetrating beyond sounds and grimaces, toward one who expresses himself in these ways. A teacher of acting, a detached observer, and one who wants quiet may attend to the cry of pain itself. Others will unhesitatingly pass beyond it, and act on behalf of what they then reach. Similar observations are pertinent to words used, sentences formed, and claims linguistically expressed. None reports a privacy. But none is merely part of a game or of a form of life. All tell us something about what was, is, and remains private.

A language, precisely because it is community-wide and

community-determined, must be broken up and transformed in order for it to be used by anyone. It needs men who are outside it. Discourse starts and ends with men who turn words, linked to one another in steady, commonly accepted ways, into expressions which expose the speaker and reach a listener. Were there only language, and never discourse, or were discourse nothing but an entering into and remaining in a language, there would never be anyone to use it. There would be no one to say 'you', no one to whom it was said, and no one to reply.

1.5. Knower and known are both private and public.

What is said issues from a private being. Since it is never entirely freed from this, whoever attends to what is said is necessarily acquainted with a privacy. It is no less true that what is said is and remains public, never allowing a man, no matter how perceptive and sympathetic, to fully penetrate another's privacy. We are always acquainted with the privacy of others, since they make this available to us in their speech and other actions; but, also, there is no place where others cease to have a public status since they are inseparable from what they make publicly available. Though there is nothing that cannot be known, there is always something that is not grasped. I always thrust beyond the point where I attend, whether this be in myself, you, or anything else. When I know, I also know that the thrust that is inseparable from the act of knowing goes beyond the content articulated, judged, and known.

Were a respondent entirely hidden or unknowable, he would answer, if he answered at all, from a beyond which no one could know was there. We are able to know something about him because we touch on what is continuous with and revelatory of what we do not then reach. Reference is here being made to a root ontological privacy, not just to feelings or thoughts which one does not happen to express publicly. Such feelings and thoughts are aspects of a privacy, impinged upon perhaps by others but also not then fully known. Since I come to myself as well as to others by beginning from the outside, my feelings and thoughts are also reached toward and impinged on by me but not then fully known.

Sometimes 'you' is used as a substitute for 'one'. The substitution is harmless when I am indifferent to anything but the fact that you are a unit, marked out, counted, located. But 'you' also has a role of its own, quite distinct from 'one'. It is a term of address, accompanying the thrust toward the insistent source and possessor of a public you. By addressing you, I make others alert to the existence of you as a source of what is present and available.

What I say is myself verbalized. Whether or not it directs me toward the depth of another, it continues what I am in depth. From that depth I begin to speak to and come to know you as one who is being privately insisted on and maintained. You may speak of your feelings, intentions, and thoughts; you may also try to keep me from learning about them. On both occasions, it is possible for me to know that they are present and also something about them by using what you say as a symptom of what you are in fact expressing behind what you say.

Both knower and known are at once private and public. Both express a privacy publicly, and both privately ground what is public. There is nothing private, if by that one means what is forever and necessarily secret, never available to any act. But there is also nothing public, if by that one means what is not privately initiated, undergone, or sustained.

A solipsist is not wholly private, though there is no one but himself to whom he can present his view. A behaviorist is moored in a public world which he privately knows. If the one is silent, he is silent in public. The other is unable to verify anything, since verifications are privately carried out and accepted. The attempt to take oneself to be wholly private is carried out by a public man; the attempt to deal with men as though they were just public objects is begun, maintained, and carried out privately.

The merely private is beyond whatever is supposed to reach it. But then, so far as something is private, must it not so far also be unknowable? Not if the private is encountered as grounding the public.

The thoughts of men are partly conveyed in their speech. That speech is not necessary. Men can express themselves and what they have in mind in other ways as well—by gestures, grimaces, and acts. Their speech, too, must be more than words made available, for otherwise it would be indistinguishable from what issues out of phonographs and tapes. There is a good reason why we do not take machines to be expressing themselves or to be giving a verbal form to their own thoughts: what they present is not supplemented by the other expressions with which men accompany their words. Nor do the machines enable anyone to move into them in depth, beginning with what is heard. They are also unable to speak to men as able to listen as well as to hear, to respond as well as to react, since that requires them to penetrate the men and not merely to act on them.

1.6. 'You' is a semantic vector.

A vector in mathematics has a direction and magnitude. Credited with a direction only, 'vector' can be used to characterize those terms which are directed toward something but which do not of themselves arrive at it. 'You' is such a vector. Directing one outside language, it does not itself terminate at anything outside. It is I who enable 'you' to terminate; it is you who terminate it. It is you, too, who enables 'you' to have the status of an addressive term, by enabling it to continue into you in depth.

'I' refers to what is more private than what is referred to by 'you', just as 'you' refers to what is more private than the referent of 'Tom.' "I am Tom" always says more than "You are Tom," starting as it does at a deeper, more private position. 'Tom' usually refers to Tom in one way in the question, "Did Tom do it?" and in another way in the answer, "Yes, Tom did it." The one is normally directed to a specific individual, but anyone might correctly reply, "Tom did it." 'You', instead, refers to you in the question, "Did you do it?" but does not occur in the answer, "Yes, I did it." "You did it" makes no sharp distinction between what is publicly available and a private source. Tom, of course, begins his act as privately as you do, but only when he is addressed as 'you' or as 'Tom' and not merely referred to as something located, do we acknowledge and move toward that privacy. And then we stop quite short of the point where the act was begun. You could answer, "Yes, I did it" because the act began with your I. You cannot refer to yourself as 'you', for though this terminates in what is not wholly public, it does not reach to the beginner of the act. One cannot here even in principle say what is meant, for 'you' is never freed from its use by an external speaker, whereas what is meant is unrelativized, beyond the referent of any externally applied term.

You enable 'you' to pass beyond the point where 'Tom' is allowed to stop. "You are Tom," consequently, always conveys information, giving 'Tom' a base not otherwise possible, thereby enabling it to become a term of address. "Did Tom do that?" is not answered by "Yes, you did it," but by "Yes, Tom did it." "Did you do it?" is not answered by "Yes, you did it," but by "Yes, I did it," requiring as it does a beginning at a point beyond where a you can be.

'Tom', when not used as a term of address, refers to a located man. 'I', when not used to give some claim an unquestioning status as in "I believe," "I am in pain," "I dreamt," or to remark a possessor as in "I have thoughts," "What I did was stupid," refers to where a presentation begins. 'You' is vectoral, awaiting termination by you and a reception by the I beyond it in order to be able to function as a term of address. Somewhat obscured in grammar, it is prominent in discourse.

There it can be loaded with and accompanied by enriching meanings.

A merely public language is a social instrument, enabling men to interchange their records of publicly available objects. Such a language has no place for semantic terms, for there are no objects for such terms until something terminates them. When someone is touched or pointed at, at the same time that 'you' is used of him, a public counterpart is provided for the 'you'. The touching and the pointing remain just movements unless they are privately made to function as additions to that 'you', helping it to arrive at you.

1.7. A discourse is an interchange of complementary and supplementary expressions.

Few know the language that all speak quite well. Men learn what words to use, the grammar to follow, the kinds of sentences that belong together by learning how to alter their speech so that what is said fits together with what others had said and done, and may still say and do. The need to produce that fitting compels them to combine and structure their sentences in only some of the ways that are in fact possible, and to use only certain words in those sentences. It does not clarify much to say of them that they transform some subterranean language into public speech, for one will still have to account for the reasons why and the ways in which they specialize and delimit the supposed common root so as to make it attain the status of the language of a discourse.

From this position, the grammar of a language is identifiable with one of a number of social structures, and is learned in the way other structures are. A child manages to make use of it through the help of admonitions, corrections, trainings, and practice. Its successes are not as great or as complete as the depth grammarians suppose, but they also are not attained by moving step by step as the associationalistic and behavioristic psychologists contend. A boy punished for biting his sister does not have to learn that he must not kick her, spill ink on her hair, or tear her dress. Punishment alerts him to an area of forbidden activities. The boundaries of what he can and cannot do are not altogether definite, but subsequent experiences, particularly with hard cases, enable him to sharpen, contract, and extend what he had already mastered. Something similar occurs when he learns to speak grammatically, i.e., intelligibly according to established patterns. He turns the words of his language at right angles to make them refer to what is outside the language. By attending to the grammar, he learns something about the use of words, and occasionally about listeners and objects.

What is said provides some evidence of both persistent and transient aspects of the speaker. A listener's response provides evidence of his own persistent and transient aspects. The sequence of their evidences is neutral to both; in discourse they complement one another. Since men usually speak to one another about something, the evidences also function as supplementary components in a reference to a common object or topic.

Complex referential expressions are produced in discourse. Because both the expressions and their components may have the same referents, men can talk about the same things. Because both expressions and their components may have different referents, the men may talk at cross-purposes. At a bargaining table, the representatives of a union and the management speak of wages, profits, and retirement. They may even use the same figures, but at the beginning and often at the end of the negotiations they understand these differently. One of the tasks of history is to find the objects of the terms—say, some crucial part of a treaty—which different users relativized in different ways.

Like gestures and cries, a recounting of your experiences is at once part of a language that others can understand, and a continuation of yourself, revealing in fragmentary and specialized ways what you are in root. Others can grasp much that is peculiar to your experience by using what is said as the beginning of a movement into you in depth. They then share in your experience without ever duplicating it or living it from your side.

Since no discourse can be entirely separated from intonations, emphases, and other expressive elements, everything in it can have a symbolic role, enabling one to move toward its source. Even a clear articulation in apparently neutral terms of what is before you expresses something of you. I usually move into you in depth, without clearly remarking on the fact, while understanding what is being said.

You and I begin and remain involved with the external world. You and I express ourselves. You and I move beyond what we confront. We speak expressively about something and may be confronted with that of which we speak. What we say is fixated somewhere between ourselves and that about which we speak. To learn what had been encountered by you, it is necessary to trace the components of what you say back to you as one who is occupied with what is external. The 'is' which is ingredient in your assertions and judgments may not be made explicit. But it is present, not only relating the terms that you provide but keeping you directed at what is behind the referent which concerns you and me.

1.8. 'You' has different roles in discourse and communication.

A discourse is about something. A communication is directed to someone. The best of conversations includes both in full measure. When lovers murmur, they communicate but do not discourse. When they quarrel, they discourse but do not communicate. When they tell one another about their ambitions, failures, and opinions, they converse. It is questionable whether one could ever free discourse from all traces of communication, or communication from all traces of discourse. Conversation is a primary fact, with discourse and sometimes communication dominating the other.

Some mammals communicate. So do some insects. Some

attend, at least to those of the same kind, through sounds and movements; some are also apparently able to interchange signals. Ants and bees direct one another toward common desired objects. They could be said to converse. What they, and other subhumans, do not and cannot do is to converse about topics, since they cannot express thoughts, and presumably do not have them. Even those which make evident what they want, or that they thirst, feel, are pleased, are in pain, fear, or are expectant, are unable to express thoughts, for to express thoughts one needs the help of centering terms and descriptions. Centering terms name topics; descriptions articulate them. Without such aids, thoughts might conceivably follow thoughts in the mind, but will not be known to occur.

The terms of an established language enable one to speak in ways that others can understand and match. The different speakings by different men are freshly united in an ongoing, created interchange, not altogether in consonance with the language of which they make use. When the men speak to one another, they together constitute a single ordered whole, not entirely dislocated from either the speaker or the listener. There, the contributions of the two are interlocked. As a consequence, the language they use differs from the language which was available for use somewhat as a set of vertical lines differs from an unbroken horizontal which they intersect.

'You' is a grammatical unit in language, a referring term in discourse, a center in communication, and an addressive term in conversation. When it functions as a centering term for you, it enables you to understand something of what another thinks of you. To make sure that it is you, and not someone else who is being referred to, it must be given the additional role of a term of address. "You are kind" centers kindness in you. The 'you' is here used as a term of address, carrying a reference to kindness with it. In the process, the 'you' begins to lose much of its centering force, with the consequence that the reference to kindness becomes more and more merged with it. A refusal to allow for that fact compels one to suppose that 'you' names a bare subject to which descriptions are referred as decorations or adjectives. But "You are kind" does not mean that you merely exhibit kindness or that kindness supervenes on you. It addresses a kind-you.

1.9. 'You' in language is without a referential role.

A public domain interconnects items independently of the roles they play outside its confines. Within it, they are variables, achieving definiteness by their relationship to one another, and acquiring specification by being used to refer to what is outside the domain.

Law, economics, and social conventions govern distinct public domains. So does a language. Like these, it is anonymous and impersonal, determining the ways in which terms are interconnected apart from their contributions or use. None tells us about the sources or possible termini of the items that are there interconnected.

It is not possible to learn from an examination of a language—or of any other publicly structured domain—exactly to what its units are to be referred. The most detailed description is framed in general terms and may apply now to this man and then to that. "The richest," "the leader," "the owner," fit different men at different times. Even such expressions as "the only child of . . ." or "the current vice-president" must be given direction and concrete backing by what is outside them. Ways of reducing the possibility of referring to someone who does not conform to the required conditions can be multiplied, but they will not entirely eliminate the possibility, since the referents exist and act outside the bounds of the domain in which the referring terms occur. Even when a part of a domain itself is being described uniquely—e.g., by "the preceding sentence"—the description falls short of the referent. The referent of "the preceding sentence" is on a page or in memory, where it has a status and career that the phrase itself does not have as part of the English language.

'You' is not yet isolated when it is part of a sentence in a language. There it is interconnected with other terms to constitute a single, structured whole. To have a referential role, 'you' must be separated from the other terms and then directed to what is outside the language. Only then will it achieve a termination and a grounding.

1.10. 'You' in fiction is a component in a single created term.

"Keep still, you little devil, or I'll cut your throat," the 'fearful man' called out to little Pip. The scene is easily envisaged. It was the creation of Dickens; it becomes ours on reading it. We attend to the man and to Pip in the graveyard, and do so only because we have read those words. The way the words are put together to form a single unity dictates the kind of situation that Dickens was able to make us participate in, despite the fact that 'you' is normally directed toward what is maintained in the world in which we exist, and kept there in contradistinction from us. When Pip is addressed as "you little devil," the distinctions pertinent to 'you' in its regular use are pertinent to it there as well, but only as part of a more complex reference.

Once we know that we are reading a story we use 'you' nonreferentially. It does not then direct us to a boy in an external spatio-temporal-dynamic world, governed by laws in which we are actually associated with others at measurable distances; instead, it is kept apart from such a world. We prepare ourselves for the difference by readying ourselves to read, to hear, or see what is fictional. The words we then use have a syntactic role.

It is not plausible to suppose that the terms of address in fiction have a semantic use which is frozen at a point where a description is directed, for the terms would then direct us to bare units, sheer, unintelligible its, unable to sustain the description. It is gratuitous also to suppose that we are initially occupied with a search for a referent for 'you' and other syntactical terms, but inhibit ourselves in order to entertain fictions. A fictional 'you' does not presuppose the 'you' of ordinary discourse, joined with a refusal to use terms referentially or to engage in a search for an objective referent; it has its own distinctive type of referent.

What we usually begin with is an idea continued into our expectant bodies in the form of a readiness to attend or to do something. If we go on to speak about you, 'you' will usually be united with descriptions. Together, they will refer to an actual present you. In a fiction, instead, the 'you' is rested with, and the rest of the story is allowed to provide the description with which the 'you' is to be united. Were there nothing more to a fiction than an imagined creation separated from all else, we would stop there. It is questionable, though, whether such a separated creation ever occurs. A fictional 'you' becomes enriched by what else is said and, with that enrichment, constitutes a single reference. If the fiction offers no more than a vivid portrayal of man, it refers to what is common to any you whatsoever.

'You' used by one fictional character in speaking to another is not a term of address for the reader. Pip never becomes the object of 'you' for him. The reader does not use the 'you' or 'Pip', or anything else in the story, to point to something outside the story. And he surely does not take a stand inside the story and there refer to one of the characters by 'you'. The 'you' is in the story as fully as "keep still" or "little devil" is. Only the entire story, including speeches making use of 'you', directs us toward what is outside the story, and then only when the story and the speeches are accepted as self-contained.

A fiction does not direct us to you or to any other finite entity, but to what subtends them all. In this respect, a fiction is like every other work of art. Even a portrait, with the name of the sitter affixed to it, is a unit in which part supplements part, neither mirroring nor referring to any actual man. It directs us not to this or that man, or even to man in general, but to the very same final reality to which every other work of art takes us when we have fully appreciated it on its own terms. This does not, of course, prevent us from using the portrait as a surrogate for the sitter, any more than it prevents us from using it as an investment.

1.11 A representative of a public domain provides model references.

Language presupposes real users and real beings to which those users refer. It leaves out many distinct items with which the users are concerned. Of itself, it can make no provision for discourse, communication or conversation. Like any other social domain, it presupposes men able to make use of it. They refer to what is independent of but capable of accommodating their references. Standing outside language, they distinguish items in it, and use what is there distinguished.

One of the characteristic marks of a dead language is that men use terms isolated there, and do so in steady approved ways. A living language's users, instead, are forced again and again to make fresh efforts to locate the terms they will use. They must succeed sometimes. Otherwise the language would not yield terms to be used in discourse, communication, or conversation. So-called living languages are languages quickened in use. Logicians and the members of philosophic schools work with artificial dead languages whose quickening they overlook because they neglect the ways in which those languages are broken up by the users, and the results then used to attend to something outside the languages.

In discourse and conversation, some terms and expressions have referential roles. They are used in common established ways, thereby making it possible to arrive at the referents which others do, can, or ought to acknowledge. If the established ways are ignored, one will risk having his expressions misconstrued and, more likely than not, will fail to mesh with the rest. Sometimes the use is backed by force, actual or threatened, physical or psychological, particularly when the reference is to something sacred or authoritative. But for the most part, all that is needed by a good user of language are habits for arriving at what is habitually acknowledged by others. The habits enable him to function representatively while he is acting on his own behalf, somewhat as a congressman acts when he frames a law requiring all to pay a tax. In the most muscular of communities, each man, in making use of a common domain, acts as the representative of the rest. A model, ideal use, a use which all the others would presumably want to have made on their behalf, will then be carried out. The situation is approximated in the practice of the professions of medicine, engineering, and law. There, men act in individual ways, with their representative functioning riding on the back of what is done.

Were there only representative action, no one would ever express something peculiar to him or be occupied with what concerns him alone. Were there only individual action, no one would act on behalf of anyone else but, at best, would be only in consonance with others. Maximizing both requirements at once makes it possible to use 'you' when confronting you in such a way that what is said and done is what ought to be said and done.

In most men, most of the time, two tempers, that of a representative user and that of an involved one, are combined. The first enables others to know to whom a reference is being made; the second enables them to address what is more than a relativized you. In daily speech there is much fluctuation. Sometimes the habitually known and public is emphasized, and sometimes the you at a freshly reached depth. When either side is neglected we speak too personally or too impersonally.

On behalf of supposedly objective, verifiable, steady, clearly formulatable results, the impersonal is sometimes insisted on, and any expression which falls short of this is dismissed as unintelligible. Not only are degrees of unintelligibility then skipped over, but in one step the legitimacy, procedures, and products of sympathy and insight are denied. Once it is recognized that the completely impersonal is at one extreme, never entirely sunderable from an occupation with what is individual, real, and expressive, the dichotomy will not only be overcome, but each extreme will be seen to exhibit part of what is grasped at the other.

Approached from an external vantage point, what is terminated at is a you, maintained from within, inseparable from your dense presenting reality. You are confronted as continuous with what is at a greater depth. As not reachable from without, as not possibly present for or to others, what is at that depth is just lived, lived with, or lived through.

1.12   The grammatical subject, 'you', is a relative pronoun.

'You' in discourse connects a speaker with someone else. It does this directly, without necessarily presupposing, replacing, or following the use of some description. But after something has been learned by attending to the referent of the 'you', descriptions help record the result and thereby enrich what is said of you.

When 'you' is given the status of a grammatical subject, its referential role is enriched by the remainder of the sentence. When you are addressed by 'you', the 'you' is joined to what terminates it. In both cases, what is said is made subject to habits and conventions, supporting an expectation of how you will respond, verbally or otherwise, directly or indirectly. The expectation is incorporated in part or whole in the way the reference is carried out. It is satisfied by being completed by what brings it to a rest.

Unaccompanied, 'you' is usually taken to refer to a person. It is, of course, not improper to use it when one is speaking to a dog or a horse or a chicken. When angry or irritated one may even use it to refer to a thing. We need help to make sure of the correctness of the reference. Without that help, there may be doubt, lack of focus, ambiguity, and surely indeterminacy.

The 'you' then does little more than express the fact that one is marking off a region to be further determined. Adjectives, contexts, appositive expressions, verbs, preceding and succeeding statements, help make evident the kind of object to which the user of 'you' is attending.

At the entry 'you', the twelve-volume *Century Dictionary and Cyclopedia* refers one to the entry 'ye'. This is said to be the original nominative with which, it is claimed, 'you' subsequently became confused. "Tarry *ye* here for us, until we come again unto *you*" is quoted from the King James version of Exod. 24:14 to show the traditional difference made between the nominative and objective cases. The 'you' in "You deserve to be better treated," "You are guilty," and "You are in the right place," despite such a supposed confusion, are readily understood today, though the 'you's' here function in the nominative case as grammatical subjects. This is not due simply to carelessness or even to the acceptance of conventions in the use of the term, but to the fact that a 'you' in the position of a grammatical subject is parasitical on other functions and other terms. Whether one says 'ye' or 'you', their use as grammatical subjects follows on the understanding of some previous expression, or of the predicate with which the grammatical subject is joined. Because of that dependence, the grammatical subject 'you' is in fact a relative pronoun, presupposing some other more informative expression, a vector, or a term of address.

1.13. 'You' and you have distinct careers.

'You' must be used in accord with the requirements of conversation if one is to speak to another about something. But the you of which it is used does not have to conform to those requirements, since it is not a linguistic entity. If what is known of that you is to be communicated, use must be made of the established grammar and terms, and of the conditions for

communication. By speaking in accord with these, one is able
to speak to one who exists apart from them.

The sentence, "Iron expands at such and such a rate under
such and such conditions" does not expand at all. And if it
could be made subject to a change in temperature and pressure, it would not react the way iron does. Words are not
things, statements are not objects, grammatical rules are not
laws of nature. 'You' belongs with the first of each pair; you
with the second. Because the rules that govern the use of 'you'
are distinct from and independent of any laws that might govern you, a knowledge of the one will not tell us about the functioning or nature of the other. Still, 'you' does have a place
and a role in the world; it is subject to whatever conditions
there be that have universal application. As so subject, it may
of course be only a word uttered or written down, not vectoral, not used as a term of address.

Sometimes it is claimed that only what is properly said can
be understood. What is intended is not entirely clear, since we
do seem to understand actions as well as words. In any case, if
we really understand what is said, we understand not the saying but that to which we are being referred. We say 'you' as a
way of letting others know something about, not 'you' but
you.

'You' may have to be constantly redirected to keep it referring to the same you. While conforming to the requirements
of significant use, it will then depend for its efficacy on how it
is kept in accord with that you. So far as you are subject to the
laws of nature, the use of 'you' will therefore have to conform
to demands made outside language, or lose connection with
what had already been focused on.

1.14. You are accountable.

Accountability is a public status having no necessary connection with intent, purpose, or desire. A man is accountable for

providing an occasion or factor in the absence of which a signal effect presumably would not occur. He is no less accountable for minor effects, but there is little reason in the rush of daily living to remark on the fact. Had a man neither depth nor power of his own, and were there no causality, he still could be held accountable, since for this he need be identified only as a point of origin, as a necessary link, or, simply as the being to whom some occurrence is credited. Though the acknowledgment of an accountable man may follow on the identification of him as one who originates a desirable or undesirable act, or who provides an essential element, it actually requires nothing more than taking him to be one who is to be rewarded or punished. He is made accountable by being held accountable, no matter what he did or did not do. By reward and punishment he is made accountable for good or bad occurrences, whether or not he in fact had anything to do with them. Sometimes men express their judgments of accountability simply by attending to others with fear, admiration, respect, or disdain. But these, too, are types of reward and punishment. Though we often look for one who brought the occurrence about or who played an important role in making it be, the search is rarely thorough or careful, and usually is made to end at a conventionally determined point.

Individuals sometimes reward or punish what their representatives do not, and conversely. Rudeness and courtesy are of interest to the one but not to the other, except in special cases. Ordinary men occasionally disapprove of the way in which rewards and punishments are officially distributed. Sometimes, ordinary men reward or punish those whom established representatives ignore, and sometimes they ignore those whom the representatives acknowledge. Where the one may take a careless worker to be accountable for having put a defective wheel on a car, the other may take the employer to be accountable instead.

One can be rewarded or punished for what was done inadvertently. Reward and punishment may be spontaneous and unreflectingly provided. No reference need be made to any consciousness, deliberation, or freedom. Evidently, reward, punishment, and accountability can be readily accommodated within a behavioristic view of human action.

A muscular account of the functioning of a society, or of some public domain distinguished within it, such as a legal system, a language of records and reports, or an industry, can be developed on the basis of a behavioristic way of dealing with men. If some set of acts be accepted as models for the rest, one can go on to produce a moral code in terms of which even the distribution and the kinds and amounts of rewards and punishments could be assessed and corrected. Accountability can stop with such public additions to and subtractions from public men. Often enough, though, men are consciously judged to be accountable, are conscious of being rewarded or punished, and make themselves accountable. An ethics, occupied with absolute universal principles of what ought to be and ought to be done, will not then be precluded.

So far as utilitarians are interested in men solely as members of a public world, they need refer to nothing other than accountability. They stand in sharp contrast with deontologists, who are primarily concerned with responsibility, a position privately assumed and maintained, regardless of men's accountability. An adequate account of what men ought to do will have to allow each its proper sphere and show how they bear on one another. That will not be possible, of course, until one knows what men are and can do privately as well as publicly, and the manner in which they can and should support the one by the other.

1.15. You are responsible for what you do.

A man is usually taken to be accountable for what can be traced back to his body as a point of origin. That body is an observable, attenuated continuation of him, at once an instrument and an agency in and through which his feelings, desires, appetites, intentions, and decisions are expressed.

As accessible to others, it is distinguishable from his feelings and other occurrences inwardly undergone. But it is not cut off from these. In Aristotelian terms, a man's body can be said to be an informed matter, an essentialized existence, the form possessing the matter, the essence subjugating the existence, though not completely. Such Aristotelian modes of expression are bound to mislead if either the body or the man be taken to be a juncture of a rational soul with inchoate stuff, for the body that is lived and inwardly possessed is the very body that is intelligibly structured, able to be known by others. It is maintained and used by one who, in a denser, more unified, nonbodily intensified form, is also distinct from it, and partially penetrated when he is addressed.

No one starts without a body, and then later somehow lays hold of one. But, also, one's bodily expressions are diversified, modified continuations of what is not bodily, and less and less accessible from without. As possessed from within, the body is not wholly reachable by anyone. By possessing it as his own, a man privately and responsibly accepts it. That which others externally arrive at and which they hold accountable, he internally possesses and uses on his own responsibility. At the same time that he provides an accredited limit for others, he himself continues into it, possessing and accepting it as that which is to have a public role. As a consequence, he is open both to rewards or punishments and to praise or blame.

A responsible man deserves praise or blame both for what he intends and for making his body the avenue through which his responsibility is given a public guise. If others are to accept him as responsible, they must therefore take his body not merely to be the referent of a credited accountability but to be a means through and by which he expresses himself. The rewards or punishments that he receives because of what he is held accountable for, will then be also viewed as public expressions of a praiseworthy or a blameworthy possessor and user of a body.

Men are not responsible for everything they do, since their

bodies and acts are not always under full control or capable of being completely supervised. Nevertheless, men may properly be held to be accountable for what is done by or with the help of their bodies. And for whatever they are held accountable, they are to some degree responsible, since they do possess and use their bodies. Even if they do and say things unintentionally or act in ways which differ from what they intended, they still deserve praise or blame for whatever they privately began.

Though a man always deserves some praise or blame, since his privacy cannot be entirely disconnected from what his body does, he is not responsible for all that is done. What he responsibly does is altered by its coming into a world not wholly within his control. He should know and guide himself by the knowledge of what the public world does to what he initiates, but he is not responsible for the fact that it alters his expressions, concretionalizes his intentions, gives his acts a setting and implications in this way rather than that. Though held accountable for the altered result, he is responsible only for providing the alterable content in such and such a way, at that time and in that place, and not for what it becomes through the action of other agents and powers.

A proper referent of praise or blame is a responsible initiator of acts, the director and user of a body, a self-maintained private origin of what is available to others. To avoid all responsibility for what his body originates or does, it would be necessary for a man to contract himself to the dimensions of a private, withdrawn unit to which no access was possible by him or by anyone else, since it would be cut off from anything that might lead to it. If he is to have no responsibility for this or that bodily occurrence—a sudden spasm or twitch which might have serious consequences—this must have a purely bodily explanation. He will, or course, still be responsible for it so far as he had placed himself in a situation where the uncontrollable bodily act had regrettable outcomes.

Animals, no less than men, express themselves. Like men,

they too have density and depth. Unlike men, though, they have no place where they can stand to accept what is done as their doing. Unable to distinguish their privacies from their bodies, if made accountable for something, they are unable to assume responsibility for it. They provide full warrant for behavioristic and utilitarian accounts. Sometimes what the animals express, the animals treat as adequate or inadequate, and adjust themselves accordingly. They do not, though, know how to assess it as right or wrong, for that requires them to occupy a position where they can attend to standards beyond bodily grasp. We hold them accountable without their being able to accept or to reject the attribution. Because only men can distinguish their privacies from what they are publicly, only they can be both responsible and accountable.

Trainers and the companions of some animals seem to know something of them that is not yet bodily manifested—their tempers and dispositions. Even those who know no more of animals than what they do and what they may be expected to do, know them to be more than what is confronted then and later. Most of us know that they are able to feel pain and pleasure. Still, an understanding of them requires only a distinction between the bodily manifested and the bodily unmanifested, between the realized and the potential. Though the privacies of animals are never reducible to anything bodily, those privacies have no careers of their own. Animals have neither selves nor persons, no I's or me's; they can make no nonbodily use of their privacies.

It is not necessary to suppose that there is a substantial, separated person, self, will, or mind in order to affirm that some items that are unmanifested by men can be maintained and utilized by them apart from all bodily activity. Even if a man were taken to be responsible only for those things for which he is held to be accountable, and for nothing which fails to come into the public world, it still is true that his responsibility is assumed outside that world, and with respect to what is initiated outside it.

An animal's privacy continues into what it publicly is. A man can hold his privacy away from what he publicly is, preliminary to a possible responsible acceptance of this, or in order to engage in some other private act. He may refuse to accept what he publicly does as his responsibility. He may even vehemently deny that he is responsible for it. But he is nevertheless responsible, and is known to be so by others. They, too, distinguish what he is apart from his body from what he is in and through that body. What they stop at is maintained and insisted on from a position further back. The insistence is the converse of the resistance which slows their advance into him.

Like animals, men possess what they express and, through those expressions, that on which their expressions are impressed. It is a possession, of course, mainly through claim and stain, lacking control, quite distinct from ownership, but sufficient to enable the men to take their bodies, and indeed the entire area where they are accountable, and make it their responsibility.

Because what you bodily are and do is possessed and expressed by you, you have a responsibility for it. Since your responsibility is private, that responsibility is evidently maintained beyond the you through which it is expressed. To acknowledge you is to acknowledge an only partially probed depth where you initiate private acts, and privately initiate publicly expressed ones. Does this give me a right to maintain, in the face of your protests, that you are responsible? Yes. When you say "I am not responsible," you are making as basic a claim as when you say "I am not feeling pain," or "I am thinking." To be sure, not every claim is warranted. Still, every time you back a claim with 'I', you are demanding that it be accepted without question. You can lie, of course. You may even misunderstand yourself. And you certainly can refuse to acknowledge what is present. You will still be responsible. And you will be known to be so, for you are encountered as both insistently expressing your privacy and exhibiting a forcefulness that is not intrinsic to what you are saying or do-ing. When you sincerely protest that you are not responsible, it is because you pay no attention to what you are maintaining and initiating and, therefore, to what might have provided you, as it does others, with the beginning of a convergence toward their source. Sometimes a man is known better by others than he is by himself. To know yourself as I know you, you must be able to go backward from what you had put for-ward. And this you do when you attend to yourself as a me.

A barking dog wagging its tail, I have learned to suppose, is a friendly dog. I do not, though, know how to use its bark-ing and wagging to begin an intensive progress toward an originating privacy. I have to be content with taking these and other expressions to be aspects of a single bodily friendliness privately sustained. To understand the dog I do not have to suppose that it has a privacy able to engage in activities hav-ing no bodily import. I discern nothing with which its body contrasts. The dog is friendly, barking and wagging its tail preparatory to leaping and rolling over. It does not express friendliness; it does not intend to be friendly; it does not know that it is friendly. All its moves are cognate with the protective colorations of insects, reacting to some external occurrence.

A dog can feint; it cannot feign. It may mislead, but it does not know how to deceive. It is not responsible, for it does only what it is geared or occasioned to do. It cannot hide its feel-ings. But a man has private powers and roles distinct from those he expresses publicly. Only he can occupy himself with what is not at all bodily—with idle fancies, mathematical truths, the objects of metaphysics and theology, with laws, principles, rules, with the ideal, with what ought to be but never is. He alone is able to imagine, plan, and speculate in ways and with results which have no bodily import.

An infant begins a bodily life as an innocent, unable either to outmaneuver as an animal might, or to pretend as an adult can. Its maturation involves the contrasting of an increasingly complicated privacy from the you another can approach, and from the me it comes to know. As it learns to feint, it also learns to feign. The discovery that some act in which it engages yields satisfying functionings by another prompts its experimentation with other acts and tentative movements to see if they too have satisfying outcomes. Once this is known, the infant, somewhat like the dog, may be able to act so as to outmaneuver others. But, unlike the dog, it will also be able to intend to function in these ways. At both times, it will root its publicly available you in a denser, more private ground, able to deceive others as to what it is and wants.

No human body mirrors a soul. Such a mirror would be set in the wrong direction. Also, it would have to transform the unextended, unarticulated, and possessive into the extended, articulated, and possessed. A human body is more like a blurred, distortive glass, manipulated by that into which it enables one to peer.

A human body is possessed and used by what is not publicly available in one sense and is publicly available in another. It is not publicly available where it is intensive, dense, and one, but is publicly available in everything it does, since what it does carries out in an attenuated and modified form what it in fact is. Because what is publicly manifested as the body and in its acts modifies whatever is begun in privacy, no one can just read off from a body what was intended, or know what a man, as more than and as contrasting with his body, is like.

Even while we attend to what is publicly located or to what might become publicly available, we are aware of something deeper in a man, more private and distinctive, able to manifest itself, not only in other bodily ways, as an animal can, but in quite a different direction. Men have privacies which are capable of expressing an interest in preconditions, truth, and promises, the remote past, the distant future, what might have been, and what could have been done. Only they have I's, occupied with whatever there be, now, yesterday, or tomorrow, with the conditions for whatever is encountered, with fictions, and with hopes. Only they are able to be self-same no matter how their bodies, knowledge, or intentions change.

1.16. The attribution of accountability is a responsible act.

A publicly accountable man is an identified precondition of desirable or undesirable public occurrences. He may be taken to be their cause, just an occasion, or even only a convenient place where one supposes the beginning of an activity, having approved or disapproved public outcomes, to occur. The attribution of the outcomes to him may be followed by acts supporting the assignment. The attribution requires one to take a private stand and to direct one's reference to what exists apart from oneself. It does not stop completely at that referent, but passes beyond it into the dense privacy which sustains and may have initiated the publicly attributed act.

Rewards and punishments, normally in the form of desirable and undesirable additions and alterations to the body and to what is achieved through its agency, can also take the form of changes in the way in which someone is thereafter approached, dealt with, and adjusted to. Taking disturbances in an existent situation to be desirable or undesirable, prompts a taking of them to require a proportionate alteration in the presumed accountable reason for those disturbances. The alteration is intended to make a man be in consonance with the new situation that he helped bring about.

Rewards and punishments are agencies by which accountable reasons for changes are altered so as to make them part of new situations just as they had been part of the old. Ideally, a hero's reward and a criminal's punishment are equal to the differences they made. Ideally, the rewards and punishments convert the men into integral parts of the situations they brought about. Since, when he rewards and punishes, as well as when he does not, a man is responsible for holding another to be accountable, if there is a reciprocity in the crediting of accountability, there will so far be a reciprocity of responsibilities.

A man knows that others are responsible when they make evident that they are taking him to be accountable. Were it not possible for him to know that they are responsible, it would not be possible for him to know that they assume that he is accountable. What was said by him would not be known to have been listened to. Nor would desirable and undesirable alterations in him be known to be deliberately bestowed by them.

A dog acts at times as if it knew it were being punished. It cowers, slinks, pulls its tail between its legs. But it does not know itself to be responsible. Nor does it know that it is being held accountable, that it is being hurt, scolded, encouraged, benefitted, because something denigrated or endorsed is credited to it. It reacts to expressions of approval and disapproval, and can be trained to associate those expressions with acts which are to be carried out or inhibited. But it never makes itself responsibly take itself to be accountable. Nor does it recognize that others responsibly take it to be accountable. There is no private area where it engages in or knows of acts occupied with what is nonbodily.

Were one to try to carry over into the world of humans the kind of interpretation that caution requires one to apply to the world of animals, one would responsibly maintain that no one else was responsible. The result would be an ethical solipsism in which others were never taken to possess and use their accountable bodies. One would then be right to blame or praise only oneself. In effect, one would be a God, and all other men would be on a footing with animals or things. There would not be anyone who could be a publicized you. 'You', as a consequence, would be a term without a referent.

If I alone can assume responsibility, I alone can hold myself to be praiseworthy or blameworthy for having made myself be accountable. If I then set myself on a par with all others, it will be because I ignore my distinctive responsible status. But, then, having no possible contact with the privacies of other men, as capable of being expressed responsibly, I would never know that I was being addressed by them.

When someone is addressed, he is responsibly treated as accountable, and also held to be responsible for making himself accountable. I know that I responsibly hold others to be accountable, for I address them. I know that they responsibly hold me to be accountable, for they address me. I address those who responsibly assume accountable roles, responsibly holding them to be responsible, and know that they reciprocate.

1.17. You have both a public and a private status.

What is without backing in an independently maintained depth cannot properly be addressed as 'you'. A dog can be talked to, and referred to by 'you', but that 'you' will not be a term of address. When one gives the dog a name or calls it by name, one marks it off, but does not honor it, take it to be worthy of respect. Its name does not adhere to it. The 'Fido' or 'you' directed at it is just a surrogate for 'this'. A term of address merges with a publicized terminus that is continuous and yet contrasts with what sustains and presents it. The fact is not in conflict with the observation that some men seem to be on more intimate terms with some animals than they are with humans, that they speak to the animals at length and believe that the animals understand them and even respond sympathetically, in well-nuanced ways. What it does deny is that the privacy of an animal is anything more than what has an incipient bodily expression. What it does deny is that the privacy of a man is completely reducible to such incipient, public expressions. It justifies a behaviorism for animals, but denies that a behaviorism could ever be adequate to account for what men do, can do, or are.

Those who address you come to rest with your public presence as merging into and being grounded in a private, distinctive unitary power. From the position of the address, you are an intensified solidification of your expressions. From the position of the unitary power, you are an embodied, publicized, partly expressed terminus for the 'you' another uses, a kind of inverted pyramid issuing from a sustaining, separately maintained apex.

'You', the term of address, is like the 'this' which is used to refer to a table or a dog in that, while relativized by what confronts it, it still has a status apart from what is confronting it. Like the 'this', it also terminates in a publicly arrived at unity for the distinguished components of a judgment. Unlike the 'this', it has a symbolic role, taking us part of the way into a privacy capable of being utilized responsibly.

The you that is known by another is midway between the possessed you and the you that is in fact confronted. In answering to 'you', you distinguish your publicly available you from what no one can fully penetrate into. Your answering sharpens the difference between another as involved with you, and what both he and you are apart from and beyond that involvement.

A reference to an actual table or dog is carried out by means of a copula at the same time that this verbally, grammatically, epistemically, and logically relates subject and predicate. 'You' usurps the copula's role in taking one toward the unity of what is being judged, leaving the copula with just the role of a connection between terms. "You are large" and "You are vicious," therefore, are to be construed differently from "This [table] is large" and "This [dog] is vicious." 'Large' and 'vicious' are attributable to you as aspects; they are correlatives of 'this table' and 'this dog'. The object of "This [table] is large" is this-large-[table]; the object of "This [dog] is vicious" is this-vicious-[dog]. But the object of "You are large" and the object of "You are vicious" is a you who expresses, possesses, sustains, and uses the large and the viciousness. That you in turn stands in contradistinction with a deeper privacy with which it is nevertheless continuous.

1.18. You are objective and unrelativized.

There are a number of distinct senses of 'objectivity' pertinent to the understanding of any you.

a) What is acknowledged in fact or in principle by a community is objective, relative to what individuals might idiosyncratically observe or claim. The 'reasonable man' in a society accepts the society's acceptances in the face of divergent observations by himself or others.

b) Sooner or later, many acknowledge that what is endorsed by their own community may not express exactly what is the case, since it fails to cohere with what a larger group of men agree upon. There are times, of course, when a single man may see what others overlook. He might not only recognize some ethical truth the rest have missed, but may have alone observed some physical or chemical occurrence. On the whole, what most agree upon is nevertheless taken to be more objective than what only a more limited number affirm, granted that they are of about equal maturity and that they exercise about the same care in forming their judgments. From this it does not follow that what all agree upon, no matter what the community, will necessarily be fully objective, for what is acknowledged may still answer to distinctive common interests, apprehensions, and needs. All that can be surely affirmed is that it will be objective for some men. But you are not only objective for some. You are, in principle, knowable by any man. All can address you; all can move beyond any preassignable point into what is beyond all relativization.

c) You are not only confronted. You are confrontable. Even when what is known of you is personalized or socially conditioned, and fails to express what anyone might know, you can be recognized to be both related to others and to have a unity of your own in which your different expressions are indivisibly one. Personal, social, and human ways of dealing with you, while taking account of different relations and laws, take account of the very same you.

d) You are objective in space and in causal relations, as well as in time. You are affiliated as well as coordinated with others. In each way, and in other ways as well, and in all of them together, you are a term sustained. We make use of this sense of 'objective' when we speak of you as a unit unrelated to others.

e) You are subject to conditions which enable you to be together with others. The conditions give you an objective status, maintaining you in relation to others, apart from all knowledge. Though you are then referred to, you continue to be objectively present, able to be referred to.

f) You, by yourself, are subject to determinations by conditions which affect everything. You are thereby enabled to be a substance and a being, to have a nature, to exist, and to have a value, as you stand away from all else. Others can be charged with misconstruing you just so far as their understanding of you deviates from what universal conditions determine.

g) One of the conditions which govern you separately and as together with all else expresses Being. This makes you and others equally real, regardless of how you and they are affiliated, classified, existent, or assessed. A you is objective because Being enables it to be related to others as one of a number of equal realities. Each you has an integrity of its own apart from all references to it, because it is objectively maintained as one of a number of irreducible beings.

h) Conditions operate over wide ranges and over narrow ones. You are objective both because you are subject to a condition operating cosmically, and because you are subject to that very condition as pertinent to some limited situation. Universal chemical laws have specialized forms when they have to do solely with the functioning of human blood or lungs. If it be supposed that the matter can be dealt with by introducing a number of constants into cosmic laws, one will still have to allow for the fact that you are also in a limited world which includes only men, no one of whom may take account of you, but all of whom are subject to the same conditions, dictating what they are and can do in relation to you and one another.

i) Like every other conditioned item, you make yourself felt in opposition to the conditions which govern you separately and together with others. You are, so far, objective, not merely because of conditions, but in the face of conditions. Were the conditions and the result of their operation known, it would be possible to infer the nature of the you that opposes the conditions and which, with them, determines the result of their operation.

j) You continue in depth, absenting yourself from all that might be available to others. You are grounded in what enables you to be available. But there is no set point where you cease and where what is beyond you begins. You imperceptibly pass into what makes you available. As inwardly possessed, you are freed from all relativizations, made objective.

From the standpoint of others and the relations which they sustain, only relativized versions of you are to be found. Starting with you as present in the world, relativized termini are that you related in specific ways. Though it is yourself in entirety who is relativized in these ways, the termini are never identifiable with you in your entirety. The full objectivity that you have as an irreducible reality is only partially exhibited in your relativized guises.

Independently of men, universal conditions qualify and relate you to what else is present. You both answer the conditions and continue to be present, independently of them and all else. You are objective because you are governed by those conditions, are enabled to oppose them, and are sustained apart from them. Since subjection, opposition, and sustaining are distinct states, characteristic of you as apart from all others, it is conceivable that you might be objective in each one of these ways and, so far, not be objective in your entirety. In fact, though, you are independent of all observers at the same time that you are sustained apart from, opposed by, and are subjected to conditions. Whether or not you are perceived, made the referent of a 'you', or addressed in some other way, you are relativized from an indefinite number of positions. This is possible because you are both objectively available to others and are together with them.

A universal relativism, which denies that there is anything apart from terms defined by relations issuing elsewhere, not only has nothing to relativize, but presupposes at least one unrelativized origin or ground for the relativizing relations. Might not that which is common to all the relativizing terminations at you just be one facet of you? Instead of being objective in your entirety, might you not be objective only because an aspect of you, additional to your other states, is distinguished from these? Affirmative answers to these questions rest on the supposition that there is nothing which is being relativized. But it is you in your full concreteness who provides terms for all relativizing approaches. The relativizing relations exhibit you in your entirety, under limitations.

1.19. Common constraining conditions enable men to be present to one another.

My reference to you as accountable is singular and asymmetrical, ending with what lacks the power to reciprocate. If you do refer to me, two asymmetries will produce a semblance of a genuine symmetry. There is no assurance that the two references will be strict reciprocals of one another. But, whether they are or not, the two of us will be symmetrically together to the degree that we have been able to terminate in one another.

For even an asymmetrical relation to be possible, items must already be together. Were the items self-contained, they would not be together. They can be referents for one another only because they are already copresent.

Men are together in a public world. They are together, too, as distinguished from what they are publicly. None could make himself be together with others in either way. All men are and can be symmetrically together only because they have been enabled to be so. And what is true of men, is also true of subhuman and inanimate beings. No unit bounded off from the rest would be symmetrically together with others, were it not that it and they are subject to a common constraining condition. A common constraining condition acts on all at and beyond the point where their separate referrings end. From the standpoint of that condition, particulars oppose and punctuate it; from their standpoint, the condition provides a field within which they are enabled to be together with one another.

An atomism is the logical outcome of a refusal to acknowledge a common constraining condition, enabling items to be together, for it takes each item to be independent of all the others, a distinct, irreducible unit. The position cannot be maintained. In the end, atomism cannot hold that there is more than one atom. In order for it to acknowledge more than one, it would have to allow that these were together. This would require it to grant that, in addition to the atoms, there was a condition imposed on them all, enabling them to be atoms together. A monism, in contrast, is the logical outcome of a refusal to attend to independent units. To account for the monist and his world, or for a supposed illusory plurality, monism must take the supposed single reality not only to produce the plurality, but to be different from it. What was not originally allowed for would then be admitted. Monism and atomism, evidently, are the untenable outcomes of efforts to cancel what is in fact essential and complementary. Every many has its one; every one has its many.

There are men, and they are together. As just men, they are coordinate. They are also together with one another as *affiliated*, *intelligible*, *distanced*, and *graded*. Each of these ways of being together is the outcome of the operation of an independently grounded final, universally applicable condition—the topic of the remainder of this chapter.

1.20. Men are affiliated.

Apart from all referring, apart from any efforts or knowledge, men are interinvolved with greater or less intimacy, are more or less in harmony, have some degree of positive or negative compatibility. They also constitute limited groups. There, a number of them are vitally together, supportively or antagonistically, in contrast with the ways in which they are together with others. Their union with one another in limited groups depends on the operative presence of a common condition. This is a limited, more specialized form of a condition enabling them to be together with all other men. That condition, in turn, is a limited, specialized form of an all-comprehensive final condition, enabling all actualities to be relevant to one another in some manner and to some degree.

Men are relevant to one another before they are aware of the fact; they have the status of affiliated 'you's' even before they are addressed. One can therefore take 'you' just to provide a means for emphasizing the fact that one of the men is already confronting another. If this is done, it will then be necessary to say that there can be no mistakes made in the use of a 'you', for one will already have terminated at its referent, and will have nothing more to do than to bring the 'you' closer to the you to which he was already related. But because there are specific individuals whom we seek to address, it makes sense to say, "I didn't mean *you* when I said 'you'." The you to whom 'you' is being supposed to address may not be the you one was addressing.

Used by one man on one occasion, 'you' not only has a referent different from that it has when used at a different time and terminating at someone else, but a different aura as well, since it is affected by the kind of relevance that the terminus has for its user. That relevance is due to the way a specialized form of a final affiliating common condition is qualified when countered both by the user and his referent. The fact is rarely noticed; because of the commonality of the condition, it is only the differences that the men make to it that are usually remarked.

The particular degrees and kinds of relevance that men have for one another may be conveyed by their tones of voice and accompanying looks and gestures. Strictly speaking, these belong with the 'you', enabling the user to address what is relevant to him in such and such a degree and manner. On each use, they enable the 'you' to be pertinent to the kind of affiliation that in fact unites the speaker and his referent.

The 'you's' employed in families, clubs, and teams are accentuated versions of those used by others within a larger, common society. Where they do not express personal stresses, they are used in some consonance with the more or less established degrees of relevance that individuals are expected to have for one another. The norm is to conform to the established ways. Men, of course, deviate from this again and again. Anthropologists and sociologists attend to the accentuated versions, taking languages and practices to be normative for the people with whom they deal. Psychologists, instead, lean toward the consideration of more personal uses. They presuppose the other approaches, so far as they accept as normative the practices characteristic of some group.

By treating men as wholly confined within a particular society, one is forced to suppose that when references are made to others outside that society they are implicitly brought within it through the use of 'you's' which are normative there. Translations of what is said and done elsewhere then become transformations, reducing what is objectively and independently occurring to a variant of what is local. This always involves some loss; the transformed had a genuine standing outside. Were this not so, no anthropologist could ever learn what the group he studies is actually doing, since, on the hypothesis, he would inescapably transform it to a degree and in a manner of which he had no knowledge. Unless one could know that something was being transformed, one could not know that a transformation occurred. Unless one could know what was being transformed, one could not know what the transformation produced.

We now face a special case of the dilemma that besets all relativizations. If everything is turned into a function of an observer, a knower, an interpreter, a translator, the fact itself must be transformed by the reporter of this, and there will therefore be nothing that he truly reports. If he can really tell us that a transformation is occurring, he has somehow escaped transforming it. For a relativist there is nothing to be known, not even that there are transformations—unless only reports of transformations are free of transformation. But why should and how could a report of a transformation be free of relativization, if reports of what resists men's acts and knowing are not? Moreover, if a man can correctly tell us why or how it is impossible to know what is the case, he surely must himself know something that is absolutely so.

Men are confrontable outside limited groups. They are faced as more or less congenial, and are addressed in ways which reflect that fact. The 'you' of which they make use, of course, was initially a term in a language common to only a limited group of men. That does not preclude it from having a transsocial use as well. Others outside one's group can be and are addressed by 'you', because those others are already connected with the speakers, not in the complex, established ways characteristic of the speakers' particular society, but in a world of men.

A lingua franca presupposes that it is possible to make contact with men in different language groups. A transsocial 'you' is part of a natural lingua franca, often understood and responded to by men who have no knowledge of the particular living language of those who are referring to them. Were there no such lingua franca, the existence and success of the hybrid languages, by means of which men in different communities communicate, though knowing nothing of one another's living language, would be mysteries, presupposing as they do that the men are already together, able to communicate with one another.

1.21. An intermediary 'you' presupposes related men.

If it is desired to speak to already affiliated you's, use can be made of 'you's' having an intermediary role. Some of these intermediary 'you's' function within limited groups; others are used in situations where both user and referent exist within common fields; still others mediate that at which attention has already come to rest and are then used to direct one toward what has not yet been attended to or is not yet in focus.

The last use is similar to that made of a 'you' or a 'Thou' by religious men when they petition rather than pray—where 'petition' is a request made to a being whom one has not yet reached, and 'prayer' is a sacramental speech by one already involved with his God. Both petitions and prayers make use of a 'you' which, while originating within a special group, is intended to refer to what exists apart from all men. But though the petition may never reach a terminus, a true prayer always must, since it is nothing less than a sacramental act which has to begin with what has been affected by the God. Petitions make use of vectoral 'you's' which had an intermediary function; true prayers are intermediary 'you's' which begin with what has already been accepted by their object and, therefore, already have more than a vectoral role. Subjectively viewed, there is no mistaking a prayer. Objectively viewed, it has no reality unless it is in fact answered in the sense of being accepted by the God. The question that remains unresolved is whether what one takes to be a prayer is one in fact. It would never be one if there were no God, or if he did not sanctify what was prayerfully said.

If there be a God who is concerned with what occurs in this world, he not only attends to the acts of men but assesses them as more or less good or bad for doing what is demanded or forbidden. The men, who are the sources of the assessed acts, could conceivably have their intentions and purposes judged. If so, they would be confronted you's beyond whom God moved to attend to the responsible sources of the divinely assessed acts. Were those men called on by the God to answer for what they had done, they would be addressed by means of intermediating 'you's', 'you's' which presuppose a connection between God and the men. Since the men would have already been acknowledged to be objects of a divine concern, or at the very least to be termini of relations originating with the God, a reference to them by means of intermediary 'you's' must be a later, subordinate, derivative occurrence. Those 'you's' either carry the weight of a divine assessment or help express it.

Sometimes men claim to have been called by a God to engage in a mission. It is sometimes said, too, that he calls to some—an Adam, a Cain, a Jonah—who then vainly try to escape his concerned interest in them. Both those who accept and those who try to avoid such a divine appeal have already been divinely attended to. The call made on them intermediates, and may incidentally record and emphasize the fact that a divine concern has already reached them. A reciprocal reference is possible, but only because it has been divinely instituted. Men lack the power to reach the divine unless divinely empowered. To be able to pray, they must first be made the object of a divine concern. It is proper, therefore, for a religious man to say, "Thy will be done . . ." since in this way he remarks on the fact that what is said and asked for has to be accepted by his God and understood on that God's terms. When a religious man adds a petition to his prayers, he in effect attaches a vector which is to terminate at his God as not yet having engaged in a desired act.

The reference that is here being made to prayer and to God is solely for the purpose of sharpening the issue. To make use of it, it is not necessary to hold that God exists. It makes sense to speak of what could possibly be done by a perfect, infinite being who is responsive to man's appeals, even if there were no such being. Nor is it necessary to hold that there are genuine prayers which in fact terminate in God in order to be able to understand what a genuine prayer must be like.

1.22. Men are intelligibly together.

Materialists take men to be aggregates of physical units, all subject to intelligible laws applicable to what in principle is not observable by anyone, since it is supposedly devoid of all taint of human involvement. Theirs is a position with methodological strengths. The fall of a man through space or his reactions to repeatable conditions applicable to all actualities can be effectively dealt with in materialistic terms. But such an approach slights or denies other equally important and even more important truths about men. It has difficulty in showing how it is possible to engage in an act of reference, to address someone, to sympathize, to think, to intend, to create, to say what experience is like, or to show how it is possible for anything to be true or false.

To understand what men do and how they interact, it is necessary to understand the laws to which they, together with what is not human, are subject. But men also behave as unitary beings with singular careers. Sometimes, too, they act in aberrational ways. Sometimes they are spontaneous; often they are unpredictable. They are accountable; they are responsible. Without ceasing to be public and together, the men are and act as individuals. None of these truths require an abrogation of a law of nature; they show only that men are not just instances of what pertains to all indifferently.

Men are more than values for variables. Laws, not men, are universals, presupposing the men and other actualities which they condition and control. What men publicly are and what they do occur within the area where laws prevail, but the men enter there from unduplicable privacies and with a freedom of which the laws take no account.

You's present to one another are together in various ways

because they are subject to common conditions; they are also apart from one another, realities with powers of their own. No matter how well we know one another, we have and maintain a reality beyond that point. There, we are still subject to conditions. Of course, there are no distinct layers in us separately conditioned or separately reacting to the conditions. Viewed from the positions of the individuals subject to them, conditions are effective enough to connect them, but malleable enough to do so in varying ways, without ever fully encompassing them. That on which common conditions operate are more or less public, more or less complex, sustained by what is more constant, intensive, and private. A man may be publicly pleasant at the same time that he is really bitter, both attitudes being grounded in him as a private, unduplicable reality with its own power and expressions.

No matter how effective a conditioning be, it is countered by what provides it with something to condition. No matter how insistent on themselves men are, there always is some condition affecting them. Were they completely under the governance of the laws of nature, or of any other conditions, they would never act. Were they the creatures of these, they would not provide something to be conditioned by them—or the conditions would have both to diversify themselves and precipitate out what is able to limit the operation of those conditions. Once allowance is made for the presence of that on which laws and other conditions operate, room is provided for what, outside the provenance of those conditions, is able to insist on itself against those conditions.

A man has a reality apart both from all that conditions him and from all other actualities. So far as he is closed off from the first, he is involved with the second, and conversely. Closed off from final, conditioning realities, he is related to other actualities as different from them. Closed off from other actualities, he is distinct from the realities which condition all. Were he wholly in himself, his distinctness from the finalities and his difference from other actualities would be inextricably joined. His distinctness and difference would then no longer enable him to be bounded off from both the finalities and other actualities, with the consequence that he would be just a nuance in some larger whole.

Turned away from all actualities, men are distinct from all the finalities. Turned away from all finalities, they are different from all other actualities. They maintain themselves by backing their distinctness by their difference and their difference by their distinctness.

1.23. A scientific knowledge of individuals is possible.

At the root of Aristotle's account of scientific knowledge is the view that individuals cannot be known. Since he made no provision for getting to individuals through acts of sympathy, love, fear, or hatred, he had to leave them veiled in mystery. The mystery is not dispelled by having recourse to genuine scientific ways of making evident what men individually are, for at the very least, the generality and impersonality of the rules and laws then employed preclude a knowledge of what is unique. Still, a scientific knowledge of individual men is possible if: a) there are laws applicable to men alone; b) the men provide translations of one type of law into other types; and c) individual emotions, feelings, thoughts, and other similar occurrences provide particular ways in which the translations take place.

a) By attending to only some specialized governing laws, it is possible to say what men are under special circumstances. They would, of course, then be known only within limitations, not as they fully are. This is another reason why psychoanalysis and behaviorism can never do adequate justice to what a man in fact is. And since they also ignore the biological, chemical, physical, historical, and other laws to which the men are also subject, they cannot tell us all that men are as publicly ruled in common ways.

Physical laws affect what is also subject to other types of law. The laws apply to men and other actualities severally and together, independently of how these function in their privacies. They are effective not merely on the surfaces of actualities but on them as full-fledged realities resisting and countering them. Even if we ignore the contributions of individuals and the difference that other types of law and other conditions make, what is governed by physical laws is far less than all there is. Chemical compounds, cells, organic beings, tribal men, historical figures, and groups cannot be properly treated as complicated forms of the physical or be set in totally separated domains. When a man falls out of a window he falls at a steadily accelerating rate. To know this is not yet to know whether or not he is careless, will be unable to work, is insured, and will leave a widow and two children in emotional shock and in difficult economic straits. Whatever may be true of him in these respects will be true of him as he falls, like a stone, in accord with physical laws. Just by walking across a room, one compels every particle, molecule, and cell in one's body to move in ways and along paths they otherwise could not. Were it possible to understand his mind as nothing more than a set of movements of molecules or other units in his brain, those movements would still be different in rate, direction, span, occasion, and effect from those which would characterize the same units were they outside his brain. A reductionism is in effect a constructionism, taking items away from the situations in which they are in fact interlocked with others of quite different types in order to consider them in an imagined domain where they consort only with entities of the same type, all under the same kind of laws.

Each of the ways in which men are governed makes a difference to the men and to the outcome of other forms of governance. To know men, both universal laws and conditions and the laws and conditions to which they alone are subject must be taken into account. All men are directly subject to universal conditions, to various physical, chemical, or biological laws, and to those that govern their societies. There is still more to know. Men are affected not only by what they are in interrelation, but by their own components and parts.

A full scientific knowledge of men is not yet within our grasp. But if it were, we still would not know all that must be known if man is to be understood. Men affect the relations connecting them; they affect the functioning of what their bodies encompass just as surely as these are affected in turn. A lie is not only uttered by a leader who moves his tongue and jaw, expels carbon dioxide, disturbs the air, and misleads his followers. His attempt to obscure what had been done, is being done, and will be done also affects his heart and breathing. These in turn affect and are affected by other organs, by cells, by smaller units, and by other activities. Whatever is said and done, no matter how one speaks or acts, depends on the presence and functioning of subordinate entities and occurrences of different degrees of complexity, and in turn affects these.

A satisfactory account of any type of actuality, from man to the ultimate unit particles, is quite complicated. Consideration must be given to different types of law applying to the different kinds of units studied by different sciences, without denying that the actualities remain single and undivided, privately and publicly. Investigations by different disciplines underscore the existence of a multiplicity of levels on which the laws operate, at the same time that they make conspicuous the truth that the individual is being ignored.

There are units with distinctive natures and relations existing within the limits of single beings, themselves involved with others in law-abiding ways. Those units are to some extent controlled by the individual. A cell is affected not only by the chemical and physical units within its compass but by the organs in which it is, by the entire body, and by the actual, singular reality who owns and uses that body. The cell itself is controlled by whatever governs both the units within it and the bodily complex of which it is a part, at the same time that it counters the operation of laws pertinent just to cells.

b) A man is the translator of what he is in one aspect into what he is in others. He translates his short body into a way of being a banker; conversely, he translates his status as a banker into a way of being smaller than most. He has a certain size, of course, no matter what he does, and he might continue as a banker while he shrinks concurrently with his growth in girth. He never is just short, or just a banker; he contributes to and possesses each in individual ways. One way may not be as important or as deeply grounded as another. But apart from the extraneously produced components of his 'accidents', whatever is true of him will be united by him both where it occurs and in a more private unity. He provides grounding and content for each of his expressions, and translates them into one another both in depth and on more superficial levels, the one as constituting a private unity, the other as terms interrelated.

The neglect of a man's role as the translator of one aspect of himself into another turns these into inexplicables. All tell us something of what he is in root, since they all express him, though with different degrees of adequacy. No matter how high or low our estimate of his intelligence, virtue, or social importance, we cannot exclude him from an equal place among humans. That place is his because of what he is, beyond the reach of those features. And what is true of these, is true also of his color, gender, and anything else, whether this supervenes over or underlies his social or ethical values, positive or negative. What he manifestly is, is a continuation of what he is in himself, but as not yet diversified, not yet qualified by components due to others.

The more persistent, direct, and complete an expression, the more does it deserve to be taken to be the term into which others are to be translated. One black congresswoman tinges what she says with bitterness; another speaks gently. They are distinguishable as individuals by the differences they allow their color and gender to make to their speech, and conversely. But often enough, what they say will have nothing to do with either their color or gender. If we are to know who they really are, we must find that agency which can translate

any of their expressions into any other. And that is either a
relation connecting apparently unrelated expressions, or it is
their unities. But the relations connecting their expressions
are as much attenuations of the unity as the expressions
themselves. Since, when the expressions are diversified, they
are also interrelated, to say that the interrelations provide rational modes of translation is but to say that they are versions
of a deeper-lying translator operating at the origin of the expressions.

The practitioners of the occult sciences know that what
seem to be idle and inadvertent features provide clues to the
nature of their common private source. A tendency to suppose that the source operates in accord with fixed rules, and
that in root it is identifiable with a set of unalterable moral
traits, however, precludes a satisfactory use of the initial insight.

c) Men have feelings, dispositions, emotions, intentions,
and beliefs. All have a bodily as well as a private role. Translations traverse the difference between the two forms.

In order to achieve a scientific knowledge of individual
men, one must first free their expressions from the additions
acquired from what is exterior to them—and which enabled
the expressions to function as terms in public relations—and
must then identify the individuals with the relations connecting the expressions. One will end with the individual as just
an articulated, thinner version of what is not yet manifest.
Such knowledge many can have; it can also be presented in
neutral terms, free from a reference to any particular observer.
But it does not exhaust the knowledge that it is possible to
have of an individual man. He can also be known through a
penetrative encounter, through sympathy, through address,
and by piecing together his autobiographical remarks. These
converge on what he is as a private being, able to express himself in public, to provide relations which translate one expression into another, and to be a unity in which the initiations of
expressions are convertible into one another. The first two are
open to scientific knowing. Since they imperceptibly merge

into the third, they allow a scientific knowledge to impinge on as well as to articulate individuals.

1.24. A public you occupies space.

You are spatially distinct from other you's in a triple way: a) you are positioned within a common space; b) your extension is part of a larger; and c) you have a distinctive distended-ness which enables you to occupy a limited extension.

a) "You are here" is short for "You, there, are here," for in order to identify you as being at a position designated by 'here', I must first locate you in space, find you *there*. Apart from an implicit or explicit 'there', 'you' would have no terminus; it would be just a vectoral term without a referent. With the help of 'there', it is directed toward you at a position in objective space. You are not merely positioned in this; you are there, filling out an extended region. As the fact of motion makes evident, that extended region is neither identical with nor inseparable from you. Because it is objective and continuous with other extended regions, when abandoned by you, it still remains connected with those other regions.

b) Occupied regions are subdivisions of a common space at different distances from one another. Each subdivision, though occupied by independent individuals, is continuous with a space beyond, where there may or may not be other occupants. The occupied regions are distinguished on being occupied, but are not sunderable from space itself. Space remains a single, undivided domain even when there are many independently occupied regions in it.

c) Men occupy space. They are real as not yet in space. And they are able to occupy a part of it. As not yet occupying a region of space, they are obviously not yet extended. But they also are not points; if they were, they would have to turn themselves into volumes when they in fact occupy a place. Despite the fact that the places occupied are never torn away from the whole of space, those places are both effectively occupied and possessed by their occupants. This is possible because those occupants, apart from all occupation, are already distensive, internally self-expansive without being able to set part exterior to part.

Because subdivisions of a common space can be occupied, there can be encountered you's within a single common space. Because men possess the extended regions they occupy, their you's are extended and locatable in a common spatial world.

1.25. You are perceivable.

There is a difference between confronting something and perceiving it, between facing it and assessing it, and between taking account of it and understanding it. Confronting, facing, taking account, are practical acts which may prove to be inadequate to what is present, but they are never true or false, since they make no claim, affirm nothing.

Perception dissects what it encounters, breaking this up into a factor marking the fact that an item is present and another marking out some contemplatable feature. The two factors are interrelated by the perceiver in a unity which purports to represent the unity in which the factors initially were undistinguished. The unifying of the features and the claiming of the whole to re-present what was objectively present is an act of judgment. To perceive is to judge the confronted.

A you is perceived at a distance. There it has three distinct, independently determined roles: a) It is affected by distinctive interests, biases, and interpretations; b) it stands apart from the perceiver as that at which he arrives and which he sooner or later finds does not act in consonance with some desire or expectation; and c) it has its own integrity, dependent on and sustained in privacy.

a) We see from special angles, intruding something of ourselves into what we observe. What we perceive through the help of sight and other organs reflects our positions and

biases. We select certain objects to which we attend; we identify, approach, examine, and interpret, in good part in terms
of what we have learned, anticipate, desire, and fear. These
facts have been incoherently universalized and absolutized by
subjectivism. No one, this holds, ever can perceive without
introducing distortions which reflect individualized, subjective, inescapable suppositions. Necessarily, subjectivism is
claiming to know what all men do, and also what it is that the
men misconstrue, or at the very least that there is something
that is misconstrued. Since so much has to be known by it,
subjectivism evidently starts from its own denial. Unless perception had nothing to do with known objects and, therefore,
could not be said to misconstrue them, it should be possible to
compare what was perceived with what was otherwise objectively known, and thereupon be able to so modify the perceptual results that they answer to what is.

Though men intrude personal notes into what is perceived,
they do this in no steady way. If they did, the notes could be
steadily abstracted from—unless their contribution could escape all efforts to discover them and they, therefore, could not
be known to occur. Men vary in what they intrude, how they
intrude it, and the weight they give it, enabling one to compare what is perceived on a particular occasion with what is
perceived on another.

Perceptions provide checks on one another. The fact, of
course, does not show that perception ever gets to what is objectively present. And, in any case, no perception or set of
them is absolutely reliable. This does not mean, of course, that
every perception necessarily misconstrues or distorts. If it
did, we would not be able to rely on the reports of scientific
instruments. Their recordings have to be perceived or, at the
very least, must be translated into perceptual content. The
most abstract formulae must be given a perceivable form if
others are to learn about them. Were perception always mistaken, we would always mistake what was impersonally recorded.

Sometimes the larger is perceived to be larger. What we

perceive is often what is so. Still, what is smaller from one angle and distance may be perceived to be larger from another angle and distance. Even when a perception is in accord with what is impersonally recorded, there will usually be some perceived features that exist only relative to a perceiver. These, though, can be utilized to tell us something true. If it be you who is perceived, it will be you with various perceivable features; it will also be you for a perceiver who is attending, judging, and, in the end, yielding to your presence.

b) No matter how much of the perceived is due to a perceiver, there is always something left over, at a distance, able to be perceived, not constituted by the perceiving. You are objectively present even though what is said of you radically distorts what you are like, and even how you appear.

Epistemological dualisms rightly distinguish between personalized perceptions and the objects that are perceived. But they set the two in such opposition as to leave one with the empty claim that an unperceivable object somehow provokes a man to produce personalized reports of it. The objects cannot be entirely unrelated to the perceiver, for if they were, they could not produce any effects in him. Unless the perceived were wholly separated from objects, perceptions must allow for some knowledge of them. The converse is also true. Adequate knowledge of what is objective provides some knowledge of what might be perceived. Distinguishable from what is perceived and from any perceiver, you are and are known to be so.

c) In itself, an object has all its expressions indissolubly together. At its surface, it has them distinguished. In perception, they are separated by the perceiver, preliminary to their union in his judgment. An object translates its expressions into one another. Since the public presence of an object depends on its expressing itself, it is also correct to say that the object's translation can begin and end with its expressed presence.

Grass translates expressions of its presence and various publicized features into one another. You provide a similar translation for your own expressions. The grass and you are, of course, more than such translators. Both the grass and you are expressive, persist, have private, intensive depths and unitary powers.

When I perceive a star over the chimney at night, it is located and has discerned features, just as you do. But unlike you, there is no actual star which can be encountered where the perceived star is located; there is no star there with which I am making contact while it is maintaining itself apart from me. To understand the actual star I must relate its presence at some other time and place to features which presumably would be distinguished were I present in the vicinity of that other time and place.

A star explosion now perceived is not the explosion I would perceive had I existed millions of light years earlier. Were I present there and then, I would undoubtedly add personalized notes to what I discerned, distinguished, and united. The explosion that occurred is what I would perceive could I not only confront the star but could observe it without introducing any personal or relativizing notes. But then it would not be perceived in the way I now perceive. My acknowledgment that something is not in fact where it is now being perceived to be, consequently, does not mean that what I now perceive should be transformed into what I would perceive were I present there. Instead, what I now perceive is to be transformed into what I *conceive* to be objectively perceivable at some other place and time.

Stars and their explosions are not perceived by me either as they now are or as they had been. No one can look into the past any more than he can look into the future. If there is anything perceived, it is perceived by a present man, confronting something in the present. Could I never know what was copresent, I would never have known contemporaries, anyone to love or hate, anyone to discuss with. All conversations would be zigzag over unmeasurable intervals. Yet it is often said that what one perceives is a feature of some past occurrence which, through the act of a perceiver or some other agent, is made available in the present. What is not altogether clear is whether it is also being supposed that what is then confronted is the outcome of a transformation of unperceived and unperceivable, or of unperceived but perceivable features of what had been present at an earlier time and place. If unperceivable, no supposed movement back in time and over space would help one know it; if perceivable, it would be subject to limitations introduced by one who perceives it, and would therefore be different from what is perceived by him now.

If all perceived content must occur later than what occurs, it is not possible to say on perceptual grounds alone how long or short a supposed interval is between the occurrence and what is perceived of it. Consequently it makes no sense to speak of shortening the interval. The interval must be eliminated entirely if one is to assert that what is, is perceived. If any interval remains, no matter what magnitude it be given, what is at the other end will not be perceivable. Were one to insist that the interval links perceivables, one would still have to allow that the past perceivable object could not be reached without moving backward, and in a nonperceivable time. That move would take place in a forward-moving time. It would also intrude into a finished past and change this from one where a perceiver was not present into one where he was.

There are no long-past explosions in the sky which one can see just by looking up at night. Were that possible, it would be possible for one to move backward in time at a speed greater than light's, and somehow be present at an event which, in fact, is no longer occurring. At best, the explosion can be conceived to be perceivable by subjecting what is now seen to imagined transformations and relocations in space and time.

An explosion that is now perceived or that might be perceived, were we present at some earlier time and in another place, has no physical effects. It is not identifiable with a cosmic occurrence taking place independently of all perceivers. If an explosion is discerned through the help of what is perceived by one who is present at the explosion at some earlier time and at some remote place, it is because the explosion that occurs is continuous with what is then perceived of it. The perceived in that case is not distant from what in fact is physically present.

An inference from perceptual content does not get me to what is entirely other than it, unless I could somehow move from a perceptual space and time into some other kind of space and time. If an actual star, as resident in another place and at another time, is what I would perceive were I transported in space and time, it must be continuous with what I would then perceive.

A perceived star and an unperceived star are both able to have distinctive careers outside the common area where they are together. When one of them is taken to be primary, the other is treated as a derivative, permitting the inclusion of only part of what there is, and then under quite narrow conditions. To do justice to what occurs, one must envisage it within the compass of common conditions. One must also recognize that objects form various subgroups, and have independent existences, private ways of uniting factors, and distinctive modes of functioning.

You, your lived body, your body in a world of bodies, what you perceive, and what sustains this are always neutrally together as affiliated, coordinated, intelligible, existent, and valuable, at the same time that they function in limited groups and in some independence of one another. Attention to them in these latter guises neither compromises nor is compromised by the way they function together within more comprehensive frames.

You, whom I perceive, are continuous with you as now being inwardly sustained apart from all perceiving. There is no reason to characterize you solely in terms that are appropriate to an astronomical account of a star. Indeed, to do that I would have to ignore the difference between a man and a thing and between what I now perceive and what I cannot. When I address you, 'you' is merged with you. 'You' and you are then forged into a single addressed you. Thereafter, you can be attended to as that which had already been noted, and can be made the object of further observations and predications. When someone attends to you for the first time, though he may not realize it, the you to which he attends and which he may subsequently address on his own, is laden with a past, a fact made evident by your readiness to accept or reject what is being addressed to you. Were he to learn that you had been previously addressed, he would know that in your depth there were nuances reflecting what had previously occurred.

Grass remains unaffected by the fact that it is attended to again and again. But from the moment a human is addressed by word or gesture, he adds to what he had been. Though every confrontation of you is new, and though there are surprising encounters, typically I make contact with you as a man who had been attended to before, if not by me, then by someone else. Though you may present yourself afresh at every moment, you can therefore rightly be taken to be already known.

By being perceived, you are made into the terminus of an interested act. You are, so far, enriched. You are further enriched by being credited with accountability, since you are then accorded the status of being relevant to something considered to be of importance. As sustained and possessed, you may be taken to be with or without the enrichments. If without, your public nature will be at odds with you as sustained and possessed. Conspicuous or persistent discrepancies between the two will lead to charges of deception, acting, pretense, hypocrisy, naïveté, narcissism, and the like.

Sometimes it is supposed that some intermediary—an intent, purpose, or will—is needed to produce discrepancies between what is perceived and what is not. Discrepancies can occur quite innocently. Occasionally men mislead by simply acting in ways which had not been expected.

A biographer tries to creatively construct a man's career out of what is known from many positions, and to have this portray what he is over time. What is imaginatively con-

structed is different from what is perceived by anyone; it captures what the man is in promise as well as in fact. There is
nothing wrong in a biographer's claims to unite coherently
what the man said and did with what others and the man
himself take him to be; but it would be quite another thing for
the biographer to take the man to be simply one who is accountable for anything and everything that he does, acknowledged or attributed, or not, since he would then be treated as
just the convergent center of a multiplicity of external occurrences. Little or no weight would be given to what the man
takes himself to be, or to the ruminations, hesitations, self-
assessments, doubts, fears, and hopes that enrich his presented you from within. Sometimes these can be surmised
from what he publicly does or from his conversations, diaries,
and notes. More often than not, they require the help of private admissions; autobiography, too, offers data for a sound
biography. The two together yield a man as known from
without, existing over a period, but never fully manifested.

One never gets to more than an enriched you no matter
how deeply one probes or how extensive and steady the re-
construction. One can distinguish less from more enriched
forms, but no one of them nor any combination of them is
equatable with the private originator of what has a possible or
actual public role.

Some psychiatrists judge a man to be deviant to the extent
that he speaks and acts as though he were sustaining a you
that was different from the one others perceive, or for which
he is held accountable. They try to make him aware of the you
he in fact is sustaining, having taken for granted that his deviant speech and acts distort what he really is and intends to
express. But when they suppose that the you which society
endorses is necessarily the better you, they risk making him
conform to conventional and perhaps undesirable and regrettable norms. "My brother married my father," the patient
says. "You mean, your mother married your father," the
psychiatrist urges. "Yes," says the patient, "My brother married my father." The patient apparently cannot bring himself

to say 'mother,' the accepted expression for the spouse of a father. He is looked at by the psychiatrist as having a you which would use only approved expressions were it not now prevented.

To know the you that ought to be sustained, one must know what you ought to be and do. That requires knowing more than what you are publicly known to be, no matter how enriched, no matter how many men agree. "My brother married my father" might have been intended to express an observed close relationship between the father and brother, or a ministerial role assumed by the brother, and so on. The statement—even the persistent refusal to say 'mother'—are deviant if one is supposed to use terms only in the ways others usually do. Granted that a man is ill and that he is having terrible fights with his mother, it still does not follow that his supposed deviant expressions reflect that fact. A man might conceivably ignore the usual ways of speaking in order to express what he ideally is in relation to his brother, mother, and father. And he will continue to have a privacy never fully expressed.

I may hold you to be accountable for past acts which played an important role in the occurrence of something now important. When I do, I transform and dislocate what I discern in the present and root the result in you as an accountable man. That attribution of accountability presupposes your continuance. If you are not selfsame over time, if subsequently you were no more than a later edition of what you had been, and surely if you were just a series of discontinuous, distinct entities, I would be able to hold accountable only what was not the origin of approved or disapproved occurrences, for such an origin, on the hypothesis, would not be present. The you I now know I hold to be accountable for what had been done because I know you to be selfsame over the course of time, even though you do not have the appearance you once had and do not provide the very same perceptual content that you had provided before. I not only distinguish and use what you make available for perception; I reach toward you as perceivable, unifying, and sustaining that distinguished and used perceptual content, knowing all the while that beyond this is a privacy resisting my advance.

The you I address is not relativized. It is not a dislocated perceived object. It is not wholly receptive. Nor is it unknowable. Mediating a discernible presence and a discernible comtemplatable set of features on one level, it unites them on a deeper level. At the same time, it is perceivable and may be perceived. One big difference between my perceiving you and my perceiving a star is that you, and not it, are now present and able to act. Because what occurred has effects, and because some of those effects are perceivable now, it is possible to take what is now seen in the sky to be continuous with what is physically occurring there now. When this is done, the difference between a perception of you and a perception of a star reduces to the fact that what I perceive of you is experienced as merging imperceptibly into a perceivable you and even beyond this, whereas the perceived star is not experienced as merging into anything. There is, though, still no warrant for supposing that the perceived star is in my mind or is projected outside it. All we have a right to say is that, unlike a perceived you, a perceived star does not tell us anything about the nature of the occurrences which are taking place where and when that star is perceived to be.

1.26. You persist.

When I say, "You have changed a great deal since I saw you years ago, playing in the sand with other children," at least three distinct things are taking place:

a) I identify the you who is now with the you in the past. Evidently, I do not stop with you as now being perceived or perceivable. Instead, I move intensively into you, the very individual who acted at an earlier time. I attend neither to the you I perceive nor to a wholly private reality outside the reach of any reference. The one is different at different times; the other is not known by me. I attend, rather, to you as a unitary terminus who is subjected to and reduced by a private power. What is selfsame is the outcome of the exercise of that power; it turns pluralities and changes into nuances of itself. I speak of that outcome as 'you' because I approach it from a position outside it. I know it to be selfsame because I thrust beyond the referent of the 'you' toward your privacy, where all that is attributable to you is reduced to a facet of you. Though that privacy is concentrated in different unities, each with different expressions at different times, it and some of those unities remain constant over time.

I take you to have the capacity to express yourself in many ways, and to possess many different items. The features you exhibit could be dismissed as irrelevant, but only at the risk of cutting you off from what is observable. Your features are partly constituted by you; your contributions to them are ontologically reduced in you, somewhat as the different things you eat are reduced to your one body. You could conceivably remain selfsame if you retained an inviolable core apart from all those features, if you never expressed yourself, or if your privacy and your public existence were rigidly separated. But then, unfortunately, the more successful you were in remaining selfsame, the more surely would you leave nothing for others to observe.

Your identity does not preclude the changes that are making a difference to you. If they did, it would not be correct to say that you had changed. You possess the changes as your own, without losing your identity, at the same time that those changes remain observable to others.

b) I attend to features that you now have, and compare them with those you once had. When I think of those you once had, I do not claim that they are now different from what I remember them to be, but claim that they are now different from those that had been yours. If my memory is questioned, I refer to present features and try to show that they are the outcome of transformations that had occurred in fact.

I could, of course, compare what you now are with what I

remember of you. Were I to do this, I would not ask myself whether or not you are now different from the you I once knew, but would just remark on the difference between what I think you looked like then and what you look like now. Though the features you had then and the features you now have are not altogether compatible, they are to be attributed to the same you, but now as having different weights and roles. Were they attributed to different you's, it would not be correct to say that I remember you, but only that I remember someone I associate with you, perhaps by continuity, name, convention, and the like.

Despite changes, you are selfsame for a period. If you were not, it would be wrong to praise or blame you for what had been done some time before. It is not enough to say that you today may have inherited a you that was in direct line with you. Your mother, too, was in that line, but you are not responsible and are rarely held accountable for what she does or did.

c) A persistent you into which diverse features and acts can be reduced is close to what some have taken to be a pure ego. But the two are not rightly identified. Distinct from what others might relativize, or what you yourself might acknowledge, you are both the locus of what others perceptually distinguish and an objective unity present for them. Distinct from what others can reach, you are continuous with this, intensified, thickened, able to express yourself as a present you.

Backed, sustained, possessed, reduced, you change and yet remain selfsame. Indeed, did you not remain selfsame, you would not change. Every change would be a distinct reality. Your identity, though, cannot be sealed off from the changes without preventing them from being changes of you. These considerations are accommodated in the affirmation that absolute change and absolute constancy are limits, each approached from the position of the other. You remain unchanged because all changes are accepted on your terms. Starting from the changes, it is possible to move indefinitely closer to an unchanging private I or to a private self. Starting from either of these, it is possible to come indefinitely closer to your changing presence in the world. In between these extremes you are neither selfsame nor different, but a selfsameness merging into discriminable new expressions which are distinguished in a public world. You persist in that world because you are a selfsame self apart from it, expressing yourself in it in distinguishable ways.

1.27. What you will be is now indeterminate.

What exists, whether known or not, is determinate, characterizable by the positive or negative of every term. Anything past is also determinate in this sense. As past, though, the inapplicable terms are just absent, whereas in the present, they are excluded. 'Non-red' is now excluded by a present object that is red. A past red object, in contrast, is just not non-red. Unlike either of these, what is not yet, is indeterminate, general, beyond the reach of either positive or negative specific terms. It is neither red nor non-red, but red-or-non-red. There is nothing in the future to separate the components so as to allow one to apply and not the other.

You are directed toward the future; that future is part of you, but a part which has no separable reality and, therefore, cannot be the object of a separate use of the 'you'. When I promise to pay you tomorrow, my promise is made to you now. Tomorrow, the very you that is here today has a right to claim fulfillment of that promise. Until tomorrow, there is no determinate you to make that claim. 'You', used to refer to the you as actually existing tomorrow, needs a terminus which it cannot now obtain. But tomorrow, 'you' will have a determinate, present referent.

I use 'you' today in my reference for what for me is only a future indeterminate. I will terminate the 'you' tomorrow in what will be determinate and present then. The 'you' used in my future reference is merged with what is general; the 'you' used in the present is merged with a determinate terminus.

The 'you', which terminates in a present you, specializes the 'you' used in referring to the future. The first 'you' is merged with what determinatively specializes the second. What is found is necessarily different from what is sought, since it is something present, always more than what is merely future.

1.28. You have a temporal span.

A present moment has an extension, separating past and future. Since different acts stretch over different undivided lengths of time, and since your entire career also occupies a single undivided present, there evidently are many presents of quite different lengths.

You are selfsame over a lifetime. But, also, you first do one thing and then another. You change in many ways. Each change occurs in a distinct, short-ranged present. You, as having such and such momentary features, must also exist a moment at a time.

To deny your identity over time is to deny your present responsibility for what you did. To deny that you change is to deny that the adventures or experiences are yours. Both must be affirmed. The two are compatible because the shorter presents, while distinct from one another, are also inseparably together within a single present. You are diversely manifest in a series of presents while you are unchanged within a single undivided present. The latter is a precondition for the former. Smaller stretches are unseparated abstractable parts of it; they also occur outside it in a temporal sequence. You are selfsame in relation to the one, persistent in relation to the other.

As persistent, you are inseparable from but not identifiable with your body. You are also more fully subject to a productive sustainer than a body could be, since the body is partly determined and limited by other bodies, while you are present for and to them. Present in and through your body, you are also expressed in and through it. The rights you insist on for your body are grounded in you as more than a body, as more than what is bodily manifest, and as more than what is bodily manifestable. You are also able to express yourself in thought, devotion, dedication, grounding these in a more basic, persistent you. Not identifiable with your body or with anything embodied or embodiable, you are nevertheless not identifiable with what is wholly private.

You persist over a lifetime as a single unit. That unit is not altogether evident, but it is also not altogether hidden. There is a thickness to it, enabling one to reach into it, beyond any preassignable degree, through emotionally quickened penetrations. Maintained from within, you are able to persist, to stand in opposition to all others, to be confronted, and to be perceived.

Strictly speaking, there is no you in the past, for the past is the locus of determinate facts, of what has been realized but which is no longer active. Nothing in it has density or depth. Were this not so, the world would be constantly being added to; in the very same location there could be any number of you's. Were these genuine realities, they would mediate action; be able to pass into the future; and do forever what is being done at a particular moment, so that the amount of energy in the universe, instead of being conserved, would be constantly increased.

You have a pace of your own and are together with others in short-ranged and in long-ranged presents. Were you, like a Leibnizian monad, just in a time of your own, there would be no present in which you could be perceived. Nor could you and others, whether quick or slow, reluctant or willing, arrive at the next moment together. But were you simply located in a time shared with others, you would be just time-toned, merely distinguished within a common time, and not temporal, living through a present moment in a distinctive way.

You live through a time of your own. You are also present together with others, moment after moment. Since your contemporaneity with them cannot be due to either of you alone, nor be due to all conjointly (since each exists in its own time and at its own pace), there must be a neutral time which encompasses all. Because you and others exist apart, you and they are able to separate out regions in that neutral time. Through the agency of your distensions, each of you adopts what you separate off, and thereby produces a distinct present. Because what you and others separate off are still part of a single neutral time, you and the others can be contemporaries, together in a common present. Were there no neutral time, there would be many noncontemporary presents of different lengths.

When you lift a chair, you engage in a single act, taking an indivisible present moment. During that interval, your eye blinks, your blood flows, cells and smaller units go through a number of moves. From the standpoint of the present lifting of the chair, the smaller-spanned events make an undivided sequence of distinguishable but not distinct units within that single present time. From the standpoint of any of the smaller-spanned events, the lifting of the chair breaks down into distinct acts occurring one after the other.

A neutral time could conceivably have distinct moments, one following on the other, regardless of what occurred. But then there would be no present moment in which a chair was lifted, unless that lifting happened to coincide with the moment of the neutral time—and then there would be no present moment in which the eye blinked. No type of occurrence could provide a proper temporal unit for others without requiring either a division of the presents of these others, or a union of them so as to constitute a new, larger present.

Newton, who took neutral time to have moments which provide the proper measure for all occurrences, Leibniz and Whitehead who took their stand with the shortest-spanned occurrences, and lawyers, historians, social scientists, and the rest of men who take some middle-sized, human occurrence to provide the proper measure of a unit of time, necessarily distort one another's insights. Since we have no evidence of a Newtonian 'equitably flowing' neutral time, nor of the magnitude of any moments it might contain, we are forced to ac-

cept one of the other views—or find a different answer. Since
the acceptance of the Leibnizian and Whiteheadean view
makes one lose the integrity of the present in which we perceive and act, and in which scientific and other investigations occur, there is no other measure left to use but that already employed in gross, middle-sized activities. There are,
of course, many such measures. The present of a war encompasses many battles, and these encompass many deaths. The
deaths, despite the fact that they occur one after the other,
occur within the single present of the war, where they form an
undivided sequence of items. When they follow one another,
their different presents sequentially divide the larger present
of the war in the way in which the present of the war divides
a larger undivided present.

Contemporaneity results from concurrent divisions made
in a common present. As contained in a larger present, the
concurrent divisions have others after but not later than them.
As outside that larger present, what occurs takes place in
separate, specialized moments. When a number of specializations of the same present have the same magnitude, the occurrences are contemporaries.

Contemporaries divide a common present at the same
points. If two battles are contemporary, they are in presents of
the same magnitude. Within the limits of those battles, a
number of skirmishes occur. When distinguished from one
another, and from the battle, the skirmishes in each battle are
in presents of their own. The skirmishes in one battle are contemporary with those in another battle only indirectly, via
their battles. Since the skrimishes occur only in the battles,
they cannot divide or specialize the present of a war.

1.29. You are a free causal agent.

You are privately possessed while you are relative to others
and while you, with them, are subject to common conditions.
As just a you, you cannot act or even be acted on, for a you is

not a distinct reality. But since you are privately possessed, you are enabled to act, and can be present for others to act on.

As long as you exist, you are accountable. You may be held accountable because you are at a certain place or time, or because you have such and such features or ancestors. No reference need then be made to any intention or act. Some societies, religious, and legal systems attribute accountability on the basis of color, family, appearance, age, or social status. You may also be held accountable for what is produced just by you or for what is taken to originate at you. Because, as just a you, relative to others, you are without power of your own, if held accountable for producing or originating something, you are evidently taken to be an avenue through which power is being expressed.

Since the future is indeterminate and is made determinate through the actions of what is present, all beings necessarily act freely, making an otherwise indeterminate outcome determinate. But only men are responsibly free, accepting as their own the you that may be held accountable for what is publicly produced. Only men govern their bodies and what these can utilize so as to bring about a realization of a prospect that otherwise would remain merely possible. They might be supposed to function in the very ways they would were they not responsible—but only if there is no reference made to the fact that they are freely making use of their bodies.

Were a man forced to act in ways which were contrary to those he could have responsibly begun, he would not be denied his *freedom* but his *liberty*, the ability to act publicly in desired ways. His responsible freedom cannot be diminished and therefore cannot be extinguished. Outside the reach of another's action, it is inevitably expressed. Liberty, though, can be so limited that a man is not able to bring about what he intends, or what he must realize in order to continue or to prosper. All the while he will be able to entertain and privately realize the prospect which the denial of his liberty precluded him from realizing in a public guise.

A man may freely *prefer* some course or object as the best

means to a goal. He may freely *choose* some combination of precondition and objective, and thereby make it his responsibility to compensate for any loss in value that the decision entails. And he may freely *will* by effectively making his body and mind function on behalf of some outcome. All three are privately expressed. None, though, is completely cut off from what is in fact done, though each occurs toward the beginning rather than toward the end of activities which continue in and through the body. Preference is bodily realized in the form of bodily anticipations of what is done; choice is bodily realized in the form of acts along some particular line; will is bodily realized in the form of a controlled body whose activity is to be completed by the attainment of some result. No one of the three, though, is purely bodily. None need come to expression in speech. But none, too, occurs in a closed-off private area.

Though it need not be supposed that there is a private duplicate of what is bodily done, or that a kind of faint or vague rehearsing precedes all bodily activity, it must be allowed that a man can privately begin some of the things that he publicly produces. Some private activities, too, have an incipient or a negative bodily role, while others seem to have none at all. The fact that the private and the public are never entirely separated, that mind and body are always connected, does not preclude their having distinctive roles and powers. It surely does not preclude the existence of a self or of a person, or of private subdivisions of these. A theory which denied that there was anything private would itself be urged as something other than a bodily activity; it would be privately entertained, could be remembered, and might be inferred from.

Theorizing, imagining, and wishing are carried out privately, but not in complete isolation from the body. All involve some degree of bodily control and neglect. At the very least, they are bodily by negation, requiring the body to act with restraint in order for them to be. A man is privately responsible for them, and necessarily, because he is necessarily the private originator of what he privately and publicly does. Held ac-

countable by others, he is himself responsible for being accountable, and also responsible for what, like the use of his I
in thinking, may have no accountable role.

A causal you is the origin of actions. These realize prospects
which are relevant to that you, and perhaps to others. The
realization may occur in the you, in others, here or elsewhere.
Were that you not responsibly governed, it could still have a
causal role; it could still be accountable for what occurs.

Like a prophet who speaks with the voice of another, the
work you do and, therefore, the acts and outcomes which are
properly attributed to you, is work to be credited to a responsible source. Unlike a prophet, though, who supposedly adds
nothing to the message he conveys, you, because of your
body's structures and habits, affect the way the work is done
and what it accomplishes. Though you are not identifiable
with your body, you are not separable from it either, and
neither you nor that body is separable from a private, persistent, responsible source of what is publicly manifest.

You are a publicly acting cause, bodily making a difference
to others, at the same time that you realize relevant prospects.
The effects that you bring about are those relevant prospects
made determinate and present through the help of what is
now present. To do this, available energy is employed by you
so as to accommodate and specialize what had been future.

You are able to be affected by the acts of others. You can be
hurt, blocked, helped, improved, weakened by them. To be
able to function as a cause, you must have already been the
terminus of causal actions. What is affected is you as partly
located in your body. What grounds and connects the distinguished sides of that body need not then be affected. But so far
as you dictate where certain causal acts come to an end and
how, and where they begin and why, you are not only present
but present relative to a past where causes had begun, and
relative to a future where effects will be brought about.

There is a difference between you, understood to be part of
a causal chain, and you understood to occupy a present place
or a present moment. An understanding of your occupation

of a place requires no reference to anything earlier or later, though such a reference is of course required if one wishes to know at what place you had been or will be. You can be an effect only if you are related to a cause; you can be a cause only if you are related to an effect. As both an effect and a cause, you keep hold of what had been and what will be, not in their full concreteness of course, but as a past cause and a possible effect. What exists in a present moment has a concreteness denied to what is past or future.

The features that you possess are the outcome of causal activities, originating both from within you and from without. Each feature is the result of a meeting of internally initiated expressions and external limitations, of external forces and inward replies. Each, too, has connections with features which are distant from it in space and time. Those distant features are not causes. Only realities and what they empower could be causes; only these face relevant prospects and convert them into subsequent actual effects. If one acknowledges only qualities, impressions, or similar passive data, causality is precluded.

Features are inert. Were they taken to be cut off from all else to constitute a domain of their own, we would have to look elsewhere for what could be causes and effects. On the hypothesis, these would be devoid of all features. If we then went on to assume that causality was confined to a mind or similar agent, the presence and nature of the features would be left unexplained. Indeed, they would not only be inexplicable but would be final realities, not features at all, since they would not belong to any object.

As a mere occupant of a region of space or of a moment of time, you are present for others. Because you are also possessed by what insists in and through you, producing different expressions in response to what is impinging, you are able to be involved in causal processes. What occurs is so far understandable as the outcome of your private answers to the impingements.

Whatever is rightly credited to you may be utilized by you. You bring the effects and actions of others to a stop, and add to them within the limits of common constraining conditions. What you undergo on your side is not known by me. But it is also not known by you, if by 'knowing' we mean what is articulated, communicable, available to another. It is also true that what you undergo on your side is knowable both by you and by me, for what we can observe of you manifests what you are undergoing. Your features, language, and ways tell us too much in fact, for they also tell something about the effects others and common constraining conditions have, but without distinguishing these from your contributions. A satisfactory knowledge of what you are undergoing is hampered by your and my lack of understanding of what others contribute to what you make publicly available, as well as by your and my incapacity to progress into you intensively for more than a short distance.

You express yourself in multiple ways. You are confronted from the position of common constraints and can be confronted by other men. You are also the continuation of a persistent, expressive, unitary power, private, responsible, possessive, more than but also inseparable from what is publicized. When you act—let us say, throw a ball—you function as a unit being who determines the way in which your arm and hand will function. The traditional view is that you then exercise your will. The account fails to recognize that the movements of your hand and arm affect your entire body, and that you can act without consciousness or intention. And unless men were without evolutionary relation to other beings, we would also have to allow for a primitive form of that will in what is not human.

All actualities make an effort to become self-complete. This effort is directed at a common possibility realized in different ways by actualities and, within their limits, by their parts. A society, an army, a mob make no such effort.

A man can be dedicated, concerned; he can be interested in

a possibility, and thereby provide some check on the way it will be realized. An animal can focus on a possibility, but cannot dedicate itself to realizing it. A thing also can be related to a possibility, but cannot attend to it in any way. Only man has the ability to make a possibility have the role of a guide and governance for himself.

The functioning of actualities requires a reference to possibilities. In the case of men, the possibilities are the object of what is distinct from their unities and from their parts. I attend to you as distinctive in this way. I take you to be accountable for what is done by you as a unity and by you as encompassing parts, because I take you to have the ability to empower a possibility and thereby to partly control what the unity and the aggregate of parts are able to do.

Your causal power, a power exercised only so far as you are involved with what is bodily possible, requires a reference to and a control by the possibility. Though the act is not observable, I know it is distinct from what is possible to a self beyond that you, for this is able to deal responsibly with the possibility and not merely to act accountably with its help.

1.30. Causation is an observable necessitation.

There is no causation if there is only a dynamic process, for then there would be no causes with which to begin nor effects with which to end. There is no causation, also, if there are only causes and effects, since there then would be no dynamic move from one to the other. Nor is there causation if there is only a law or structure between cause and effect, for then there would be no production of an actual effect. And, of course, there is no causation if there are only detached inert items. But if there were no causation, if there were nothing produced through activities begun earlier and able to realize possible effects, there would be no one who could act responsibly. Anyone taken to be accountable, also, would have the status not of a source of effects but only of an identified point of origin, or of an identified object of a reward or punishment. One would then have to allow that no man might ever act, make, produce, or create, commit a crime, work, play a game, reward or punish, or affirm anything about the nature of causation. The situation is not remedied by supposing that causality is a category, for that does not enable one to take care of the fact that different men bring about different outcomes in different ways, at different paces, sometimes responsibly, always with some accountability, and perhaps without knowing that they are active, or that anything is being produced. Nor is a remedy provided when it is supposed that what is subsequent preserves what had preceded it, for this still leaves untouched the fact that actions are begun before they are ended and often enough begun in order to be ended in such and such ways by what comes later. Causes have effects in which nothing of those causes may be found.

At least six factors must be considered if causation is to be characterized satisfactorily: 1) There must be an actuality able to initiate acts artd to do this before the effects can be actual. 2) Time must pass. Produced effects follow initiating causes in time. 3) There must be a possible effect relevant to an actual cause. Actual effects must first be possible; and they must be possible for their causes. 4) An actual cause and a possible effect must be linked by necessity, if it is possible to rationally conclude to the nature of an effect once the cause is known. 5) There must be an actual process of causation in which the possible effect is converted into an actual effect, replacing the cause in a new present. 6) Finally, the effect must be detached from its cause, if it is to be able to function as a cause or part of a cause, independently of its own cause or the necessitating process that brought the effect into existence.

Causation occurs within the limits of a formal necessitation linking an antecedent cause and a possible effect. There the formal necessitation is given a dynamic role. Consequently, for causation to be known, it must be possible to know the cause, a relevant possible effect, and the way that possible effect is dynamically converted into an actual effect at a time subsequent to that in which the cause began to operate. Because I know my weight, I know some of the things I can do. Because I know the nature of the wooden step, I know some of the things it can do. When I am about to stand on the step I envisage the possibility—I-standing-on-the-step—which the step and I together face. If I stand on the step, I realize that possibility in a specific, not altogether predictable, way and enable the step to have it realized in another correlative way. I cannot, of course, perceive possible effects; nor can I perceive the conversion of possible into actual effects. Possibilities are not perceived; nor are actualizings of possibilities. But I can and do think of them. Otherwise I could not rightly say that I know what might be if I did so and so, or that I sometimes know that what could have happened did in fact occur.

When we attend initially and primarily to what seems steady and unchanging, or whose role seems to be minor, we often speak of causation as though it were the work only of other factors. We may wrongly ground it in just one actuality. Whether or not we do this, we should recognize that every effect involves the realization of possibilities that are pertinent to many causal powers. For practical purposes, it may be desirable to emphasize those pertinent to only one or a few. The landlord says that I broke the step, while I remark that I fell because the step was worn down. The effect, my-falling-through-a-broken-step, requires the step and me to realize a common possibility in distinct but conjoint ways. What the step realizes is a delimited version of the very possibility I realize in another form. Both realizations occur at the same time and thereby constitute a caused effect involving the step and me. Before the actual effect occurs no one knows just what it will be in its full specificity, in part because that full specificity is constituted then and there as the outcome of the realization of the possible effect. No actions are mere logical products. To be, they must be produced, not deduced.

1.31. You exist.

As at once spatial, temporal, and dynamic, you are an existent, mediating between the features which owe their presence in part to others and imposed conditions. What is
perceived may be quite unlike that existent. There can be
perceptual errors. But what a perceiver knows when he
perceives you has a constituent which was expressed by you
apart from the perceiver. That constituent continues in depth
into you as inwardly possessed and maintained in opposition to all else, at once existent, individual, and real, with a
nature and value. These are independently present. If any is
taken to exhaust your essential nature, the others will be
reduced to arbitrary or adventitious factors. Were you essen-
tially only an existent, you would not be a genuine individual, an independent being, or have a rationale or status of
your own.

1.32. You have value.

Animals are held accountable by men, not by themselves.
They can also be accountable even if not held accountable; accountability is then taken to characterize them for making
possible what benefits or injures themselves or others. They
will be good or bad depending on what goods or bads are due
to them. Warrant for such an extension of the term will allow
one to hold that things, too, are accountable for what benefits
or injures them or others. It is better, therefore, to restrict accountability to what in fact is held accountable. This will
still—though at infrequent times—be found to include
things. Even if these be eliminated, accountability will have a
variable range. Value, in contrast, is a constant, expressing the
degree an item approximates the state of a final excellence.

What deserves to be held accountable has a status higher
than that which could not be so held. To be responsible is to

have a still higher status. This is man's privilege. Only a man is to be blamed or condemned for responsible acts. If also rewarded or punished, it is usually for the purpose of altering him in such a way that he will have a value in the new situation expressing the fact that he is its indispensable precondition.

A value is the worth of something, marked out by its place in a hierarchy of greater and greater excellencies. The holding all men to be intrinsically equal in value attests to the recognition of them as occupying the same rank within the hierarchy. Each there has a value equal to that of every other because of what he is in himself, a being who can express himself responsibly, controlling and accepting as his own the you that he presents and the body which he lives through and uses.

The rewarding and punishing of men and animals normally testifies to our understanding of them as able to act, to be present over a period of time, and yet to be alterable through benefits and disabilities produced in consonance with the increases or decreases in value credited to them. They, and things as well, have values no matter what our evaluations, or whether we evaluate them at all. Each has a place in a hierarchy determined by the degree to which it conforms to the demands of a final excellence. According to the degree to which it can become part of that excellence without having to be altered, each has a higher or lower position relative to this. Were there no such hierarchy, we would have to be content with taking value to rest on the questionable supposition that because men find something to be good, it is good.

Because a final unifying excellence is itself subject to other conditions, it also has value. The kind of value it then has, of course, is different from the kind it enables others to have, since the values it obtains from other finalities merely mark the degree to which it must be altered if it is to be reduced to them. Since it is independent of them, its value is not high; since it is compatible with them, it is not negligible either. We do not usually speak of these values. 'Value' as a rule requires a reference only to the position which something has in a hierarchy governed by a final, excellent Unity. It is hard to determine just where something fits in that hierarchy. For the most part, we must be content to attend to the comparative place an item has in relation to a few others, and to do this in a rough and ready way. Little harm, though, is to be expected from this practice, particularly if the evaluations that are important are persistently maintained, are widely accepted, and rarely need be precisely distinguished from one another.

A man has an intrinsic value because of the kind of standing he has in an objective hierarchy. He has other values depending on what he does to make other items have a higher or lower position there than they otherwise would have. Though his features have no intrinsic value, they accrete value from his intrinsic value. When we take some of those features to be congenial, repugnant, attractive, ugly, likable, and so on, we incidentally evaluate them. The evaluations tell at least as much about us who attend to them in these ways as they do about the beings to which the features belong. When we differ from one another and from other beings in our assessments of the features and of the actualities to which these are ascribed, our positions in an objective hierarchy of value are not seriously affected. An objective world of values allows for many relative and fluctuating assessments of abstractable aspects of what we confront. What is done because of those assessments, of course, may make a great difference to the values that are objectively present.

The assessment of a man varies from time to time, and from assessor to assessor. All the while, he has an objective value because of his place in an objective hierarchy, and an acquired value because of what he does. The objective value can be made pertinent to the assessment by understanding the objective value to function as a means for so transforming the assessed that the result is equal to the objective value.

1.33. Your value is absolutized.

Your objective value permeates your substantiality, reality, nature, and existence. Conversely, that value is individuated, maintained, given a rational role, and endowed with an insistence, all permeating the value. Possessed in an individualized and persistent form, that value is enjoyed from within and is so far absolutized, merging with other absolutized, intensified facets of you, in a single lived through, centered unity. Made manifest through a multiplicity of expressions, most of which are bodily, and some of which continue on into the common world of language, societal action, and causality, you can be confronted from various positions. What is expressed in and through your body, and therefore in and through you as conditioned by other actualities, is an intrinsic value come to expression in transient ways in the form of multiple claims.

1.34. A value is implicated in the use of 'you'.

As confronted, you are distinguishable from you as abiding. In the one guise, you are relative to those who confront you; in the other, you are the derelativized locus of all the relativizations. The latter grounds the former; abiding, you are more than what is confronted, but less than what is outside all relationships.

A proper name adheres to its referent. It reaches to you who abide, and is accommodated by what is beyond this, centered and dense. 'You', used to substitute for such a proper name, is a term of address, and is intended to be accompanied by a respect for the individual addressed. Inevitably, it carries an imputation of responsibility and an implicit acknowledgment that inwardly sustained values had been initially derived from a position in an objective hierarchy. When not used in this way, 'you' serves just to mark you off, to point you out. It then becomes a mere sign, unable to adhere and thereby to become one with that to which it is referred.

You have an objective value because of what you are in an objective hierarchy. You have a social value as well, determined by what is traceable back to you as an origin of publicizable expressions. Once there is an awareness that you are more than such an origin, and that you continue and are backed by what has an objective value and is able to initiate many other occurrences in a career extending over considerable time, 'you' may be used with a sense of that fact. And though no outside agent can reach the absolutized value you inwardly maintain, once it is known that there is such an inwardly maintained absolutized value, 'you' will take one toward it, beyond any preassignable point.

We usually speak considerately to those we meet for the first time, not because we make a quick analogy between them and others with whom we had been acquainted, or between them and ourselves, and then unhesitatingly attribute to them the values which had before been acknowledged to belong to others. Such analogies presuppose a knowledge of ourselves and others, require some reflection, have little warrant, and are surely hazardous, for we do not know much of others when we first confront them, and rarely have clear enough knowledge of ourselves or of others to ground a comparison. We deal with other men immediately, with confidence, using adherent terms successfully. Even when we speak to someone whom we do not know, we may use 'you' to refer to him as having an absolutized value. We proceed at once to use the 'you' with some of the meanings which accreted to it when we spoke to those with whom we had already been acquainted. Departures from such use in the direction of less penetrative references deviate from the norm.

Though we tend to take 'you' to function like an effectively adherent term, we still do not, for most purposes, wish to reach much below the surface of those whom we confront. We restrain ourselves, refusing to allow the term full play and thereby, while remaining alert to the fact that another has a depth and is worthy of respect, minimize the adherent role of the 'you'. Consequently, while the values that men have ground the adherent terms by which we address them, those values are not always acknowledged to be in all those to whom respect is due.

The titles and proper names that are used for the first time on meeting bureaucrats, officials, new acquaintances, and even strangers, are accompanied by intonations and gestures which give the terms an import approximating those possessed by 'you', when this is not allowed full play. As a consequence, respect is indicated without attention being paid to the reality to which that respect is due. It is correct, therefore, to say that we then ascribe values which are a function of discourse, provided that it be added that the discourse acquires the power from beings already known.

A porter, waiter, or bus driver is usually not dealt with as an individual with a value confronted and absolutized. We speak to them to mark them out, to make them attend, and more likely than not ignore their status as men. But it is not entirely correct to say that there is then no awareness of them as men and therefore of the fact that they have objective values confronted and absolutized. Should they stumble, cry out in pain, or bleed, they are responded to at once as men having the kind of values possessed by others with whom we are on more familiar terms. Should they suddenly seem to be in serious danger, the responses we make will more often than not bear on their objective values, and we will deal with them in ways we do not deal with animals or things.

When we see men being denied rights that others are enjoying, we may attend to them as having the rights, and therefore take them to be men who are being unjustly treated. Such responses are not always forthcoming. Rarely are they precise or free from prejudice and distortion. But just as surely, they are guided by values reached and glimpsed, if only for fleeting moments. It is doubtful whether anyone is ever entirely oblivious of the humanity of other men—even of those he seems not to notice. 'You', used when speaking to enemies, the despised, or to men engaged in menial tasks, inevitably comes to rest beyond merely located entities. It insensibly moves toward what has confronted and objective values. Those values may be ignored; one may try to reduce them. But no one succeeds in separating them off or freeing them from all relationship to individual absolutized values, themselves actually if only faintly discerned. Even the Nazis did not deal with those whom they abused as though they were devoid of all value. On the contrary. They took their victims to have accountable negative values for having supposedly brought about public evils; to have objective negative values for having a negative rank in a hierarchy in which the Nazi members of a state or nation alone could measure up to a final standard of excellence; and to have absolute negative values because they were supposed to be inwardly what they had been outwardly credited with being. The Nazis misconstrued, not the accountability or responsibility of their victims, but what it was they were justly accountable or responsible for. Nor were they mistaken in thinking that their victims had a negative value within the Nazi hierarchy of values. But they were viciously wrong in acting on the idea that this hierarchy could be absolute, despite the fact that it was incapable of allowing for the truth that all men are equally men. The Nazis took their victims to have absolute values, but not the ones they in fact had, and then brutally acted in terms of the wrong assessments.

It would be callous to accept the implications of some recent philosophies and say that the Nazis' cruelties were due to linguistic errors or to a failure to think, that they were merely intentional and confined to the mind, that they just went counter to conventions, or that they simply opposed the private hopes of their victims. It would be wrongheaded to take the Nazis to have been so inured to evil that its presence no longer affected them. The Nazis properly used such terms of address as 'Jew' with great skill, and they were most acutely aware of the negative value of what they wanted to eliminate. They had a devil theory of the origin of evil, leading them to take what they deplored to be the outcome of the presence of wicked spirits. These, when present in men, were thought to make the men inescapably corrupt, the source of public evils. Having given up the idea that the devil could be exorcised, the Nazis found no other recourse but the destruction of those he had supposedly corrupted.

The devil, for the Nazis, worked through the course of history, ruining both the spirit and the genes of some men while leaving others entirely alone, pure and good. If the Nazis assumed that their victims provided just residences for the corruption, they also incidentally supposed that the corrupted and the corrupting were so far different. If so, that consequence was ignored. All men were fixated by the Nazis as being either positively or negatively toned. Stopping short with what had been fixated, the Nazis took this to be the locus of absolute values, and thereby precluded themselves from understanding what their victims were in themselves. The absolute values that those men in fact had were then not only misunderstood but were not connected with what the men were publicly seen to be.

If a term of address, with its tacit acknowledgment of the humanity of the individual addressed, necessarily entrains respect, should this not have precluded the Nazis' unspeakable treatment of the Jews? It would have, had the terms of address not been kept from their proper termini, had the values reached not been obscured by an emphasis on the supposed negative values for which men were being held accountable, and had these values not been identified with absolutely negative values set in an objective hierarchy.

1.35. 'You' may have a fixated referent.

In contracts and other official documents, even when the proper names of men are explicitly used, reference is made, not to what the men are in an objective hierarchy of values, or to what each is privately, but to them in a social world where they are required to function accountably in specific ways. Social security numbers would have served just as well. The documents, in effect, use 'you's' impersonally, as having referents riding on the surface of what the men in fact are. But because you are sustained responsibly, what is required by a document can be brought about freely, from within, without having to have recourse to externally produced enforcements.

The referent of 'you' is you. If you were not grounded from within or fixated from without, you would not be able to provide the 'you' with a referent. Since an impersonally designated you is rarely maintained steadily at a constant position, or in such a way that all others are able to attend to it, the you to which the 'you' of a document refers has to be further determined. Because convention and custom have ill-defined borders and requirements, the determination requires a controlling of the reference. One way is by using rules which are backed by an enforceable, viable, legal system. Documents thereby become instruments determining how and where 'you' applies. Since the 'you' in documents is legally used to refer to units in a public order, when the rights and duties that the legal system and its documents impersonally ascribe fail to do justice to what men are themselves sustaining, the legal system will prove to be indifferent to or in conflict with those for whom, and perhaps even by whom, the system is instituted.

The United States Constitution speaks impersonally of many men and sometimes impersonally of individuals who may occupy particular offices. The rights and duties that it specifies refer to them, not as they are in themselves, but as within an area defined by a legal system. Strict constructionists of the Constitution are content to take the rights and duties of men to be completely and exhaustively expressed by that document, and to require only the determining aid of the legally enforceable system. These strict constructionists could be strong defenders of a legal democracy, where this is understood to be a state in which laws are interpreted and applied with rigorous impersonality. But their position fails to do justice to a human democracy in which public meaning and support are given to some of the rights that men have acquired over the course of history, as well as to some of the rights men natively possess.

Strict constructionistic Nazis were not wrong to interpret their laws in the way they did. But they failed to see that their laws could not be applied without going counter to the warrant for a state. In effect, their laws had to do with men in limited roles; the laws conflicted with what men objectively are, with what they are responsible for, and with what they make available for public designation and control.

1.36. 'You' can be anticipatorily ascribed.

The Nazis were consistent when they used the physically and mentally defective for experiments, since the defectives, like the Nazis' political enemies, were defined to be outside the world to which whole, genuine men belonged. These unfortunates are better seen to be deviants who could conceivably be brought into intelligible connection with the rest, and perhaps helped to become normal. No one who had ever been involved in the human community, particularly if he had engaged in discourse, should ever be taken to have lost all contact with it.

Would not such an approach be so arbitrary that it justifies the view that animals have the same rights men have? Indeed, some animals—particularly those which are responsive to what is said to them—seem to be even better candidates for an admittance to the human community than the congenitally idiotic. This consequence can be avoided if we accept as crucial the acknowledgment of the existence of a human that takes place at birth, or even earlier, at the first feeling of a quickening. If we take idiots to be inwardly human, we can and should treat them as incipient members of the human community, hoping that eventually a way will be found by which one can convert them into full interplaying members.

These considerations have some bearing on the current question of the nature of the difference between men and machines. A machine exists within a world of present physical entities, with a structure reflecting something of men's interests. A man has a reality in himself; his structure, unlike a machine's, is not introduced by other men in order to make a sequence out of the operation of various parts. Men and machines differ, too, in the manner in which they reject various items. A machine rejects what is not accommodable by it. A man, in addition, can dismiss what is not compatible with some possibility. Where a man dismisses with the help of a possible outcome whose realization the dismissed precludes, a machine simply rejects what does not fit its structure or functioning.

Men reject some things because there is an incompatibility between those things and what the men are and do, but men also dismiss some things because, unlike a machine, the men bring prospects to bear, with which the considered items are not compatible. Men engage in acts which are partly determined by the way they accept various possibilities. When 'you' is used to address a man who differs considerably in behavior and appearance from those to which 'you' is usually ascribed, it is in anticipation of the discovery that he will, like us, bring possibilities to bear to determine what he does—the anticipation itself being an instance of such a use of possibilities. A complete account, of course, must attend to other conditions besides possibility, which he uses effectively. But these are rarely to the fore.

1.37. 'You' has a collective and a distributive use.

A number of people may be addressed at the same time by means of 'you', usually with the help of a reference to some shared characteristic. "You cadets . . . ," "You writers . . ." begin references to a number of unspecified individuals dealt with in terms of common features. The plural 'you' is also used distributively. "You—Mary, Tom, and Sarah—go to the blackboard" refers to them individually. Neither of these uses is altogether separate from the other. A group is addressed, but as a group of individuals, some of whom are usually held accountable. And when different men are referred to by means of the distributively plural 'you', they are attended to at the same time, sharing the common fact of being so attended, and perhaps also of being directed to the same things.

Because of the distributive component in the collective 'you', the various distinctions appropriate to a 'you', used with reference to a single individual, are pertinent there as well, though usually in minor ways. So far as the collective component is dominant and operative, the objective and absolutized values of the individuals are forced into the background.

1.38. You have a predominantly bodily role.

As an individual, you think, feel, hope. You cannot be identified with a body; you cannot even be identified with the capacity to express yourself bodily. When you are held accountable, to be sure, it is primarily as an active or activated body, and when 'you' is used collectively, it is usually of a number of living embodied or bodily beings. Though for most purposes, 'you' refers to what has a bodily role, that role and the body are privately sustained by what is able to express itself in other ways as well.

A human body is complex. It is a unit, extended but undivided. It also encompasses a number of organs operating together, a multiplicity of cells interrelated regardless of the organs in which they are found and where they have distinctive roles, a multiplicity of smaller chemical units which are related to the cells as these are to the organs and to the unit complex, and a multiplicity of physical particles which have a similar relation to the chemical units that the chemical units have to the cells. As confined within the limits of some subdivision of you, items are related to those subdivisions as parts to wholes; as just confined within the limits of your body, they are parts of it. You have various types of parts within a physical, chemical, biological, complex body.

Some of your organs are known. Occasionally, you might attend to a cell or even to a smaller part. But you do not know or deliberately act with reference to the ultimate physical particles which are within your body. Yet these play an inescapable role. It is they which dictate the rate of your fall, which sum to your weight, which make you subject to cosmic physical laws. The functioning of your body cannot be understood if their presence and influence are ignored.

Though often enough you are occupied with what is not your body or its parts, you are also unavoidably involved in the realization of conditions which are diversely, independently, and partly realized by both in specialized forms. Possibilities and other conditions are used by you to control your activities. They then incidentally provide a common area for realizations by the body and its parts.

You help make your body be a whole for parts, and smaller units be parts of that whole. If you did not do this, your body would stretch over the region where the parts were, but not be their whole, while the parts would form a merely arbitrary selection from the entire set of all such items, most of which have nothing to do with that whole. There are parts for just that whole and a whole for those parts because the parts and whole are related to one another through the agency of the conditions that you help realize.

Though there is no human body without parts and no parts in the absence of the body, the parts and the body have distinctive natures. They also satisfy common conditions in distinctive ways. But you are more than either, and more than both together. You have a privacy, only part of which is bodily expressed. Because of that privacy, it is possible for you to know yourself as a me.

CHAPTER 2

You and Me

2.1. A me is partly coincident with a you for another.

THE QUESTION, "Who is there?", we are taught, is properly answered by "It is I." The French know better. They say "C'est moi." We, too, answer with "It is me" when we answer the question in daily life, for we, too, know that what is being asked is who is present in a public world. We want to know if it is a member of the family, a friend, a messenger, or a delivery boy who is there. We are not being asked a metaphysical question about what is beyond all public guises, perhaps could never be fully known, and surely is never publicly encountered, and we do not try to answer such an unasked question.

In the exchange, "I would like you to take that package." "You mean me?" language is used quite well to express what is intended. Yet the respondent, in the attempt to confirm who is being addressed, shifts from a reference to himself in the role of a you, addressed through the use of a 'you' by another, to a reference to himself by means of a 'me' used by and only of himself. The you to which a reference was made by another is effortlessly replaced by a publicly approached me which the individual takes himself to possess.

It is possible to imagine oneself attending to oneself from the position which another occupies. I do something like this when I make an effort to free myself from a personal bias so as to grasp the objective import of my speech and acts. Neither

then nor at any other time do I succeed in occupying the position of someone else. I cannot become you, refer to others by
means of your 'you', or know you as a me. I cannot make use
of 'you' to confirm or repeat what you are doing when you
refer to me. What you take to be a you when you attend to me,
I cannot take to be a you at all. And what I take to be a me
when I attend myself, you can face only as a you. If I am
to attend to what you do, I must, on imagining myself as
attending to me from your position, refer to a me even though
you, at that position, refer only to a you. The you to which you
refer does, though, coincide, in part at least, with my me. But I
alone can attend to me. The you you know is not the me I
know. Like that me, though, the you is confronted as continuing into a dense depth. To know that you are referring to me in
the guise of a you is to know you to be penetrating toward but
not reaching as far as I can to what is sustaining what each of
us terminates at. The coincidence of the depth at which you
arrive, with part of the depth at which I do when I attend to
me, grounds a partial coincidence of the you at which you
arrive with the me at which I arrive. I know of the coincidence
of the you and me at which we severally arrive, so far as I
know that you are reaching into a depth that I pass beyond,
via the me.

Both the you at which you arrive and the me at which I do,
are blocked by the same resistance. We both can know that resistance. We both can experience it. But only I am able to provide and undergo it, and only I can penetrate it maximally.

I can say to myself, "You need a shave." "You are not looking well," "You are not very considerate." When I speak to
myself in these ways, I hold my publicly confrontable me
apart from the rest of myself. I distance it, and therefore leave
some doubt about the relation that holds between it and what
else I am. I could take the me, which I might roughly identify
with a you to which you had referred, into an extension or
phase of my privacy. Indeed, to see that to which you do or
might refer, I must allow my me to be alienated from my privacy, and so far to cease to be a true me, a me which is wholly

mine, a me to which I both refer and meet insistently from a depth another never entirely penetrates.

Having heard another say, "You need a shave," I do not say, "Me need a shave." The child must be corrected if it says "Me am a Jew," "Me am a girl." All are to say, "I," because the you to which another refers has been transformed by each into a possessed continuation of an irreducible referring private power. This is not dependent for its existence on a reference being made to it, nor does it have to be available for such a reference.

Though a me is in a public setting, it continues into what possesses it, alters its import, and determines its career. That possessor will defeat the closest scrutiny, even though it is penetrated toward by others who confront it as a you, and penetrated even further by myself who confront it as a me.

Though I am never directly and entirely known by myself or by another, I do provide evidence of who I am by what I express. There is no item that is necessarily and forever hidden, but there also is no knowing which exhaustively captures all that is. At the very least, the living through of the knowing will remain outside the knowledge of it. This result is not due to human weakness. Even an omniscient being must stop short of the inward being of what he knows, for his knowledge too is distinct from what is known. At most he knows that what he knows is fully in accord with that of which it is the knowledge. If it is men who are known, they will insistently live in depth what he or others grasp as grounded you's, and which the men themselves grasp as grounded me's. The grounding in both cases is beyond the reach of an approach through either. Both the fact that it occurs and the nature it has can be known speculatively, by reflecting on what must be if there are to be you's and me's.

The you to which you in fact attend, when you attend to me, I can partly identify with my me. If I do not do this, the you at which you terminate will remain remote, relativized, strange, and perhaps defied or denied. But I cannot make a complete identification of the you and the me, because the you will always remain oriented toward what is distinct and distant from myself, while the me is always oriented toward the very being who attends to it.

2.2   A me faces in two directions.

You, as reached from the standpoint of another, may give way to your me, also reached from beyond you, but now by you. You are attended to by another who is distinct and distant from you. Your me, instead, is attended to only by yourself, though it may be reached only after something else was attended to and used as a pivot, making it possible to turn back from there, with or without accretions, to terminate at what is sustained at a deeper, denser level, by the I which refers to that me.

When accompanying an indication of the public role I have, 'me' has the status of a grammatical subject; when it does not, it is a grammatical object, primarily what denotes the inwardly sustained end of a self-reference. It has that self-referential role even when I speak of me as the object of an act initiated by another. "You hit me," "Give it to me," "Don't stare at me," all make implicit use of some such additional expression as ". . . the one whom I both know and sustain." I refer to the terminus of your act, the additions make clear, as that which I possess in my own way.

A me is reached by the very I that accepts it as continuous with itself. I, not another, terminates in me, and I do so only because I continue to sustain it. That me, consequently, faces in two directions, toward a public world and away from this. The reference of 'me' to a me, which is both approached from without and sustained from within, stands in the way of a complete identification of 'me' with 'you', or of me with you.

A man holds on to the you to which others refer, and thereby modifies the import of the you for himself. He may exaggerate or minimize the status that the you has for others. Rarely will he get it exactly right. Acknowledged from without, his you is public; accepted from within, it is transformed. What is true of the you is both like and unlike what is true of the me. Both are acknowledged from without, but the you is acknowledged by another whereas the me is acknowledged only by oneself. Both are transformed. But the you is transformed into me-as-known-by-another, whereas the me is transformed into I-as-known-by-myself.

2.3. 'Me' inescapably addresses me.

'You' may be used when you are not present, and even when you are not reachable. The mother calls out to her child, "I need you," but the child may not be within the reach of her voice. The same situation cannot occur when use is made of 'me'. 'Me' never lacks its proper terminus. It is not merely referential. It is the verbal part of a reference which always and necessarily reaches me.

'Me', to be sure, is a word in language. Since the words in a language remain words even when not in use, 'me' evidently exists even when not directed at me. It can have a role in a story, and could be used to address a mirror image or picture. Apparently, in opposition to what was just said, it is not only distinguishable from me but is sufficiently independent of it as to require an act by which it is hazardly referred to an actual me. That conclusion is avoided with the recognition that 'me' in use is distinct from 'me', a word in our language. The latter cannot be put to work except by being modified, since it is impossible to use it without having it immediately arrive at and be attached to its referent.

A referential 'me' is a perfect proper name. The terminus which it infallibly reaches and adheres to is both possessed by and is continuous with an I, an object of respect. Even when one despises oneself, speaks of oneself as empty or unfathomable, or tries to withdraw from all public activities, one honors oneself as the referent of a proper name. But though a perfect proper name, 'me', unfortunately, is not a very useful one, since it cannot be used by anyone other than the man to whom it is addressed. It would be ridiculous for you to say 'me' and, instead of pointing to yourself, point to me.

The necessarily effective semantic role of 'me' brakes its syntactical connection with other words and allows it to function outside discourse. Its departure entrains departures by various clarifying expressions as well—". . . the butcher," ". . . the man, with whom you just spoke," and so on—by means of which others can know what public aspects I am emphasizing.

Orthodox Jewish theologians say that God's name is known only to himself. It must, therefore, be some variant of 'me', since this is the most proper name of a being who refers to himself. It should not then be said that God answered a question by Moses with the gnomic, "I am that I am." If he referred to himself, he should have been recorded as answering, "I am me." That certainly is no more informative than the other but it, not the other, could be enriched by having it carry meanings which tell what is encountered at the me and which, presumably others might be able to note. If, as orthodox Judaism maintains, God refers to himself by a secret name that no one else can know, it will be by a 'me' secretly elaborated and enriched. That 'me', though, could be used by him only if he came to himself from without. A creating God would presumably do this by pivoting at the world beyond him. He would, to speak with Spinoza, come to his *natura naturans* via his *natura naturata*.

2.4   The referent of 'me' is a sustained me.

The me at which I arrive when using 'me' is an integral part of myself. I make it that with which the 'me' is joined, while I penetrate beyond that point toward what continues to function and to be apart from it, the I. There is, of course, not first a 'me' and then a limit set for the me. The me is sustained by the I at the very same time that that I refers to it by means of 'me'.

I come to me from an outside position at the same time that I sustain the me from within as an attenuation of that I.

When the me functions as a terminus for 'me', it is also possessed from within. Possessed, it is *mine*, myself continued, not just the termination of a reference. It is the limit of an expression, the point at which I responsibly hold myself accountable. I may well deserve reward or punishment for public acts traceable to me. But because the determination of my accountability for what in fact occurs does not suffice to determine my responsibility, even for that accountability, my deserved rewards and punishments may diverge considerably from my deserved praise or blame.

The you I am for you and my me are reached independently, from different positions, with different intentions, entraining different auxiliaries and means. The you is sustained at a point where public interactions end; the me is sustained at a point where I responsibly assume accountability. In order to know myself as others know me, I must abandon my private approach to and my sustaining of me and try to look at myself as though I were just a sustained you. I never succeed; I cannot come to myself exactly the way others do, for I never can entirely free my me either from its sustaining I or from a reference by that I. Inevitably, my me is referred to from a distinctive position and is sustained at a distinctive point, both with an emphasis which is determined independently of what is reached by you.

2.5. There are three ways to determine accountability.

Others and I may take me to be accountable for different things. Neither attribution may coincide with what I responsibly make accountable in the very act of sustaining me. Since all three determinations may coincide, two may coincide but be discrepant with a third, or all three may be different, five cases are possible:

a) "I do not only accept as right the decisions of my superiors," says the subordinate, "but I know no other duty, no other right or wrong than that." A public determination of his accountability is accepted as being at a me which he sustains.

b) "I know that I am innocent," says the indicted man, reporting his intentions. "You are guilty," says the judge, fixing him at a different position, where illegal acts are accountably begun. "What I did was inadvertent," he replies, fixing himself at still another place, but in the very public world where the judge had taken him to be.

c) "You are a hero," the others say. "I did not know what I was doing," the honored man says to himself, "but I must admit that I did not shrink from facing the onrush of the enemy." The point at which he is identified by others, he does not take to be the proper point, but he does take it to be one he in fact sustained.

d) "I live up to my public duties," says the conscientious official, "but I have my own opinion whether what is done is right or not." He acknowledges his me to be where he is held to be accountable, but still sustains it elsewhere and differently.

e) "You can avoid paying those debts," Sir Walter Scott was told. "I am responsible for them," he replied, "and I will pay them." He both sustained his me and set it in contrast with a legally defined accountable you.

The first of these achieves the coincidence of all three determinations—an accountable you, an accountable me, and a sustained me—by refusing to provide independent determinations for what is sustained. A full coincidence could be brought about, though not as easily, by one who produces all three determinations. The second tries to avoid not only an identification of a public terminus with what is privately sustained, but even with what he himself arrives at as his me. But, like it or not, he belongs to a public world where he is accountable even for some of the things he does unintentionally and inadvertently. The third allows for a coincidence of a public determination of accountability and a responsible sustaining of it, but accepts himself at a different point. The fourth cuts off a sustained me from the you and the accountable me, and thereby allows no adequate public role for what is ethically decided. The fifth expresses high principles, but is not well adjusted to the customs of a commercial world where the debts were acquired and where they ought to be repaid in accord with its customary rules.

Ideally, all three determinations should coincide. This result is properly achieved, not by taking one of the determinations to be the measure of how the others should be understood and carried out, but by according all of them their rightful roles. This sets a task: In each particular case one must try to harmonize all, with a minimal sacrifice of what each would otherwise independently produce.

2.6. I make myself into a moral being.

When the me at which I arrive is not at the place to which others refer, the discrepancy between what I take myself to be publicly and what others acknowledge can be overcome only by some concession being made on my side or theirs. If the others are many and more powerful, there is little hope for a concurrence of the two. But if I deliberately take my me to be at the point where I am being fixated as a you by others, my public position will be backed by a self-acceptance. I will then not merely conform to a determination of my public presence but will adopt it as part of my publicized nature.

A publicized nature is a public status privately accepted. When I take me to be at the point where I take myself to originate public acts, I take myself to be accountable, usually at about the point where others fixate me as a you. I do this in my own way and on my own terms, thereby making myself into a *moral* being, one who has accepted a position in the public world. I am not then necessarily in accord with what I am *ethically*, for to be ethical is to be concerned with what ought to be done, regardless of how accountability is determined.

2.7. 'Me' addresses my-me.

Without attending to anything else, I say 'me' and come immediately to me. The 'me' that I express is initially directed outward; the me to which it is addressed is sustained from within. For the 'me' to bear on me, it therefore has to have its direction reversed in the course of a single, immediate involvement with me. If I look at a mirror image or at a piece of work that I made, I can use this not only to enrich the meaning of 'me', but to provide a position from which the 'me' can have its outward thrust reversed and made to refer to me.

If I look at my hand with detachment, somewhat in the way I might look at the hand of another—as I might well try to do if my hand is numb or if I try to draw or paint it—I block out references to anything else. I then approximate the position where I attend to the hand as though it were an alien, distinct object, despite the fact that it is attached to the rest of my body. The fact that it is mine is set aside. Were I instead to attend to it as mine, I would make no claim to attend to it in the same way that I attend to the hand of another. Though I might still observe it with considerable detachment and objectivity, so long as I see it to be mine, I will terminate in it as that which is inwardly possessed as my-me, a me which belongs to the very I who is attending to it.

The me I know is my me. I do not ask myself whether or not I both possess and attend to it from the same position, what possession and attention are like, or whether there is something beyond both which engages in these acts. I just attend to me or to the hand as part of this, as that which is inwardly possessed. It would be absurd to follow Wittgenstein and maintain that on feeling a pain, if my eyes were closed and I touched someone else's hand while undergoing all my usual kinesthetic changes, I would feel a pain in him. I can feel only my own pains, no matter what it is I touch. And his hand, precisely because I do not possess it from within, I never feel to be in pain. Were I to feel pain on touching his hand, it could be said that I was pained by that hand. But the pain would still be mine, at once felt within and located from the outside. If I do not know whose hand I touch, I still can know that the pain is mine. If I do not touch my hand and yet feel a pain while touching a hand, I know that the pain is mine but the hand is not.

When, instead of directly attending to any part of my body, I refer to it as 'mine', or use it as a referent for 'me', the words themselves have a double role. *I* use them, and I use them to refer. Because *I* use them, 'me' and 'mine' can become one with me and, therefore, with what at once faces outward and is inwardly possessed. Because I use them to refer, 'me' and 'mine' change from words uttered into adherent names, integral parts of what faces outward at the same time that it is sustained from within.

The situation is not changed when I hold my hand before me and say, "It is mine." I do not then direct the 'mine' to the hand that is before me in the way I direct it to the typewriter or to the pen that I am holding in that hand. If I did, the hand would be viewed the way the typewriter or pen is; it would not be something that I inwardly sustain. 'Mine', 'my', and 'me' cling to the hand to become, with it, part of what has a side away from that which another might acknowledge. They become part of me. They are therefore not just words uttered or claims which might be justified. Merging with their referent, they are sustained with this by the very being which uses them.

When I look at myself 'with the eyes of another', I deliberately use the you, where he could arrive, to serve as the locus of the referent of 'me'. To do this, I first make him be a pivotal point, enabling the 'me' to make a return journey toward the I which initiated the looking.

You function in a different way from that in which my hand
and 'me' do. My hand is a pivot by nature, facing outward and
being sustained at the same time. 'Me' is a pivot in use, going
outward and returning in one undivided move. You, in contrast with both, can be turned into a pivot of which I may
make use. When I arrive at you I may or may not come back
toward the sustainer of what I can reach from the position of
that you.

This hand is midway between what is seen and possessed.
The 'mine' which adheres to that hand is necessarily sustained, together with it. As a consequence, I am able to see my
hand from a position external to myself. At that external position there can be a you for me. Or it could be where I imagine
such a you to be .

When I look at myself with the 'eyes of another', I do not
first try to attend to him as a you for me. If I did, I would fixate
him there in the guise of a terminus of my reference, charac-
terization, and act. Instead, I try to view myself in the way I
take him to be viewing what is a you for him. I do not then
know whether or not I am successful. Nor do I know if or
where he might set the you I take him to be, or the you that I
am for him. I am content to use him for a moment as a pivot
enabling the 'me' to be referred to me. The return to me may
or may not be begun at the very point where he may have
presented himself; it may or may not be begun at the very
point from which he attends to me. The return may or may not
be in consonance with the manner in which he attends to me.
It makes little difference. All that has to be done in order to try
to look at myself objectively is to turn at him on the way to an
arrival at me.

I need not, in order to be able to attend to me, have to pivot
about an actual man. I can imagine him. Or I can abstract from
him, taking him to be just an impersonal or anonymous pivot.
Or I can ascend to a collective, or to some representative of
this, and come back from there by a reverse move. In the first
way, I risk idealizing the position from which I approach myself and, therefore, may miss what I might in fact be like for

another who attends to me as a you. In the second, I try to approximate the position which I think anyone might adopt with reference to me, and where I might persistently attempt to begin a return to myself. I never succeed, though, in achieving a position from which I can confidently return to myself unaffected by what I encountered at such a pivot. In the third way, I make an effort to see myself from the position of a group, society, state, or mankind, with which no individual can be identified. I here pivot about what is on a different level from me, rising to it on the way out and coming down to myself on the way back. This is a desirable and may even be an unavoidable move, but it needs supplementation by an arrival at me from the position of actual men.

An ideal, individual pivot, imagined or abstracted, is untouched by the distinctive nature of the man who grounds it. One tries to make use of such a turning point in order to be able to face oneself impersonally, as just standing in contrast with all others. Inevitably, the self-reference accretes content and meaning from what grounds the pivot, so that one returns to oneself with an enriched 'me'. One then sees oneself, not as just a me, but as a 'you-ified' me, one which is not simply referred to and sustained from within but is also public and relative to another.

When I take someone to be a you for me, I am *conscious* of him. When I use him as a pivot, I become conscious of me. If I do both together, I become conscious of him while I am conscious of me. It is not entirely correct to say that I am then self-conscious. *Self-consciousness* requires a beginning and an ending with the I; a consciousness of me stops short of the I who is conscious.

If I am conscious of you while I am conscious of me, I have a doubly directed consciousness. I do not then feel any embarrassment—as well I might when I am self-conscious—since you, of whom I am conscious, are not necessarily aware of me, nor do I look at myself as you might look at me. If I am conscious of you, not only as a terminus, but as providing the beginning of a return to me, my consciousness of me will be inseparable from my consciousness of you and from your presumed consciousness of me in the role of a you. Though I then will not be self-conscious, I will be conscious that my you and my me are being independently determined. I may be embarrassed, annoyed, indifferent to, or challenged by the fact. I will feel ashamed, conscious that I am somehow found wanting by you, only if I identify the position from which I am a you, with that from which I return to me, and then find that the you which I am for you has a lower standing than that which I take my me to have.

2.8. Me and you are publicly together.

There are conditions to which every actuality is subject, enabling them all to be together in space, time, causality, and to be equals, affiliated, intelligible, and of value. By assuming the position of one of these conditions, one can envisage a number of individuals whose me's share various persistent traits, making possible scientific and other accounts of any one, freed from references made from particular positions. The use of such conditions deserves examination. But before doing that, it is desirable to attend to the way in which a man may see himself, not only from the position of this or that individual, but as just together with others.

It is possible for another to provide enrichments for the 'me' which I address myself. If I keep the enrichments distinct from the 'me', I am able to terminate in me as having the role of a you for him, without having it lose its status as a me. Instead of being just a you to which he might refer and which I might sustain at the same or in a different place, I then make the you coincide somewhat with me. At best, though, the you and me can be only partially identified, for the me is still independently determined and rooted and can take on roles without regard for that you.

The use I make of another is not dependent on what he does. It is not necessary that he know that I use him as a pivot. But should he attend to me later, he will face a you which partially coincides with me. He might do so, though, in a way that differs considerably from that which I followed when I returned to myself, qualified by what I had derived from him.

Though I might come to know me as I might be known, I do not necessarily know myself as I am in fact known. By speaking, I make my references public. Heard by another, they could help him learn about what is behind the you which he confronts. I may discover from his speech and actions that he does not know what I am or what I intended. I may conclude that he misconstrued me, or that what I publicly am is to be altered. Since overconfidence encourages the first of these approaches and lack of confidence tends to veer me toward the second, an adjustment must evidently be made between the two.

The you that others know and the me that I know must be brought into some consonance if I am to know myself as others do, and the others are to know what I take myself to be. The adjustment need not take account of what else I may be or what I suppose to be true of myself. As long as others and I both agree on what is public, without either of us simply submitting to the claims of the other, my status will be that of an accepted public being. Were I cut off from the world and then lived only within the area of my intentions, I would neither be able to come to rest at another nor have him as a fellow man. There would be no world in which we both were.

When I take myself to be a you for another, it is for one who could be a you for me. The second of these you's is maintained apart from me while the first coincides in part with the me which I sustain. The two, strictly speaking, are not copresent, symmetrically related, since they are both dependent on what I do. So far as you are just a pivot for me, you do not interplay with the you that I am for you. Copresent you's are maintained by independent individuals, related through the help of common conditions.

2.9. Another can have knowledge of me.

A me is individually and privately arrived at. Even when I
reach me by pivoting about something external, the pivoting
is accomplished privately. The fact would seem to preclude all
possible knowledge of me by another, unless he could somehow become me—and that is impossible. Nevertheless, there
are a number of ways in which another can know me:

a) He can hear me say 'me'. He will then not share in the
addressing of me, nor will he experience the way in which the
'me' and the me are united. But though he will not know me in
the very way in which I do, the 'me' which I use he can see is
addressed to me. Observing where and how the 'me' terminates, he will so far know me.

b) He can observe the way in which I alter the you I present
in order to adjust myself to the you to which he or others attend. He may see me try to present a you like the you he takes
me to be. Watching me, as alert to him, changing the you
present for him, he comes to know what I take my me to be.

c) He can know that when I use him as a pivot I also add to
the 'me' which I then direct at myself. I may show in my
speech and acts that when I refer to me I do so with a 'me'
which he enabled me to enrich. I might be oblivious of what
he in fact is like. But he can see the change that comes over me
in the course of my referring to me via him.

d) I may present myself to him again and again in the same
or in a different guise; I may also make him aware that he is a
you for me. I speak to him or act on or for him. As a consequence, he becomes aware of me in the form of a presented
you. Because he can distinguish between what is being
presented and that at which he terminates, he is able to note a
difference between what is being independently grounded
and which could be my me, and what is relative to him.

e) In sympathy and concern, he may penetrate beyond my
public guise toward a deeper, denser, darker, more intensive
privacy. In that penetration he will use the you that he reaches

as part of a proper name, i.e., as a symbol operating in depth. He can note its merging into a more private, centered possessor, and can come to understand how this might pivot at him when making use of the same name that he does. He will know what my me is like just so far as he takes account of the fact that I, too, use that name properly.

f) I can perceive myself. The perception, like most of my perceptions, is rough and ready, not altogether reliable. But it is possible to perceive with care. Doctors, biologists, and psychologists sometimes report on what they perceive when they look carefully at themselves in somewhat the spirit in which they look at another. When I imitate them, I am able to perceive what they do—and, conversely, they are able to perceive what I do. Though their perceptions of the you I am for them can agree with my perceptions of me only in part, that part is continuous with my objective reality. The perceptual content for all of us may be identical, permitting them to know the me that I perceive—but only, of course, in the guise of a you for them. What they perceive, so far as it agrees with what I perceive, can be said to be a you or a me indifferently, the same item perceived by them and therefore as a you, and by myself and therefore as a me.

2.10. I can know me.

The immediate rejection of observational, behavioristic, mechanistic, materialistic, and physiological accounts of oneself, which is exhibited by almost everyone on first hearing them, is rooted in the awareness that no matter how complete and accurate they be, they necessarily deal with what can be only an aspect. Such an aspect may be all we may wish to know about some others. We may therefore for a while find considerable satisfaction with these accounts, even though they do not do full justice to what is occurring. When we try to take similar approaches toward ourselves, we are usually not satisfied with what we then discover, even where this coheres with what the scientists say, and we are pleased with it.

A detached account of ourselves satisfies only to the degree that we are willing to suppose that what we can publicly know of ourselves exhausts what can be known of us. But what is publicly known merges into what is not so known. The perceptual knowledge we have of ourselves is inseparable from what absents itself from the perceptually known, at the same time that it sustains and possesses it. We feel uneasy with what we learn of ourselves when we assume the position of a detached perceiver, in part because when we focus on the distinguished items we make available we are also aware that we are sustaining what is observed. We do not then reflect on the limitations of the perceived, or look at something deep within ourselves. What we observe is just accepted as being midway between two limits, ourselves as observing and ourselves observed.

A me, though publicly arrived at when perceived, is not wholly detachable from I, its possessor. I give it an orientation, career, and meaning beyond the reach of perception. Consequently, as perceived it is both part of a perceiving and continuous with what is more private, intensive, not perceived. When I take a stand at another so as to face me from his position, I can know me not only to be a terminus arrived at by taking him to be a pivot and a source of an enrichment of 'me', but to at least partially coincide with what is a perceived you for him, terminating a reference made by him from his position. What I face when I see myself to be coincident with such a you is not myself as a you, but myself as a me, subject to determinations produced from the position of another. From that position, I arrive at a different terminus from what he does or can.

"Give it to me," I say, and at one and the same time understand myself to be reachable from the position of another, and to be able to possess something on my own terms. The point is emphasized by my use of the Golden Rule in the form: I should do to or for others what I would have them do to or for me. To consider what I would have done to or for me, I envisage what begins at him and which arrives where he might, but as inseparable from an inwardly maintained depth he cannot reach. The rule would require what is impossible were I not able to imaginatively assume the position that he occupies and there face not only the you to which he attends but the me to which I alone can attend.

My assumption of the position that another occupies involves no displacement of him, but usually only the unreflective, unconceptualized acceptance of the meanings he supports or uses, and making them terminate in me. If I make use of concepts, it is with respect to a terminus at which he might arrive. Since those concepts can also be used by him when attending to others, different from him and me, I can look at myself in terms applicable to any number. I do not, though, look at me in the way I look at any of them, for when I look at me I necessarily merge what I see into its sustaining possessor.

The concepts employed when I know myself could be applied to others as well. It is possible even to use them when trying to understand things. I then use them to help me know both what cannot be or have a me, and what necessarily does. Evidently, the difference between these will not be expressed unless refinements are added, or the same concepts are applied differently in the two cases.

The attempt to think of myself as a complex machine is up against the fact that concepts, used in knowing myself, inescapably apply to content that is pulled inward and grounded in the very being who is making use of those concepts. Even if I were to use the very same concepts when knowing me and when knowing a machine, I would still know different kinds of entities. The content which I provide when knowing me enables my concepts to be possessed by what lies beyond that content. I am then not only the user of concepts but the possessor of the content to which they apply.

My perception of myself from the position of another makes

use of my sense organs. You perceive me by using yours. Apparently, I use senses similar to those you use and in the same way, allowance being made for the differences in our acuity and positions. But if this were so, are we not back to the position rejected before, that one might look at oneself just as one might look at another? I do not think so. When you and I perceptually terminate at the same content I have made present, you rest there, fixate it for your own purposes, while I sustain as well as perceive it. I give the perceptual knowledge that I have of myself a different grounding, role, and career from what you give to the perceptual knowledge that you have of me. Still, I can look at least at part of myself, and perceive what is present from my distinctive position, under limitations which are similar to those under which you operate. If I look at my hand in a bright light, I will see what you and many others see in such a light. Though the angle that I assume when I look at the hand is not identical with the angle from which you and they see it, and may be overlaid with factors peculiar to me alone, I can make a shrewd guess as to just what can be discerned of me, particularly when we are not at a great distance from one another. Though I do not actually ever take up the position of another, it is one which is occupiable by me in principle, with results convertible into those I obtain from my own position, abstraction being made from what I add through my sustaining.

2.11. The perceived is grounded beyond the perceiving.

It is sometimes contended that I can attend to and even know another only from a private, unique position, and with unduplicable outcomes. Instead of looking at myself as another could, I am then supposed to look at myself in an individual way, even when I pivot at a public reality at which others might also pivot. It would then be maintained, with a solipsist or a subjectivist, that I never escape from dealing with everything from a position radically different from what some conceivable other might entertain. Where the Kantian denies that I can have a distinctive knowledge of myself, it is now denied that I can have any knowledge at all, where 'knowledge' is understood to embrace common, impersonal truths which others might also possess.

A number of considerations stand in the way of the acceptance of such a view:

a) I can know myself when I know other things, and can do so under the same limitations and in the same way. I can see my hand holding a pen, the pen slip from my grasp, being picked up by you, and being given to me. There surely is a difference between what I know when I have the pen in my hand and when it is being picked up by you, but the conditions under which I see both are the same, and are no more restricted to what is part of me than to what is not.

b) My perceptions terminate in what can be used symbolically by me in one way when I attend to myself, and in another way when I attend to someone else. If, when I attend to you, I also attend to myself, I am aware that I know us in distinctive, penetrative ways, for the perceptual contents and approaches are grounded differently in the different places.

c) The you that I know is maintained apart from me, as you make evident when you act contrary to my expectations and interests. Whether I wish it or not, you present me with what I do not sustain. The opposite is precisely what I can say of the content I perceive when I attend to myself. It may be quite unlike anything I would like to see, but I nevertheless possess it, have it as mine, enjoy it from within as having a distinctive tonality, maintained apart from my perceiving.

When I attend to you or to myself, I find that I am defied, blocked, faced with content which continues to absent itself in depth. But only when I attend to me do I continue toward the very I who is attending. From one side I present myself, and from the other distinguish what I perceive of me from this I. Since what I perceive of me is between a perceiver and a presenting sustainer, unless I could somehow be divided in two, the perceiver and sustainer must be specializations of a single reality able to perceive from one side what is sustained from another. The perceiving, though, apparently begins at a position different from that where the sustaining is begun.

Though my perceiving of me moves past the point at which another might arrive, it is slowed and eventually stopped, denying the perception further content. What I perceive of myself, consequently, is a me which continues into a more and more intensive defiance, having a depth, grain, and career that neither I, the perceiver, nor my perceiving can exhaust or control. I know, therefore, that what sustains me is not identical with what is engaged in the perceiving of me. Nor is the latter identifiable with what is able to engage in other acts. Since the perceiving is countered by the sustaining, the two must be distinguished as opposed, leaving no other alternative but the acknowledgment of a more basic reality having these two roles. The perceiving is *my* perceiving, and me is *my* me, both presupposing what can both express itself and possess them. The examination of the question as to whether or not this being can be known, what its nature is, how it can have multiple roles, and related questions is an inescapable task for an enterprise such as this. They will be faced. For the moment, though, it is necessary only to observe that I can perceive myself by making use of the same concepts that are used in perceiving you, and that what is beyond my perception of me is different from what is beyond my perception of you.

2.12. Perceptual conditions constrain.

Each individual looks out at the world from a distinct position. He colors what he sees with his own memories, expectations, and bias. How could this be known by me? Each individual looks out at the world in terms similar to those that others employ. He can see what others also see. How could this be known by me?

I know that you perceive something different from what I

do, for we report different things about what we are calling by the same name, and on which we are acting in similar ways. If it be denied that what is called by the same name and is acted on in a similar way is the same object reported on differently, all the more surely is it the case that we two perceive different things for, on the hypothesis, we do not and can not attend to the same objects. Were one willing to go this far, one would then have to say that the common observation that men act and speak of the same objects though they engage in different acts of perception is mistaken, despite the fact that they can readily agree on what they see, particularly when they take account of their different distances, angles, histories, physiologies, and interests. At the very least, men can note how differences in their perceptual results can be made to increase or decrease by increasing or decreasing the differences in the approaches they take toward something before them.

Is this conclusion disturbed by the fact that each attends in an unduplicable way to the outcome of perceptions begun at different angles and distances and with different preconceptions, expressed in different attitudes, actions, and speech? No. If one holds that different perceivers necessarily face different contents, he tacitly supposes that he already knows what it is that other perceivers can know. This is not yet to claim that no one could perceive what another does. Were this maintained, it would be hard to find justification for it. At the very least, the justification would require quite advanced knowledge about men's different abilities and the kinds of perceptions that are possible to them. Could one know this much, it will be because he has been able to know certain truths. If those truths are also available to others, the most that could be reasonably claimed is that it is possible for a number of men to know that some are not able to perceive what the rest can, and that it is possible to know what it is that the divergent ones are unable to know.

Whether or not one perceives exactly what another does, the other is perceived under various conditions of perception which remain constant, even when distances, angles, interests, and speech vary. Since what is confronted is resistant, setting a limit to perception, what is perceived will be maintained apart from, at the same time that it terminates each one's perceiving.

Perceiving makes use of constant, universally applicable, conditioning structures which give a place to the perceived content. The structures it brings to bear match what is present in what is confronted. We need not subscribe to a theory of innate ideas or suppose that there are specific items of knowledge that can be obtained apart from all experiencing in order to affirm that in perception we all make use of factors which are also present in the objects perceived.

In perception we make use of structures which are also present in what we perceive. Were there no such structures each of us would grope in the dark, perhaps forever, for some appropriate way of grasping what is present. But each of us applies the structures in special ways, in particular situations, and from special positions, with the result that what is confronted is both known and distinctively qualified. If the perceived is also a perceiver, he will be subject to the very structures he uses in knowing himself and will also be outside the reach of them, as that to which they apply.

What exists is too limited, dense, and independent, at once too narrow and too deep for perceptual conditions to encompass fully. That fact is discovered when we symbolize and act. I know another as more than what he is perceived to be, because at the very least I apprehend him as absenting himself from my intrusions.

Conceivably, there might be only one person who perceives. Only one might be awake or attending. This does not affect the fact that the conditions used could be used again in other circumstances and with respect to other objects. To say that another also makes use of these is but to add that the conditions are indifferent to the nature of the user, not only as he is at a particular time but as he might be at any time and under any circumstances. Evidently, they are prescriptions for any possible perceiver.

The conditions of perception set limits to what one can perceive. They constrain both the perceiver and the perceived. Since these counter and diversify the conditions, the conditions are evidently distinct from and yet involved with both perceiver and perceived. Locating them in a Platonic realm of universals independent of and indifferent to what is, will not help one understand why or how they are operative. Nor would anything be gained by supposing, with Aristotle, that they are part of an active, universal mind which hovers over and governs each individual mind, for one would still leave unexplained how each man can know independently of the others.

The remarks of solipsists and subjectivists are addressed to men other than themselves, whom they seek to persuade. Rightly remarking that each knows himself in a distinctive way, they ignore the common structures all use, and the role these structures have in what is known. In their justified defense of personalized factors in knowing, which Aristotle ignored, they overlook the Aristotelian truth that by incorporating the forms of things men become informed about those things.

2.13. My me is multiply differentiated.

It is desirable that I try to see me from the position of another perceiver, for in this way a perceptual bias can be counteracted. That other, of course, may be perceived with a bias. If his insistent presence counteracts this, I will be able to perceive me by means of perceptual conditions used as a neutral observer might use them. On returning to myself, I will then be able to know myself in the way another might and, so far, as not yet distinguishable from what is a you for him. But unless I can also manage to pivot at the exact point where he counteracts my emphasis with one of his own, I will inevitably return to me as not coincident with what has the role of a you

for him. Whether this occurs or not, I will perceive me as inwardly sustained beyond my perceiving.

A *me perceived* is a *me that I perceive*. This is not identifiable
with a *perceived me*. A me perceived is maintained outside the
perceptual conditions governing my perceiving; a perceived
me is united with perceptual content. The second differs from
the first as a known object differs from an object known.
Where the one is confined within the conditions by which it is
apprehended, the other is independently maintained. A perceived me is only when perceived; a me perceived is what perceptual conditions made it possible to perceive.

Perceptual conditions and a me perceived together constitute a perceived me. They also continue to be outside it, since
they are able to come together again and again and thereupon
produce perceived me's at other times. Even when the perceived me is identified with my body, it is distinguishable
from the me perceived, since this is inseparable from the living of the body from within. The perceived me is inseparable
from the body so far as this is distinct from the living of it.

I know I am an intending, thinking, believing, hoping,
expectative, remembering being. These activities are not observable by others. This does not mean that they are unknowable, or entirely private, without any possible public role. Intending and the other acts are no less public than eating is,
and eating is no less private than they are. We can see someone take food into his mouth, chew and swallow; we can also
see him hesitate, blunder, attend, persist, get ready, correct
himself. In both cases, we fall short of their active source; but
in both cases, too, we know something continuous with the
source of them.

In the course of experience, it becomes evident that what I
say and do are not as clearly and as completely a part of me as
various features I perceive myself to have. What I say and do
slip so quickly into the world beyond that it does not seem
right to say that I possess and sustain them. My words and
acts are due in good part to powers outside my control; again

and again, I do not say or do exactly what I intend. But since even then they are mine, they are evidently held on to as continuations of myself. I do not then enjoy a privileged position or a private access to myself in any sense in which I do not have one when I directly look at the hand I also feel. It is, of course, true that my sayings and doings are quite different in kind from my hand. Not only are they transient while the hand is more or less constant, but the hand is continuously maintained from within, roughly at the same time and in the same manner in which other parts of my body are maintained. What I say and do are mine by claim, responsibility, and accountability, but not, as my hand is, also maintained as a bodily part of me. If, as is sometimes said, my words and deeds are me, they are so only so far as they are not yet separated from me, detached by what is external to them.

When I touch my hand I am sometimes dimly aware that it is then being sustained in a way which differs from that in which my felt leg or other parts of my body are sustained. These differences do not often interest me, except when I am in pain, or when I notice something unusual about those parts. From the position of their common source, more limited sustainings are so many differentiations of it. Similarly, different parts of my body, different perceivable features, and many things for which I am accountable are so many differentiations of me.

2.14. Some things are mine by right; others are mine only through possession.

As we have already seen, others can know the me that I know, but not exactly or surely. Others, too, can know my hands, legs, deeds, and speech, sometimes even better than I do. What is not possible to them is the single sustaining of my hands, legs, deeds, or speech and, therefore, the having them all as merely differentiated.

What sustains me is accessible only through the agency of me. To move toward it, it is necessary to pass beyond feelings in my hands and legs, and the thoughts and intentions expressed in my speech and acts. What is then met can be said to be either me or I, or both. It is properly taken to be me, for it is continuous with what has already been publicly encountered. But it can also be taken to be I, as well, for it is an attenuated version of this, the inward, dense possessor of feelings, thoughts, intentions, speakings, and acts. It is also properly taken to be both at once, for the me is the I in a public role, at the same time that it provides a mediation for a reference to that I. My thoughts, intentions, and the rest, are me in a more unified, sustained form. Equally, they are my I in a diffuse, superficial guise. I make present what others might divide and relativize and to which I can refer, at the same time that I am able to face both the presenting and the referring as my acts. Whether I take account of my me or I, or both, one thing is sure: no one else can make use of the one or use the other.

My thoughts, like the feelings in my hand, are accessible only through me, not because there is something hidden or blocked off from others, but because the thoughts are mine, inseparable from the act of possession, itself inseparable from their possessor, I. My clothes are mine, too. They are my possessions in somewhat the same way that my hand and speech are, but only when I am actually laying hold of them. My hand and, under some limitations, my speech as well are mine by right and also mine by possession.

Whatever is known, whether it be a thing, me, or I, is subject to the conditions governing knowledge, and counters these with some insistence. I know me under the same conditions which govern the knowledge in which others engage and in which I, too, engage when I know other things. I continue, nevertheless, to remain outside those conditions. If known, I am known by applying structures governing all knowledge, while still remaining outside the reach of these, where I sustain what they reach to and govern.

I may have lost all feeling in some part of my body and may not therefore be able to counter the addressing of it with a felt sustaining. I will then not be altogether sure that what I am attending to is actually part of me or merely that which had once been so. What I attend to then will still be different from what another attends to when he focuses on that part of my body. While there is an ambiguity for me as to whether or not the unfelt is part of me, there is no ambiguity for him, since he rightly takes it to be part of a you relative to him. And when the ambiguity is removed, it will be in the direction of making even more evident that a me is differently grounded from the way in which a you could be.

The sustaining of me could conceivably continue into some object acting on that me—a fact recorded in such common expressions as "I feel the shape of the ball," "I feel the roughness of the wood," "I feel the quickening of my child." There is no confusing of the felt, in such instances, with me. My feeling as terminating in me is countered by my external reference to that me; my feeling as terminating in anything else is countered by the insistent absenting of the sustainer of that terminus.

My you and me, though distinct, may have common content which is sustained in different ways—accommodated if it be my you, and constituted if it be my me. The content contrasts with what is accommodating or constituting it. My you may coincide in part with me, but I never make it into my you in the way I make me mine. I relativize that me in approaching it from without and compensate for this by possessing the me—and that I cannot do with the you I am for another.

2.15. Thoughts and feelings are knowable.

It is hopeless to try to match what can be learned through detached observation with what I can know of me. No knowledge of physiology, brain processes, stimuli and responses, or behavior, will enable me, or anyone else, to know just what I am undergoing, what feelings I have, or what I might be thinking, believing, and the like—unless these could be grasped as denser forms of what is publicly reachable. But then one will have moved beyond detached observation.

A doctor may look at my hand and find some odd occurrence there whose fluctuations are in some accord with the pain that I report. Though he may sympathetically share in that pain, he can not know that pain as it is being undergone. To know it he must attend to what I report and take it to pertain to what he knows, but as lived through and sustained in a way he cannot experience.

What I report to a doctor helps him know the hand that I alone feel. I may look at what he is pointing to, but I then and there also face it as inseparable from a feeling of pain. He, relying on previous knowledge, can surmise that some act by me or by him will perhaps increase or decrease my pain, but he must wait for me to tell him that it does or does not do so, and to what degree. The hand that I know coincides only in part with the hand that he knows. In asking me whether or not I feel pain, he makes evident that he is aware that there is something I can but he cannot note. His pressures and his use of remedies are affected partly by his awareness of a depth beyond what can be noted detachedly, and in part by his acceptance of the role that my actual and possible subsequent pain have in a hand that he can know only as part of a you for him.

My thoughts and feelings are not beyond all knowing, particularly when they provide constituents for my speech, reports, and behavior. To know my thoughts and feelings, one must free them from what has been added to them by my body and by what is publicly encountered, and then recognize them to be expressions and continuations of a dense, unitary privacy. If the feelings and thoughts are taken to be just the underside of me, they will be understood to be continuations of what is publicly manifested. If taken to be expressions of an I, they will be understood to be continuations of what privately produces them. They are both, and at the same time.

Terms like 'pain', 'thought', and the like, Richard Rorty has suggested, should be taken to be merely ill-defined markers of the presence of purely bodily states in somewhat the way in which 'the devil' might be taken to be an ill-defined mark of the presence of some illness or germ. He thought that one might eventually dispense with their use altogether and that, thereafter, one might refer only to this or that observable brain movement. But if there were no inwardly undergone feeling, a pain would be mine only in the way my blood is. Conceivably transferable to another, it would not be a continuation of the I or of the me.

If I were to look at my brain, I would see nothing of my thoughts or feelings, not because they do not exist, but because they are not observable bodily occurrences. Thoughts and feelings are publicized, but only as combined with what originates elsewhere, to constitute speech, reports, and acts. Held away from what combines with them, they provide evidences for what is privately undergone.

An account of brain movements stops short of the being who is making himself manifest. If he could be taught to speak exclusively in the objective neutral language of brain movements, he would also have to give up a distinction between what he knows of himself and what another could know of him. If he said he was in pain when there was no discernible, supposedly appropriate brain movement, he would have to be taken to be wholly in error, somewhat as a child is who calls its shoe 'daddy'. But when we ask who makes the error, the answer would have to refer not to some brain movement, but to the private being who responsibly says, "I am in pain."

Movements may be irregular or incorrect. Statements may be false or wrong. Perceptions may be distortive or misleading. Only one who knows, a private being, can err.

2.16. Me is a person publicized.

The you that is known by others is approached from the vantage point of perceptual and other epistemic conditions. These are given specific, limited ranges and colorings by those others and by the circumstances under which they are used. That very same you is more objectively and constantly confronted when approached in terms of *final* conditions which govern all things, known or not. You are then faced not as having a side just relative to others but as objectively interrelated with them.

The same conditions in terms of which I can attend to you and other things, I can use to attend to me, making it possible to deal with me in the same terms that are used for you and others. The me will then be faced in a neutral spirit. The categories in terms of which I know that me will themselves be grounded in and affected by those conditions. Otherwise the me could conceivably be only the counterpart of or be constituted by the categories by which it was known, with the consequence that when I was not attending to me, the me would vanish. But though I cannot know me without knowing, and therefore without conforming to the principles governing knowledge, I can know what that me is apart from these.

As just sustained, a me is present, available. As just the terminus of a reference, it exists only so far as it is being attended to. As present for such reference and maintained apart from this, it is a subject for conditions. These need it for content and to be diversified, as surely as it needs them in order to be known.

Though I make no mistakes in knowing that this to which I refer by means of 'me' is me, I can misconstrue its nature and read into it what is not there. I try to protect myself from such prospects by trying to assume the position of others, where my biases would not be operative. I do not succeed. If I did, I still would not know the me which alone provides a standard in terms of which I can learn of my misconceptions of me.

A *perceived me* is affected by conditions governing perception. What is not so affected is an *available me*, a me which, though not then referred to, can be referred to again and again. As inseparable from a component which helps constitute it, an *available me* is identifiable as the outermost limit of a *person*.

A *legal* person has viable public rights specified by an enforced legal system. A *private* person has only native rights. In an *historic* person, public and private rights are distinct from one another. In a *complete* person, public and private rights are distinguished while connected. A me is evidently a part of all, except the wholly private person, the person as not yet publicly present.

A person differs from a *self*. This does not, like a person, ever have the me as a component. Also, unlike a private person which, through publicly determined supplementations, can help constitute a legal, historic, and complete person, a self never becomes a component in something that is also externally oriented, though epitomizations of it in the form of the I or mind, of course, do affect and are affected by bodily and extrabodily occurrences.

A sheer *privacy* is the common base for both self and person, the two not distinguished. It therefore lacks both an I and a me. A *human* is able to have a self and a person, and an I and me; he has a privacy able to ground an identity and rights, the one privately maintained, the other publicly viable. A *mature man* is at once a self and a person, with a distinctive I and me; he has private, publicly viable rights and is able to possess changes and pluralities without endangering his constancy and unity.

In the course of our unreflecting life, we often use these distinctions steadily and accurately. Not only are self, person, me, I, human being, and mature man rarely confounded, but the references to them are used by all with considerable precision. We can and do use them loosely at times, sometimes even interchangeably. But when we must distinguish them, we do so rather neatly and well. Rarely do we say that a self has rights; rarely do we say that a human and a mature man are one and the same.

2.17. I know that my me is like another's me.

When I know that another is attending to himself, I know that he attends to a me which is like the me to which I attend. I could not learn this by making an analogy between myself and him, for that would require me to first know myself, then to recognize similar features in him, and finally to go on to transfer what I know about myself to him, paying some regard for our differences. I know that his me is like mine, and that it is known the way mine is, without taking such care and so much time. And I surely do it without having much knowledge of myself or of him. Nor do I infer that he knows that he has a me. Inference requires premises and conclusions, and sometimes makes use of rules, but I know that he has a me without making use of such machinery. Nor do I jump over to where he is and look at him the way he looks at himself. That I cannot do, for his me is available only to him. It is the recognition that he, when attending to himself, terminates in what is subject to the very same conditions to which I am subject when I attend to myself, that makes it possible for me to know that what he confronts is a me, related to what he is in depth the way my me is related to what I am in depth. The outcome is distinct from what I might know when I confront him in the guise of a you, when I perceive or otherwise judge him, or when I watch him attend to himself. In these ways I can know that he is present, not what he is to himself; that he is known, but only so far as he is being judged; or that he is a me for himself, possibly with a nature quite unlike that of any other me.

To account for the ways in which your me and my me are together, reference has to be made to what applies to both of us. When I know what these conditions are, I will not yet, of course, know you in your privacy, but only what you are as governed by those conditions. Because you and I are subject to the same conditions, your me and my me will be together in ways neither of us determines. Our togetherness is pre-scribed to us, controlling, incapable of being a function of one or the other.

Were my me not in a public world, I would be cut off from all else. Were it equatable with what is known through a de-tached observation, it would be only an aspect of myself. Were it identifiable with what others might know, it would be identical with a you for them, or with what they might be able to infer about what they cannot confront. Were it only a delimited portion of some universally expressed power, it would belong to a distinct common source of what is publicly done. Though my me is unduplicable, and can be faced by no one else, it has a role in a public world. There it has dignities and burdens distinct from any that might be privately as-sumed, though the standing it then has may not in fact be respected or be known by anyone. My me is in a public world at the same time that it merges into what I am privately.

2.18. I know that another can know himself as a me.

Without denying or obscuring the sustaining of my me or the feeling of it from within, I can sustain it as a unit which is to-gether with others in a public world. I then do not allow the me to play any role other than that of a point of orientation and possible locus of features. Another might confront it, tak-ing it to be a you for him. If he also noted its disaccord with his me, he could become aware of the fact that his me stands in contradistinction from mine, under the same common condi-tions.

Another and I do not become just two you's for one another—that loses our separate self-references. Each of us knows himself at the same time that he knows that the other knows himself. Nor do we become just two me's set in a common world—that loses our references to one another. Nor are we just me's acknowledged by one another. Each of us knows only his own me. Because I know that I a common condition is imposed on my individual me, I know that it can be imposed elsewhere as well and that, as a consequence, another can also know himself to be a me. He and I can both know that the other can know himself as a me, because we both can know that we are conditioned in the same way as we stand apart from one another. If this be denied, the knowedge that we both have that each of us is a me becomes inexplicable, if not impossible.

Animals and things are also subject to whatever conditions operate on everything. Yet they are not credited with a knowledge of themselves as me's. Evidently, it is not enough to remark on the fact that there are common conditions to assure a knowledge that there are other me's. I must know that the others can come to themselves in the way I come to myself and this, we have already seen, is known only because I know them as you's, inwardly sustained by privacies able to act in the public world.

We are now in a position to examine once more the remark that no one but a black (woman, immigrant, prisoner, or blind man) can know what it is to be a black (woman, immigrant, and so forth). The claim is at once too bold and too timid. If it is not possible for another to know what kind of life this or that individual has, then it is not possible for this or that individual to know that another does or does not know it. If you know that what is known by each is known to him alone, you already have knowledge about everyone. Consequently, one must hold either that there is a common knowledge that is available only to certain groups of people—and that would have to be justified—or that there is knowledge available to all, and therefore that what one man knows another also might. Still, since a me entrenches on what is beyond such ostensible features as color, gender, and status, each member of a group will undergo something that others do not. Conceivably, it might be known only by him. If so, each will know what others cannot. But no one can maintain this without claiming that he knows something about others that confessedly cannot be known by him.

If one can know the distinctive difference such a feature as color makes to oneself, it should be possible to learn how other traits might also make a difference, and the kind of difference they might make to anyone else who might possess them, a variant of them, or opposite forms of them. If it is possible for one black to know that other blacks can know themselves in the way he knows himself, it is also possible for him to know how any other human might see himself when he attends to what he is. He will be able to know that nonblacks know what he and other blacks know—unless being black necessarily makes what is known accessible only to the possessors of that color.

Color, gender, and the like are part of an individual me, and are knowable when this is. Each makes some difference to the me. If they can be known to be present, the difference they make can be understood. One way is by imaginatively transforming one's own individualized traits into the individualized traits of another. It is not easy to do this, but it surely is not impossible. Novelists manage quite well; so do physicians and biographers. The actual encounter that each has with his own me, of course, will not then be duplicated. Each will sustain the traits and his me in a distinctive way. And each knows this, because each knows the difference between a you and a me, and the fact that, beyond all public qualifications, there is a private sustaining by each from within.

For most purposes, I attend to another simply as a you. Too often I am content to suppose that some conspicuous features there are revelatory of his character, promise, or intentions. I am not always wrong when I do this, but I am not always right either. And it need not be done. The noted items can be understood to be part of his me and so far not to be exactly what they are when taken to be part of him as a you. You and me, too, can share content, and this can be judged, reported, communicated, and made common knowledge.

Court psychiatrists would like to find out just what a defendant thinks of himself for having brought about what is
widely condemned. He is not to be just observed, for though
this will allow him to be looked at with somewhat less bias
than might be expressed otherwise, it will not let one know
how he sees himself. Nor will the thoughts or beliefs that had
passed or are now passing through his mind, though they
might throw some light on how the act came about, necessarily make evident whether or not he responsibly takes himself
to be accountable, and for what. The defendant is held accountable for acts traceable to him, but what is not yet known
is whether or not he holds himself to be accountable, and to
what extent. It is not known to what degree his me coincides
with the you that the legal system and its agents acknowledge.

What a man does might have been initiated in the secret recesses of his being. It may not be known to him. He may have
used his own body solely as an agent for carrying out a responsible decision. What one wants to know when dealing
with him apart from a social or legal frame is whether or not
this occurs. And one would like to learn whether or not, and
to what degree, he accepts for himself what is socially or legally attributed to him—matters to be learned partly from his
own reports, asides, and casual remarks, partly from his behavior, and partly by knowing what it is for him to face himself as a me.

2.19. Each me is irreducible.

Conditions applicable to everything are distinct from every
thing. I get to know them when, pulling back from the public
world, I see myself becoming more and more involved with
controlling, prescriptive governances. Or, when attending to
myself in a world with others, I distinguish all of us from what
constrains and relates us. To make use of these conditions, I
subordinate my judgments, principles of knowledge, and at-

titudes to them. I am thereby able to deal with myself and others in the same terms. These are quite general, abstract observations. It is time to attend to the conditions so as to learn what affects everything and, particularly, you and me. The conditions are reached only at the end of a difficult journey, emotionally sustained and speculatively pursued. I have engaged in that venture elsewhere. To understand the role that the conditions play in the constitution of whatever there be, and particularly of the me, it is fortunately not necessary to engage in that venture again. All that is needed now is a knowledge of their functioning. That knowledge is not easy to obtain. Difficulties and misconceptions quickly arise if various obstacles are not removed:

a) When I attend to myself from the position of a condition, I face a sustained me. But what sustains me has power of its own. We would have to hold that this power is split into two oppositional forces unless we recognize that I as facing the me, and the me that is faced, are both continuations of a single, more basic I.

b) Were conditions to sustain me, or were they part of the I which is sustaining me, they would provide a limit for any reference I make to myself. But then they would not be used in order to attend to me. Instead, they would be what blocked or interacted with whatever was so used. Conditions are imposed from beyond the me and the I—indeed of every item—and are encountered by each in a distinctive way.

c) Primary conditions affect all actualities. They are imposed on each with the same force. The result would be the same everywhere, were it not that they are countered in distinctive ways. Each condition is an attenuated continuation of what empowers it and is specified when, where, and by that on which it operates. To attend to it, or to its source, as not yet involved with anything, I must withdraw into myself. I then am able to face me as that which is being neutrally governed in the way other entities are.

My me is known through the use of the very conditions I

use when attending to anything. Did this not occur, the knowledge I have of my me would not be knowledge like that which I have of anything else. But neither the me, nor any other entity, is ever wholly within the control of conditions. If it were, it would not oppose them, qualify them, or specialize them.

Schopenhauer spoke of an absolute will which came to expression in the claws and fangs of the tiger and in the beak and wings of the eagle. That will was a primary power, manifesting itself everywhere, nonrationally and vitally. Later, Jung spoke of a collective unconscious which came to expression in common myths and symbols. Both referred to what was not only present everywhere, but was effectively present in everything. In different ways, they not only attended to a single primal conditioning power but tried to explain observable combinations and dissociations in terms of it. Unfortunately, they did not make clear how this one power could manifest itself in many ways, or why. They neither made provision for the existence of the various individuals on which it operates, nor showed how these make a difference to the outcome of its operation. I never grasp me in its completeness at any one time. I note only sides of me from particular angles. Nor is that me ever altogether in perfect focus. There are half-hidden tendencies which belong to it. All the while, I come to it as an indivisible, internally possessed unity. I subordinate every distinguishable part to it, and maintain a hold on it from a dense depth outside the limits of the public world.

Easterners are inclined to overemphasize the power of a final condition or its empowering source; Westerners, instead, over-insist on the irreducibility of the individual. As a consequence, the one usually minimizes radical differences, while the other usually minimizes what is present for all. Were the former alone to prevail, everything would be an illusion except an unreachable One; were the latter alone to prevail, men would be monads, cut off from one another, irreducible and possessive of what is distinguishable only within or for them, sharing nothing, not even the character of being monads.

2.20. Men are affiliated.

When a man attends only to himself, he is able to know how he in fact accords with what intrudes on and is countered by him. To the extent that he effectively counters it, he is alienated from it; to the extent that it constrains him, he is at home with it. Ontologically viewed, his is a constant state, the outcome of what he is as an actuality and of the operation of constant, impersonal powers. Empirically viewed, he constantly changes the degree and manner of his acceptance, resistance, interplay, and accommodation.

Did a condition just act on men, they would share common features, but they would not yet be interrelated. Yet this they are. At every moment, men are in some degree of harmony with one another, because they are related by a final affiliating power which is resisted by each independently and in its own way. That power is too insistent to be equated with Tao; too impersonal and cosmic to be identified with a subterranean will; too transcendent to be identified with an unconscious, individual or common. It is not to be equated with an intellectually discerned Platonic receptacle or an Aristotelian primal matter, for it is directly confronted and is more effective than these are said to be. It does not fully own anyone. But it cannot be disowned, avoided, entirely defied, for then nothing would be more or less affiliated with others.

A common, affiliating condition interrelates men, and is embodied in each actuality in a distinctive way. Each individualizes it in the course of an adoption of it. The source of that condition can be discerned while one is reacting to it, for the condition merges into it. Many have reported that they have reached that source or have at least moved into it at great depth. They have difficulty in persuading others, and usually take refuge in admonitions, dark sayings, myths, strange tales, and the repetitions and stories of revered masters. They say that if one is to get to it, one is to give up thinking, reflection, interest in oneself, the lessons of experience, and an involvement in daily affairs. There is no guarantee that one will then arrive at what is final. Still, were there no truth at all in what was being claimed by those who speak of it, one would not know how men come to be more or less harmoniously together even with those they had not encountered or with whom they had not shared experiences, background, history, or ancestry.

2.21. My me thinks.

Among the many questions that are raised by Descartes's famous, "I think, therefore I am" is that of knowing whether these two 'I's' refer to the same entity and, therefore, if he was begging his question in assuming that there was just one I, before he went on to claim that it had a being of its own. More relevant to the present discussion, but no less important, is the question whether that which was engaged in thinking was just an I, and not a self, a person, or some condensation of these, other than the I. When Descartes went on to explicate what he meant by thinking, his illustrations seemed to point to what was known by his coming to himself through his me, since he spoke of beliefs, true ideas, intentions, and other involvements with what presumably had a reality apart from him. There does seem to be little question, though, that Descartes also wanted to consider these processes only so far as they were occurring in his mind, regardless of whether or not there was anything outside that mind which matched them, or toward which they were directed. This is not possible. Like the rest of us, he came to a knowledge of himself as thinking, believing, and so on, via the me at which he arrived by attending to himself from an external position.

"Methinks me thinks" would have been a more cautious statement for Descartes to make than "I think, therefore I am," since it starts with an element of dubeity about an ac-knowledged me which thinks. Did he wish to affirm that the me not only thinks but is, he would have had to make a sec-ond move, going from a me which thinks to a me which is, and this on the ground that the me thinks only so far as it has a distinctive being of its own. This is the very supposition that he does make with respect to his 'I' in his "I think." If his thinking functioned somewhat as a hand does when made to hold a pen, he would not have been able to infer with surety that when thinking occurs there is a distinct I that engages in it. Thinking, he supposed, was carried on by an irreducible, distinct reality. But, as he went on to observe, that might still be dependent for its presence on another, more ultimate reality—'God', he called it. One need not go that far. When I seek the source of my thinking, I need refer only to a self, or to a mind or to an I, which epitomize the self. However, since the self, mind, and even I, might conceivably be agencies for another reality having thoughts of its own, we do not neces-sarily arrive at an aboriginal source of a thinking by referring to a self, mind, or an I rather than to a me. If the self, mind, or I could conceivably be an expression of a more original source of thinking, the me would be dependent on such dependents. Conversely, if self, mind, or I, despite possible grounding in a more basic reality which itself might engage in thinking, could have independent beings and therefore could think on their own, the me, despite its grounding in a more basic re-ality, might similarly think on its own.

Could the thinking, which Descartes credited to his I, be a thinking carried out by God or some other final reality? Not unless this could think fallibly, sometimes make mistakes, have trivial, foolish, and finite thoughts, and join with various finite beings in a hesitant, confused inquiry. Could thinking be carried out exclusively by a self, mind, or I? Not unless the thinking was not dependent on experience, was not knowa-ble through the agency of the me, and was never manifested in a public world.

I know that my me is whenever I attend to any of my acts

and see that what I am approaching from without is both sustained from within and is subject to common conditions. Sometimes I deal with my me in terms of principles and rules I deliberately apply. But because that me is approached from without, and because the conditions are prescriptive and intrusive, I still know that the nature of me depends on what is not me. Like everything else that is objective, the me that is known does not depend on its being known. But that me does depend on the meeting of a private sustaining and common conditions.

The present distinction between a me and an I has associations with Aristotle's distinction between the passive and the active intellect. It does, though, differ from this in important respects. Most likely—though it is not altogether clear that this is what he meant—Aristotle thought that the active reason was identical in all men. If this is what he held, he supposed that there was an impersonal power, conceivably identifiable with an expression of Being itself, which makes it possible for each man to think and perhaps to act. But such an impersonal power could not operate on anyone in a distinctive way. My distinctive thinking shows that I also contribute to the presence and nature of what is thought.

2.22. The being of me is part my total being.

No one is just a me. This he cannot be, for the triple reason that he approaches himself by starting at a deeper level, that it is he who arrives at the me, and that he does so only if and so far as that me is sustained by what is not a me. Nevertheless, the me functions in society and state in the guise of a self-contained irreducible, with a career in time, maintained in a world with others. Were the me to be taken to be just an abstraction, or to be irrelevant to what I really am, in one move the me which I know so well would be denied a public role, and the origin of my accountable acts would be canceled.

Empirically minded thinkers are right to insist on the me, but are surely mistaken when they deny that beliefs, thoughts, intentions, and the like are part of it. A me is not a sheer surface. Nor is it exclusively bodily. It both incorporates and mediates what is begun on a more private, more basic level, and has an integrity of its own in a public world, with a distinctive nature and career.

Each me has a being to the same degree that any other has. This would not be possible were the me wholly closed within itself, for then it would not be comparable with anything else. And since a me is attended to, sustained by, and is continuous with a private being, the being of the me is evidently part of a larger being. If the me and the I were self-contained, there would be two beings separate from and presumably able to function in complete disregard of one another. The consequence is avoided with the recognition that the being of the I and the being of the me are inseparable parts of a single being.

I and me are persistently and pervasively qualified in a number of independently produced ways, only one of which enables them to have beings. Still, when I and me have beings they are also substantialized. The being and the substantiality pervade and qualify one another. Since, as will become evident, the I and the me are conditioned in other ways as well, they are also subject to other pervasive qualifications.

2.23. Each me has rights.

A right is a claim made by a being or subdivision of it, against anything that could preclude the satisfaction of the claim. The claim is that the being deserves to be preserved and to prosper. It is *native* if it is an inseparable part of the being; *bestowed* if it is credited and supported by an authoritative or possessive power; and *acquired* if it is attained in the course of history. A me has rights in all three senses. As available for reference, it is an essential dimension of a man with the native right to be present in the world, to have a distinctive role there, and to be enriched by what is available. Made the object of a reference, the me has bestowed on it the right to be in contrast with what sustains it. Modified by experience and the uses to which it is put, the me acquires rights answering to crucial changes. Each man can know that he has these rights if he knows himself to be a me. Their presence can be surmised and even taken into account by others, just so far as these know that my me is copresent with their own.

The rights of each me are claims made by what is in the world with others. They are rights to which one appeals when protesting against what are taken to be injustices of a social or political system, for though possessed apart from any acknowledgment by others, they are claims that one be taken to be equal with others in a common world. There are other publicly significant rights besides these—among others, the rights of the you (which may or may not be acknowledged by a group or institution), and the externally defined rights of the legal person.

"I know my rights" may mean either that one is aware of the rights that are established by law, or that one is aware of the rights one has apart from these and other guarantees. The former are the rights one has as a legal person; the latter the rights one has a private person. My rebellion or resentment against the conduct of a state or against the warrants provided by a legal order may be on behalf of the rights possessed by me as together with others. These rights might be publicly accommodated. I would so far have no complaint about the way a public system functions. But I might still hold that the system fails to give adequate public meaning and support to expressions of the rights known to be my own, apart from others or any public acknowledgment.

A me is a locus of inalienable rights, i.e., rights which ought not to be alienated. A private person is the locus of inalienatable rights, i.e., rights which cannot be alienated. The rights I have as a private person are inalienatable; unlike the rights of my me, they are evidently beyond the capacity of a public world to promote or hinder. Those inalienatable rights achieve only a partial translation in the form of the inalienable rights of the me. The rights of that me in turn receive only a partial translation in the form of the rights of a you, since this is that me limited and made referential by others, or by the system in which all men are publicly together.

Understandably, everyone more or less both exaggerates and minimizes the inalienable rights his me has; an exact knowledge of the nature and boundaries of a me are not easy to obtain and are even harder to exhibit in practice. Both the exaggerations and minimizations can be limited by recognizing that the me of each is objective, present with the other me's in a common world and, with them, subject to the same conditioning.

The right to be me, so passionately urged when young, is not extinguished when one grows older. It is a right, of course, which can be so exaggerated that it can be insisted on in such a way for oneself as to preclude a satisfaction for others no less deserving. The price that is then paid is a loss of friendship and respect in the course of the effort to increase power and control, presumably for the sake of achieving a position deserving friendship and respect.

2.24. My being continues into the being of my person.

If in the course of a reference to me, not only 'me' but whatever might be encountered along the way, is brought to bear on the me, they will be made part of it. The fact will be misconstrued if stimuli and sensations are taken to be encountered items which are reduced to effects suffered. When empiricists speak of impressions, objects experienced, sense data, and the like, they rightly try to avoid that reduction and to hold that the acknowledged stands away from oneself at the same time that it is experienced. But insufficient attention is given by them to the brute resistance that makes it possible to encounter what exists apart from oneself. Did what was acknowledged not always have a status apart, it could not be encountered, for encountered objects are maintained apart from encounters with them. Beyond them it is possible at times to discern the presence of a more powerful, impersonal Being on which the being of a person and consequently the beings of the me and the objects which are oriented toward this me eventually depend. The fact becomes more and more conspicuous, the more I become aware that my full being is a specialized version of what is specialized elsewhere as well.

The being of my me continues into the being of my person. Both depend on Being. This comes more and more into view the more there is a withdrawal from a concern with what can be publicly encountered. The being which my person has is then seen to continue beyond the point where it can be identified entirely as *my* being. I may then become aware of it as remote, receding, never entirely within my control, a being continuing into Being itself.

When I withdraw from the public world, Being becomes both more and more insistent, and absorptive of what yields to it. In the East it is often said that this fact cannot be grasped except experientially, and then only after considerable training and practice. Claims have been made in the West that a shorter route is available for those who take special drugs. Neither is necessary. One can effectively move toward Being by deliberately withdrawing far into one's privacy, beyond the point where a person is distinguished. One then directly faces Being, the very finality one may have already deliberately, speculatively, or appreciatively attended to.

The divergence between person and Being is undergone as *dread*. As Heidegger has remarked, this has no specific object. Unlike *fear*, it reflects the fact that one is losing the contact one had with Being. *Anxiety* also mediates person and Being, but in such a way as to allow for a contrast between them. Reaching from person to Being, at the same time that it characterizes the complex in which the person and Being are together, anxiety is necessarily relational. Since it is felt by a person sensing a separation from a counteracting Being, anxiety is evidently quite different from aimless terror.

2.25. Me has a general meaning and a singular role.

My life and interests are mainly practical; they resolve about things which are important for my continuance, welfare, pleasure, and ease. When I attend to me, I am usually aware that I then am doing something distinctive and different from what I usually do. To turn toward me and what is behind this, I have to restrain a tendency to focus on what I encounter along the way. Usually what I focus on is qualified by that about which my attention pivots. But it is possible to ignore this and to just return from a position distinct from and so far indifferent to me.

Though faced and known by no one else, my me can be thought about and made intelligible to others. It is, after all, not only my me, but *a* me, one instance of a kind, a me like others. Though only I can attend to it, I can communicate what I then learn. Also I can sometimes predict what might next become evident, on the basis of what I there observe. And I can come to understand how it is related not only to what is external to it but to my person and to my self.

The awareness that I am encountering my me from a neutral position makes possible the awareness of myself as *a* me. I do not then, of course, see myself as something general, duplicable, like any other. The me at which I come to rest is mine, and mine alone. But it is still *a* me which is one of many me's. When I emphasize the singularity of my me, the many other me's are ignored, at the same time that the generic nature which all me's instance is incorporated in the me to which I alone attend. When, instead, I emphasize the nature of the me, I abstract from my peculiarities. In the first way I know that it is possible for me to have many different guises over the course of my career; in the second, that the me's which others confront are like my own.

2.26. I locate me with certainty.

A child has to learn how to use 'me'. One who knows no English will not use it properly. The learning in both cases is rough, schematic, involving errors. It would seem, therefore, that it makes no sense at all to speak of using 'me' in ways which differ from the use of other words. This would be true were the issue the *word* 'me', rather than the referring to the me by means of the word. 'Me' is used with the same meaning by all who both conform to ordinary ways of speaking grammatically, and who take the word to be singularized in the course of being applied. That singularization is an essential part of 'me's' use when different men speak, address themselves, and embody within their unduplicable me's what they say and use.

Were there no commonly understood 'me', with its core of common meaning, it would not be possible to know that another can and does terminate in a me when he uses 'me'. Yet, did each not use 'me' in a singular way, the commonly understood term would not terminate in unduplicable me's. Training in the use of English consists in part in learning to singularize a 'me', whose meaning many understand in the same way.

'Me' is used in accord with conventional rules. One of these requires each man to use it to refer to himself and no one else. The requirement, though, is stated in general terms. It does not tell one that he is a singular being, nor how he is to give the 'me' a singular application. Did one do nothing but follow rules, one would not yet use 'me' in a singular way, making it terminate where it should.

Eyes closed, a man who has had his leg cut off says that he feels a pain in it. Granted that he is using language in the usual way, it must be allowed that he has felt a pain, but has not been able to come toward it by attending to an observable part of his me. He has a phantom leg.

Can the reverse situation be imagined? Eyes closed, a man reaches out, touches his desensitized leg, and says "Me!" Granted that he knows the way to use the word, has he arrived at what he does not sustain from within? No. 'Me' requires such a sustaining. Since he is conscious, he has some feeling, but it is not in his leg. His is a phantom feeling. Both phantom leg and phantom feeling lack a factor essential to a known me. The one phantom lacks a locatable factor, the other an encountered one.

I arrive at me from a position external to myself. Sometimes I use an external object as a pivot or as a source of enrichment. I can also place one of my hands on the other. I do not then think or say "Me touches me." I say "I touch me." Yet both hands are part of me. They are also severally sustained. I would, of course, be divided against myself were it not also true that both of these sustainings are continuous with a single sustaining of the hands, and of other parts of the body as well. In any case, I know where to find me. Should I make the mistake of supposing that some severed portion of myself is still part of me, it would still be true that the mistake will be known when I contrast what was severed with what is still part of me.

It seems odd to say that any matter of fact is a certainty. Yet it is certain that I know where to find me without error, always—though not, of course, if one takes the finding to require a precise determination of the distance and direction that the me has from some other position in public space. The me, to be sure, is in a larger space and I must locate it there. But when I locate the me with certainty, it is not as in a position related to other positions, but as the referent of 'me'. When I say 'me' I thrust it into the world which exists apart from the being who is saying it. When I use 'me' properly I make it terminate in me.

I confront myself by approaching myself from without; yet I

cannot meet myself coming toward me. Despite the paradoxical sound of the conjoined contentions, no one ever questions either. A commonsense man attends to neither, and since they do not express primary truths on which a multitude of others hang, a commonsense philosopher does not take them to be important. But they surely are basic truths.

A me does not await the arrival of 'me'. The use of 'me' instead presupposes me. I may even know me before I refer to it. If so, when I refer to it, I make the me more evident and distinctive than it had been before I had made it the terminus of 'me'.

2.27. The conditions for meaning can be meaningfully expressed.

'Me' has a special meaning; it requires a speaker to use it as a proper name addressed only to himself. The more general meaning—it is a first-person pronoun, must be addressed to one who approaches himself from without and sustains it from within—depends in part on limited conditions which govern 'me'. If one were to speak of conditions which are operative everywhere, the nature of nonlinguistic factors which govern all words, and other items as well, would be expressed within language. This, of course, is what is being done here. It is also what is done when one speaks of whatever there be.

When we speak either of the limited conditions which are pertinent just to language or of those more universal, final conditions which govern whatever there be, our terms acquire meanings in the very act of being used. It is therefore right to maintain that we always mean more than we say, since what we mean is in part the conditions which are outside of but which govern everything. But it is also right to maintain that we can mean exactly what we say, since our meanings can be imposed on and carried by what is being said. It is also correct to say that we always mean less than we say, for there are layers upon layers of meaning that are present in what we say but of which we are not aware, never did intend to express, and may have nothing to do with what we are or know.

The inferences of historians—accumulative and stressing the preponderance of evidence within the limits of common-sense judgments—as well as the inferences of other inquirers, occupied with what is concrete, ongoing, extended, and possessors of values, are all within limited frames. Together with the inferences formulated and used in logic, they are under the governance of meaningfully expressed conditions for intelligibility. Those conditions make it possible for anyone to know what is meant by what is said, whether or not this is meant in fact, and whether or not its meaning is understood by its user. Such conditions are partly caught within the frame of the unit expressions and inferences approved by logic, as well as in richer expressions and other modes of inference. 'Me' is one such richer expression.

2.28. 'Me' carries an intent as well as a meaning.

'Me' is singularized just so far as it merges with its terminus. Before that merger, it retains a core of generality, making it possible for anyone hearing it spoken to know that it has the same meaning for different speakers. Many can know that it is available for anyone to use with a distinctive singular result.

Like any other word, phrase, or sentence, 'me' incorporates a meaning. Like any other, its meaning enables one to understand it. For the meaning, one sometimes turns to the history of the word, sometimes to conventions, sometimes to its referent, sometimes to the way it functions, and sometimes to more general, pervasive conditions. Its full meaning includes all. Like every other term in discourse, 'me' also incorporates an intent.

An intent is not an intention. Often enough, it is not even intended. If 'me' is used to refer to someone other than its user, the user will be known to have an unusual intent, perhaps one expressing a loss of a sense of identity, for in its normative use, 'me' carries an intent to refer to me. Deprived of its intent, it would be just a term in language. In discourse, though, one expresses oneself, intrudes an intent, and thereby partly exhibits what he is. Were the meaning there ignored and only the exhibition noted, the word and other parts of a language would be just loci of intents, symptoms of feelings, attitudes, beliefs, or prominent states.

Made deliberate and conscious, an intent becomes an intention. There are times when a man has an intention to speak of himself in such a way that others will attend or do things he wants done. Even prosaic observations, such as "I am not feeling well" or "My finger hurts," are understood not simply as meaningful because used in conformity with the rules of language and established conventions but as carrying an intention to have others attend to oneself with concern, and perhaps with remedies. These will not be forthcoming in the desired form or ways, however, unless the listeners locate the intention in the speaker. Did they, instead, content themselves with just grasping a meaning, they would understand the assertions, make note of them, report them perhaps, but would not act because of them.

Because of a concentration on just meaningful expressions, it is sometimes supposed that language is wholly public, that there is nothing private which individuals undergo, or that this could be known only by using public expressions as criteria of their presence and nature. But in discourse private intents are already incorporated in the public terms, to be read back into their sources.

As 'living', a language has a minimal intent, what is common to all users, and a minimal meaning which results from its domination by grammatical rules determining the placement and ordering of its words, and combinations of these. So far as they carry minimal meanings and intents, the words, and the larger units composed of them according to rules, are translatable into the words and units of other 'living' languages. As carrying more, the additional meanings and intents must themselves be capable of translation into other additions having similar roles in the other languages.

A used living language mediates between intent and meaning, minimal or more. Each part of it may function as an agency for translating some limited meaning into some limited intent, and conversely. The language is then identifiable as the totality of such verbal mediators or translators, set in an ordered whole.

2.29. Both me and 'me' unite meaning and intent.

Me, no less than 'me', has a meaning. It, too, embodies an intent. Though the me is not a word any more than a word is a man, like a word it can be understood to be not merely a locus of a meaning and an intent but to provide a distinctive way in which a meaning and an intent are mediated and inter-translated. As united in me, intent and meaning have a more intensive, purer form than the content and meaning united in 'me'. And beyond the me there is an even more intensive union of intent and meaning. The me merges imperceptibly into that union at the same time that it exhibits its own distinctive union of meaning and intent.

The presence of meaning makes 'me' intelligible to anyone who attends to it from the vantage point of the conditions to which it is subject, and makes it have the role of a penetrative symbol for anyone who uses it properly. Just as I can know what another means by attending to what explains the words he uses, so I can know what I really intend by attending to my own speech as expressing a deep unity of meaning and intent.

A me is both individual and subject to common conditions rooted in a final meaning. That final meaning is countered by and united with individual intents. In the course of the day and over a lifetime, the union varies in strength and evidentiality. No meaning is ever entirely caught within an individu-

al's expressions; it always remains tied to an explanatory condition. No intent is ever entirely embedded or united with
meaning; it always remains tied to an individual source of expressions. Still, there are moments when a man approaches a
state of intellectual isolation, when he feels that everything intelligible is irrelevant, abstract, sterile. He is then aware of
being alone, merely present, evidently meaningless. Sartre
and other existentialists have brilliantly portrayed this state. It
is never reached, of course, in its stark purity. A man retains
some hold on meaning even when this is turned away from as
irrelevant; he is subject to it even when he moves away from it
toward complete aridity and unintelligibility.

A mathematician's acceptance of an endless store of meanings rationally connected and free from intent is but the other
side of a self-involved or irrational man's movement away
from meaning. Since meaning and intent are never entirely
sundered from one another, the mathematician, no more than
the other, ever loses all grasp of the factor he is inclined to
neglect.

Why should a mathematician be joyous as he moves toward
sheer meaning, while a self-involved man is more and more
miserable as he approaches his intent? Does not one always
continue to remain oneself, uniting both components? The
questions are connected. A man is the locus both of meaning
and intent, able to pass from one limit toward the other. His
movement toward his intent is toward his unduplicable, expressive individuality; his movement toward meaning is toward an impersonal finality. In neither direction does he get to
one of them all alone. All he can do is to get intent or meaning
to increase its dominance, without ever extinguishing the insistent presence of the other.

A mathematician finds joy in his progress toward pure
meaning because he finds himself to be involved with what is
eternal. A self-involved man, instead, finds himself to have
meaning more and more submerged in himself as a transient
source of expressions. The rest of us avoid both extremes. But

we are not poised neatly between the two. We fluctuate about the midpoint, sometimes verging more toward meaning and sometimes more toward intent. Inevitably, the more constant, steadier conditions come persistently to the fore, to make us normally aware of ourselves as having meaning.

2.30. I know me intropathically.

The Peircean view that a noun is used in place of a pronoun, and not conversely, does not normally hold of 'me'. No noun or proper name is used in place of 'me', unless one is joking or misunderstanding himself—or what perhaps is close to the same thing, unless he is pompous or self-important. The me to whom I refer may be just myself when speaking—"Me? Over here!" Usually, though, it is a more inclusive, mainly bodily, voluminous whole within whose limits myself speaking and engaged in other acts can be demarcated. If another were to name, address, or even touch me, what he provided would not become part of me until I gave it a backing by a possessor.

A machine could be programmed to write or verbalize "Are you looking for me?" When appropriately questioned with "Are you Sam Browne?" its program might enable it to follow this with "Yes, that's me." It might even be furnished with an arm which accompanied the last expression, and be so geared that it extended a finger toward itself. It would still not refer to itself as a me, since it would not provide a possessing sustainer for what was being directed toward it.

Were there no way in which a cleverly contrived machine or some strange creature from outer space was known to be capable or incapable of possessively sustaining anything from within—and, therefore, if one could not know whether or not it was organically one; could feel; that the words it produced did not just follow one another but served to articulate a judgment; that what it presented had both meaning and intent,

and so on—one would have no other recourse but to abandon
the attempt to treat it as able to present a you and have a me. If
one could not make contact with it through love, hate, sympathy, repugnance, condemnation, appreciation—all special
instances of *intropathy*, a penetrative participation in the
depths of others—one would have to say that there was no
way of reaching toward what could have a you or a me.

The fact that one may not be able to say whether this or that
is a machine does not stand in the way of the truth that the
words produced by a machine are not wholly identifiable with
those made by a man. Though the two could be equally meaningful, only man's speech has an intent ingredient in it. Were a
machine to function aberrationally and produce incoheren-
cies and oddities similar to those that a man does, we would
look for defects in its program or in the ways in which its parts
were put together. If we could find no defects, we would be
perplexed. But when we attend to the aberrations produced
by a man, we can explain them even when no such defects can
be found. If a machine were to produce 'glove' where it would
be appropriate to have 'love', we will look for something
amiss in its design, parts, or operation. When a man makes
this substitution, there might not be a discoverable explanatory defect in his body. He might have made the substitution when his body was functioning well, since he could have
produced an intent strong enough to distort the pattern of the
discourse which he was physically equipped to carry on. His
substitution of 'glove' for 'love' might then betray the fact that
he preferred to keep hidden the hand that he had in some af-
fair.

Without intropathy, or a knowledge of an intent present in
what is said or done, there is no way of knowing that another,
no matter how closely it resembles a man, can face a me, for
we will not know if what is arrived at from without originates
with what could sustain it from within. If we know that someone could engage in such a sustaining we still, of course,
would not know that he is in fact doing this, and what it is

that he then learns. Should we come to know that he faces himself as a me which is being internally sustained, we will then know that he is a man, even if his appearance is radically different from any we now know. A man is one into whose depths we can directly penetrate to some degree, with whom we can be allied, who can make an intent override the role of meaning in what he says, who can internally constitute the termini of what he addresses to himself—and who can know that some others have me's.

'Me' is under the control of intent. Though it may fit well within the pattern of a meaning dependent on a governing condition, it accommodates and subordinates that meaning in a way no other terms can accommodate and subordinate theirs. Exclamations and various standard statements about my feelings offer additions to, variations on, enrichments or extensions of 'me', alerting those who hear them to recognize that the you to which they attend is being made part of me. If I have no other way of knowing that another faces his me, I grant the point as soon as I find that I am dealt with by him as one who can deal with himself as a me. I know which beings are men when I know which take me to be a man having an available me, or take themselves to be me's. Beyond that point I cannot be sure.

There are many men who claim that they make intropathical connection with their pets, and even that their pets make such connection with them. Some hold that master and animal are linked by means of more basic felt sustainings, and that the pets sometimes exhibit neuroses and other disturbances traceable not to anything peculiar in their physiology but to their psyches. Were all this accepted, we would have to say that their pets possibly have you's, but not yet that they have or could have me's. Only if the animals could conceivably know that what they reach from without is being sustained by themselves from within could they be properly credited with me's. That knowledge would require them to know that the reaching and sustaining both express the same I.

An animal has feelings; it can express hurt and pleasure. It can publicly attend to places where an injury or disturbance occurs. But it cannot merge the termini of its attention and feeling into a single me. Fortunately, it does not have to have a me nor to credit me's to its young to deal effectively with their needs.

An animal may lick its injured foot, or even hold it out, as though it were the public side of an internally felt pain. We rightly hesitate even then to credit it with a me because it has not shown that it knows that we have me's. Because it does not show that it knows that I am a me for myself, I do not allow that it ever knows that what it can grasp of itself from without is known by it to be continuous with what it is sustaining from within.

One whom I take to be a man may, of course, not care to attend to me, or may do so in violation of what, by following the clues of my intent, he discerns is being felt by me. But precisely because I know him to be one who knows that my grimaces, gestures, outcries, and various standard ways of expressing distress and need are sustained from within and are radically affected by intent, I condemn him for not caring, for his neglect, and for his brutality. I do not condemn an animal for not caring, because I do not expect it to care, and I do not expect it to care because I do not know that it knows I have a me. When I respond to an animal's squeal of pain, I undoubtedly intropathize, but this is not yet to know that it faces itself as a me.

My me is paired with a you which coincides in part with your me. This me of yours, in turn, is paired with a you which coincides in part with my me. No machine or animal can make a you, which is paired with my me, coincide in part with its me, for it has none. I therefore do not condemn either in the way I condemn a man for acting without regard for my feelings, or for his brutality or violation of my rights. Conversely, a man is condemnable when he tortures, humiliates, or enslaves other men. Since he is aware that they are men, even while acting on them in inhuman ways, he does not act as a beast. He is condemnable, as a beast is not, for having acted counter to his intropathical grasp of other men.

2.31. Any me can be dislocated.

Another can know where to look if he is looking for me. He will, of course, not find the me that I constitute from within, but only what is a you for him, held away from him. Though that you is not identifiable with me, it may be coextensive with it. The extensions of the two nevertheless differ in kind. The you is oriented toward him; the me is bounded off from all else.

My me and the you I am for another are both connected with other spatial units at a distance, the one as a maintained, bounded, disconnected portion of a larger region, the other as a delimited portion of that region. Both are bodily, but also more. The you is a designated origin of accountable acts, and the terminus of another's intent; the me is part of my person, is approached only by myself, and is filled out by various feelings not reachable from without.

Another finds me at a distinguished portion of a common space, in the guise of a you for him. I maintain me at that place in opposition to what else there is in the rest of space. The located you is a nuanced subdivision of a larger space; the very region where the me is found is an integral part of it.

When I sink back into myself, instead of finding myself there, I feel more and more disoriented, lost, dislocated, unable to grasp myself in the space where others also are. The awareness of that state tempts the belief that in myself I am unextended, merely spiritual, an unlocatable reality. The awareness that I am in the same world with others helps keep this belief tied in with its opposite. Whitehead remarked that it is wrong to say that one is lost, for one has lost only the other places and always has himself. Not so. I am lost, and feel lost when I cannot determine just where I then am. I feel lost, too, in a related sense when I do not know how to connect myself with others. To be sure, I do not then lose all hold of my me. And when I speak of being lost, I do not lose all awareness of a larger space and the places there, but instead fail to take them to be part of my environment or milieu. To know that I am lost is to have the other places, but not in the guise they ought to have for me. When I know I am lost, I sometimes know a great deal about others, but do not know just how we fit together.

The more deeply I retreat into myself, the more I become dislocated, without ever entirely losing hold of myself as spatialized and therefore as related to places beyond. Also, the space that is occupied by me, even while it is made my own, is not entirely sundered from a larger space within which it is a delimited place. Though I cannot separate me from the place it occupies and therefore cannot hold the me entirely apart from the space beyond it with which the place is continuous, both the place and space can become less and less involved with my needs and interests. I am dislocated because I do not keep a complete hold on them; my me, as part of my person, is always maintained in some opposition to the impersonal extension of space. To be me fully, the place occupied, and at least the spatial milieu beyond it, must be held on to.

2.32. Each me is in an indivisible present.

No moments elapse between the start and the terminus of a reference to me. The stretch between these limits does not reach from a past to a future; it occurs within a present. Were this not so, there would be a moment of time when I was using 'me' but had not yet arrived at me, with the consequence that 'me' would not address me, but instead would accompany a concern which conceivably might be frustrated, and in any case would at some time during the act of referring not yet be involved with me.

Like 'seeing' and 'believing', 'me' is what Ryle called an "achievement" word. These have to do not with starts and stops, preparations, struggles, but with single, final states of affairs. 'Me' in use is one, for it is inescapably part of me, its terminus. Both 'me' and me are in a present moment, one end of which has the ending recessive, and the other end of which has the beginning in that status, the entire present moment being spent in the indissoluble passage from the dominance of the one to the dominance of the other.

As soon as it is used, 'me' is united with me, with the 'me' decreasing in distinctness over the undivided course of the present moment. This has beginning and ending together in different degrees throughout, but in such a way as to preclude the setting of one degree earlier than the other, and therefore as exterior to and sunderable from it.

Did the present moment not have a stretch to it, it would be followed by another point-present, and this by another, and so on without end. But an infinite number of points cannot make even the tiniest extendedness. As a consequence, did the present not have an indivisible stretch to it, where beginning and ending were inseparably together, there would be no time at all. That present is demarcated within the whole of time. It is not identifiable with what would be a moment for Aristotle, just a number marking a period of change or motion; with what would be a moment for Newton, an arbitrary cut within a single, equable flow; or with what Einstein took to be a moment of time, a unit scientifically determinable through the use of light signals. It is a unit, present, occupied stretch, preceded and followed by other unit stretches of indefinite length.

The attempt to deal with time in terms appropriate to inanimate objects about which we learn through light signals has misled some to suppose that one attends only to a you that is already past. A consequence of such a view is that no one could ever know a you which was partly coincident with a me. Nor would one ever be contemporary with anyone he knew. And there would never be an encounter or interplay, but only external pasts in linear relations to private presents.

Each you occurs in a present, flanked by an indifferent past and future; each me occurs in a present which is bounded off from a relevant past and future. The present moment of both is evidently achieved by occupations of distinctive sorts. The you I am for you occupies an extension within a larger; my me, instead, possesses a filled-out present, relevant to the rest of time.

2.33. You and me are contemporaries.

The you which another knows me to be is given standing by me in its present moment. That you, though, has a relation to the rest of time different from what the equally present me does. In different ways, the you and me fill out one differently approached, publicly knowable division of a common time.

The me to which I attend is in the present. But I did attend to it earlier and I may attend to it later. Even now in memory and expectation I refer to it as in the past and in the future. But it is in the past and future only in relation to a present. Were I no longer to exist, there would no longer be a me which existed or will exist, since there would be no one who then could approach it from without while sustaining it from within. The me I now remember is a me only so far as it is sustained—and that can be only in the present. I know that I privately persist over time because I now know that I had been a me, and therefore had sustained it as I am sustaining it now. The me I expect to have is just a possibility, not a true me. It lacks the determinateness of a past me. But I expect it to become a true me because I face it as that which is to be sustained as I am sustaining me now.

A paired you and me are together in the same present moment. That present can be looked at in a number of ways: it is a public present which spreads from me to you; from your me to myself as a you; from the me's together; and from the you's together. Terminating in each of us, it is bounded off by each one from the common present moment in which we both are.

While in present moments of our own, we are contemporary with one another. Were we only together, we would not have our own privacies. Were we each in our own present moment, filling it out in a distinctive way, we would be monads, unable to interact or be concordant in time. Each of us would then have to be content with knowing himself from within, or would have to suppose that, in the act of referring to his me, he left himself behind.

In myself, as Augustine observed, I am distended. I am inwardly stretched out, without a publicly determinable magnitude. In attending to me, I bound a present moment off from its relevant past and future. In attending to you, I operate in a public time in which the two of us are together, but do so within the limits of a present moment that is being filled out by me in one way and by you in another. And what is continuous with my me and what is continuous with your me are also together with one another in the same contemporaneous moment of present time. Since each of us has a status independent of the present moment, each of us also privately lives in some disregard of what goes on without.

Animals and plants have rhythms of their own. Both have bodies, and some of the animals, at least sometimes, make evident that they also have feelings. Since some animals can attend to injured limbs, feeling from within what is encountered from without, their outward and inward sides evidently meet but are not dealt with as solidified, single units. The time that the animals fill out from within, like the time of each one of us, is bounded off from contemporaries and from a past and future, without being sundered from them. But the animals live only in an environment and not, like us, in a milieu as well. They are involved with what is pertinent to their continuance and welfare and not, like us, also involved with what is relevant to thoughts, interests, and beliefs.

When time is pictured as a line, much besides the passage of time is neglected. One fails to portray its present spread between those who attend and those who are attended to. This is what Newton and Einstein do. Their characterizations are pertinent only to a supposed time which encompassed physical objects that existed long ago and others that will exist much later. Such a time is a distorted version of the time through which men individually live and share in together. This does not mean that physical entities do not exist in an appropriate time. One can even take the time pertinent to them to be primary, hardly affected by the things it encompasses, affected somewhat more by plants and animals, and considerably by men, individually and together. Whether this be done or not, provision must be made for the fact that men are contemporary with animals, plants, and things as surely as they are with one another. However, they are contemporary with each kind in a distinctive way, at once setting subhumans outside the limits of a human vital time and taking them to be in a time characteristic of an environment or a cosmos.

2.34. The past and future are operative in me.

The present separates the past from the future. It is also present for the past and for the future, one determinate but frozen, a tissue of facts supported by what is present, the other indeterminate, merely possible, depending for realization on the acts of present actualities. The present, characteristic of things, has both the past and future outside itself, excluded and distinctive, at the same time that it grounds them. The living are burdened with a past; the present of each not only grounds the past that it lived through but is affected by it. As now excluded and sustained by the present, the past of the living is also within the present in the form of an effective modification which compels the whole to function in ways it otherwise would not. The future, too, though excluded and supported, bears upon and is operative within the living being, determining the kind and direction of the activities in which that being will engage.

If the beings have memories and expectations they make connection with a past and future. Human traditions and ideals are types of social memory, enabling many men to become involved with what had been and what will be, at the same time that they make themselves felt in the present. To avoid the traditions and ideals, one would have to extract the men from their settings in communities with their histories and programs, from the teachings of experience, and from the influence of myths and ideals. None of this, of course, is evident when a man approaches another as a you or himself as a me, though both the you and me are affected by his memories and expectations, and by traditions and ideals.

When sustaining me, I bring to bear what I have accreted from the past and have taken in from the future. I thereby make the me big with both past and future, at the same time that I occupy the present. Consequently, though what I confront of me is wholly in the present, I attend to it as reaching into, absorbing, and insistently making use of a past and a future.

Held away from all involvement with what is outwardly encountered, the present of my me is indistinguishable from a sheer duration. Because human time is both privately and publicly undergone, each affecting the other, that state can never be attained. My me is never entirely separated from what is available and encountered in a public world.

2.35. Each me is now partly detemporalized.

As outwardly arrived at, a me is bounded off from both past and future. Though never wholly sunderable from its sustainer and, therefore, necessarily connected with a past and future, the me is therefore also partly detemporalized, fixed within boundaries, made tenseless. It is then not simply present, excluding a past and future, but is also *now*, indifferent to the existence of what is no longer or of what will be.

It never occurs to me to say "Now, there's me again." Even while the me is in successive presents with changing appearances, ways, and aims, I remain in one distinct, bounded, constant now. So do you. I know that you also are now so far as I know that from your side you too are a me. I do not share in your now. But my me, while now by itself, is also now with you and others, themselves now.

Once separated from an outwardly produced constituent, the sustainer of me allows for a distinguishing of a deeper base which reaches into the past and future and uses these to turn a privately oriented now into a temporal present. The more I withdraw into myself, the more surely I make that separation, and the less and less intimately do I find myself involved with an objective temporal world. Though the separation is never complete, it moves closer toward a limit, the more there is a stress on my person. I approach quite close to that limit when I am seriously perplexed, so bewildered that I cannot make use of what I have already learned or of what it would otherwise be sensible to expect. I do not then escape into eternity. I remain confined to a now, able to become temporalized again. I become fully me, approached both from within and without when, once again, I occupy a present related to a past and future.

2.36. Each me is both free and necessitated.

Freedom is exhibited in every act. It provides private determinations for possibilities then and there realized. Liberty, as has already been remarked, refers to the comparative absence of constraints. Necessitation, in contrast with both, is a compulsion, logical or ontological.

It is possible to be free and have little or no liberty, for while expressing one's unity, all attempts to exhibit this in undisturbed speech, motion, rest, or other efforts and actions may be hindered. It is also possible to have considerable liberty and little freedom. The wild duck flies as it pleases; it expresses its own nature when doing this, but since it privately provides few determinations in the expression of that nature, it has little freedom. It is also possible for something to be subject to necessitation and have minimal freedom. Stones freely express themselves by adding minimal unpredictable determinations to possibilities. It is also possible to be free without being subject to a necessitation. I freely express myself and can freely subordinate others to myself. When I sustain me, I limit the reach and force of the necessitation to which the me is subject.

Expressions begin freely, and are progressively denied liberty under the governance of a necessity connecting the multiplicity of items into which the expressions fragment. A me, consequently, is free in relation to its accountable acts, in relation to its possible effects, in relation to a 'me' addressed to it, in relation to a you, and in relation to whatever else it accommodates. At the same time, it provides necessities for what is distinct from it.

Necessity has a number of forms worth distinguishing: a) In a *constitutive* necessity, the condition and conditioned are joined. I freely introduce a constitutive necessity when I produce *my* different expressions. b) In an *articulative* necessity, expressions are kept together and are intertranslatable without reference to their unitary source. I express myself in an articulative necessary whole of expressions. c) In a *situational* necessity, items distant in space and time, and in abstraction from a common underlying unity, are interconnected. A paired you and me are related by a situational necessity. d) An *obdurate* necessity exhibits a control of a plurality by a unity. The resistance of parts to absorption by me reveals an obdurate necessity in those parts. e) Formal items are interconnected by a *structural* necessity. The 'you' and 'me', isolated by logic and grammar, are united by a structural necessity. f) In a *causal* necessity, a possible effect is transformed into a present necessitated effect. My acts exhibit a casual necessitation.

Freedom does not require the exercise of choice or will, any more than necessity requires the exercise of physical force. An expression may be freely begun, without consciousness. But preferences, choices, and willed decisions are freely made by conscious men.

Both the me and the you are accountable so far as they are at
liberty. Neither ever exercises a preference, choice, or will.
When we admonish, encourage, and criticize some of those
whom we encounter, we do so in the hope that they will attend to themselves and reform their ways. Evidently, what
we are then trying to do is to prompt them to make certain
private decisions.

2.37. Neither you nor me originates acts.

You are the terminus of a reference by another; me is the terminus of my own. You and me are origins to which manifestations, expressions, and actions can be traced, but you and me
are not their causes; you and me have no power, are not able
to do anything. Were it not that you and me continue in depth
into more powerful, free privacies, what occurs would have to
be credited to the action of an impersonal, cosmic force rear-
ranging the ways in which you's and me's are related to one
another and to other items. It is not surprising, therefore,
that those who attend only to what is observable or scientifically manageable, should conclude not only that there are
no free acts, but that each particular serves only to channel the
passage of a cosmic force. But if particulars can do no more
than make possible a change in strength and direction of a
cosmic force, they need be no more than concentrates of the
force itself, simply modifying its normal monotonous, universal exhibition. Though neither a you nor a me originates
acts, neither just modifies the manner in which a cosmic force
is being exhibited. Actions pass through both the you and me,
carrying the burden of preferences, choices, and wills, and
therefore also of the thoughts, aims, purposes, ideals, and
dedications which are involved in preferring, choosing, and
willing. Detached from their origins, viewed solely as packets
of energy pointed in a definite direction, no actions would be
due to a responsible man.

Might it not be the case, though, as Kant suggested, that action is begun and carried out by a free being who intersects but does not affect the indifferent ongoing of the physical world? One would then allow for freedom, and even have it terminate in the world. Such freedom, however, would not enable anyone to act in accord with that ongoing nor to introduce into it divisions, directions, and values by means of which consideration was shown for what others need or deserve.

"You gave this to me," in the light of these considerations, is to be understood to have two quite distinct referents: a transaction occurring under the physical, social, and legal conditions in a public world where you and me are terminating points, and distinct individuals outside that public world who express themselves through a publicly available you and me. A behaviorist and a lawyer will be inclined to emphasize the first, the one attending mainly to the terminals and the changes undergone, the other to the departures and arrivals of some public item at those terminals. A personalist and an ethicist, instead, will be inclined to emphasize the second, the one occupying himself with what each individual is by himself, the other with what all ought to do.

Buber tried to combine the positions of the personalist and ethicist. He urged men when they confront one another to remember that beyond each you there is an individual, as irreducible and as important as any other. He also urged each to give something to himself in the process. It was good advice. But it needs supplementation by a concern for you and me as termini in a public world, responsibly accountable for what they publicly originate.

2.38. Each me has some liberty.

A me is approached from without in a setting ruled by necessity. As subject to that necessity, the me, though it does not act, makes a distinctive contribution to the nature of what ensues. At the same time, it is free, both in the sense that it provides a unitary starting point for the accountable and in

the sense that it is an integral part of a private source of expressions and acts. But as only at liberty, it is ineffective and,
in comparison with itself as involved in causal processes, impotent. This is not the impotence of one who is being effectively constrained, faced with obstacles in the way of his expressions. It is rather the impotence of one who is outside the
area where he is able to act—the impotence of the enlightened
man of the East, not the impotence of the frustrated man
of the West. Like the latter and unlike the former, however,
it is the impotence of an individual, radically distinct from
all others, and not of one who has lost himself in an all-
encompassing spirit, eternally calm.

I must withdraw into myself if I am to make choices and
to will. I must withdraw if what originates with or passes
through me is to bear the marks of my intentions and desires. I
must withdraw if I am to constitute a linked set of expressions.
The more I withdraw in these ways from an involvement in
the world, the more impotent I make myself be. If I content
myself with just making choices, I will so far limit my freedom
to the making of decisions which may not be carried out in action. If I withdraw beyond that point, I ignore the world of
particulars.

The further I withdraw, the more I move toward myself as
unrelated. I do not then merely hold myself in reserve but effectively disconnect myself from the area where action occurs.
If I could thereby become a member of a kingdom of ends, I
would not yet be one who legislates for himself or for others,
for I would have lost connection both with the world and with
the other members of that supposed kingdom. It is not, therefore, a state which I seek, nor one at which I can ever completely attain. Usually, as soon as I come to a stop in my
withdrawing, I turn about to become involved with what is in
the world, mainly on my own terms. The effort is rarely conscious, being an almost reflexive attempt to escape from a position where I am not able to affect what is happening.

The further I withdraw into myself, the more by myself I become, uninvolved with what else there is. Though I never ar-

rive at the point where I am entirely disconnected from everything, there is no point where the detachment comes to an
end. Throughout, I have some awareness of a world outside
me that, precisely because I am still involved with it, threatens
and may hobble me. My retreat into myself leaves me exposed
to more impersonal, more insistent, more inescapable forces
than those to which I had been previously subject. The more I
unify myself with those forces, the more are my free expressions interwoven. I am free, not when I understand or accept necessity, but when I make it part of myself, able to con-
stitutively necessitate some occurrences. My preferences,
choices, willings, and actions are then in consonance with
what is necessitated to occur.

2.39. This is me, therefore I am.

Descartes arrived at his "I think therefore I am" too quickly.
The ultimate point he reached in the course of his effort to
doubt all things was a state of doubting. He had no warrant to
move on to a 'thinking', which for him was a miscellaneous
number of mental activites, such as believing, hoping, inferring. Instead, he should have tried to show that a doubting
required a doubter, and that this required an I who doubted.
This he did not do. In fact, well before the time he doubted,
like the rest of us, he was already in possession of indubita-
bles, on which his own awaited. One of these is: "This is me."
That entails "Here I am," for the me continues into the I which
possesses it. "Here I am," in turn, entails "I am." This is inseparable from an affirming I, and that is inseparable from the
I as able to engage in other acts. The first needs the others to
complete itself, not as the two sides of a triangle need the
third, but as a part of one side needs the remainder of it.
    "This is me, therefore I am," attaches what is outwardly ap-
plied to what is inwardly operative. So far no reference is
being made to any thinking. I do not, of course, understand

any of this without thinking. But I can say "This is me," not even knowing that I say it. If I do, the saying will still be grounded in the I; I will be expressed in that saying.

The existence of an I is continuous with the existence of a me. Both the me and I are united in a private existence, itself an internalized specialization of a more primary and controlling existence. The specialization is precariously maintained; eventually it comes to an end. The me and I do not then necessarily vanish, for apart from the more primary existence to which they are subject and the portion of it which they have internalized, they are involved with other finalities.

As long as I am connected with a conditioning existence, no matter how tenuously, I remain in existence. Only when I become submerged in the existence of others, or in Existence itself, do I cease to exist. If this is true, must we not conclude that the more surely I exist, the more surely I must cease to be? Yes. The paradoxical sound of the affirmation vanishes at once, if after "exist" we insert "within an alien existence," and add after "cease to be," "a separate existent." The result is a tautology: "The more surely I exist within an alien existence, the more surely I cease to be a separate existent reality."

2.40. Each me has a value.

In attending to myself, I deal with me as a unique terminus. If I speak in the course of the act of addressing, I use 'me', or some substitute or limited form of it, to end in the me. That me possesses a special dignity as an ultimate, distinct unit. Yet I might have come to myself in an attitude of contempt, hatred, despair, or self-destruction. I might despise myself and both say and mean that I am worthless in myself and in relation to others. It is no consolation to know, but it is nevertheless true that I have then marked myself out as having the special dignity of one who sustains these characterizations. Did those regrettable and perhaps even correct characterizations exhaustively express what was persistently true of me, that me would have only a minimal or negative value. But they only presuppose me. My me has the dignity and power of being able to carry and give those determinations a resting place. I cannot sensibly condemn (or praise) my me for being a me, but only for being or exhibiting itself in a special way. What is hateful (or admirable) is not the me, but only an aspect of it. Since my me is always more than what it is being characterized as, when it is despised as the accountable origin of what is regrettable, in addition to being credited with the status of having a negative value, it is also held to have the positive value of an origin. A me has a value that is not only superior to the features of it, but to any acts or outcomes for which it is accountable.

2.41. 'Me' entrains relativized and absolute assessments.

In the course of the use of 'me' (even when no explicit use is made of any verbal expression) a momentary stop is sometimes made at another. I can then return to myself in terms of values supposed to be present at that other position, and the judgments that might be made from there. It may then appear at times that I have allowed my value to be minimized. "You are a model for me"; "You are right, and I was wrong"; "You make me ashamed of myself," so strongly reflect my acceptance of another as a locus of value or a source of judgments that they tempt a denial that the me has a value of its own. But I had already assessed the other; he was arrived at, not as one objectively evaluated—though this, of course, does occur—but as providing a base in terms of which I assess myself. Were I to evaluate him objectively, and not on the way to an evaluation of myself, my evaluation would be made partly in terms of a standard which applied to both of us. I would then not deal with myself in terms of assessments which were relative to a man to whom I attended in a particular way and whose supposed judgment or standpoint had me in a state of reduced value. Instead, I would have reached a position from which I was able to assess myself objectively.

There are times when I am ashamed of my impulses, thoughts, and prejudices. My irritations, selfishness, and conceit make me think of myself with distaste. At other times I am ashamed of what I had been, and even how I look and act when I am selfish or conceited. Most often, I am ashamed of myself as the source or locus or some things I take another to have discovered about me. Rarely do I stop to find out whether or not he is in fact evaluating me, or to learn just what his evaluation is. The shame I feel expresses an immediate, unreflecting acceptance of what I take to be his evaluation of me, and which I accommodate in the course of my reference to me. I credit myself with a minor or negative value as a consequence of the application of a standard which he is supposedly incorporating.

Philosophers sometimes bedevil themselves by seeking a necessarily true answer to the question how anyone could ever know that there were other men with minds of their own. Like the rest of men, the philosophers know that there might not in fact be another at a supposed position. No more than the rest of us can they rightly conclude from "I feel ashamed" to "There is another." All they, like anyone else, have a right to conclude to from "I feel ashamed" is "I have a mind."

Nothing in principle is in the way of knowing that there are other men with minds. The knowledge depends on an ability to discern something that requires a sustaining. This their shame provides. One knows that there are others with minds if one knows that they are ashamed. Could it be known that they are ashamed? Yes. The blushing, cowering, flustering, which accompanies their noticing that someone is looking at them, is grounded in a consciously maintained shame. They do not then provide a criterion or mark of some inward hidden act. The blushing and other exhibitions are the shame itself as its outward limit, continuing in depth into the shame as lived through.

A man may blush with a quick flush of shame if he notices

that he is being critically viewed when he performs some ordinary bodily functions, but he does not usually feel ashamed when he is so emotionally involved with another that he reveals himself and his weaknesses to a degree that he had not even allowed himself to know. Should he think he is just being watched, or if he becomes aware that he is being overheard or being seen by an outsider ready to assess him unfavorably—or even if he just thinks he is—he usually feels shame at once. Evidently, shame reflects a consciousness of the fact that without conventional protections, privileges, and disguises, and the good will of others, one will suffer the denigrating judgment of another. Though a surgeon's eye may be just as unsympathetic and cold as any bystander's, one does not usually feel shame on becoming alert to it, for it is not supposed that it will be accompanied by an assessment of one's relative place in the world of accountable men. But were one dissolute, overweight, with the liver of a drunkard, and the like, one might not be able to free oneself from a sense of shame when scrutinized by a surgeon.

It is not the coldness or the dispassionateness of the look of another that disturbs, but what one takes to be the accompanying or prospective judgment of one's comparatively low worth. In any case, a feeling of shame does not await a determination of whether or not anyone is in fact noticing, but only on a conscious acceptance of another's supposed actual or prospective evaluation of one's worth as a man relative to others. When the outcome conflicts with the judgment a man had entertained of himself, he will often keep the two separate, recognizing them to have different bases.

The determination of the objective value of a me is achieved by adopting an absolute position on the way to a termination in that me. When this is done, 'me' is used to carry a measure of value. I condemn and praise others for the ways in which they have reduced or enhanced my and other values, judged in terms of an absolute, universal standard as available to them as it is to me.

I try to maintain myself persistently against all intrusions and, therefore, inevitably, against any evaluations and the values in which these terminate. The more successfully I do this, the more I remain untouched by the evaluations of others and the more I become involved with what determines the absolute value I have as together with all else. Eventually, I reach a point where I turn in the opposite direction. The fact has been underscored many times by religious thinkers of different persuasions. To share in the kingdom of final evaluations, they have insisted, it is necessary that I both tear myself away from an involvement with the world of every day and abandon a concern with myself. But I will not know that it is myself who is being saved if all hold on myself is lost, any more than I will know that there is a kingdom of final evaluations if I am not now affected by it to some degree.

CHAPTER 3

The Self and I

3.1. A self encompasses an I and other distinguishable sources of privately initiated acts.

'SELF' AND 'I' are often used synonymously. But there are times when one is and should be used rather than the other. I say "I did it," not "my self did it"; "I try to be true to my self," not "I try to be true to my I." I usually involves some claiming and responsibility; self, in considerable consonance with its philology, refers to what is wholly private, embracing a plurality of unit origins and roles, only one of which is referred to by 'I'.

An I is a representative condensation of a self. Once a distinction is made between self and I, room is made for the acknowledgment of other epitomizing condensations of the self. Unaffected by bodily changes or acts, a self is able to engage in various activities through the agency of these different condensations. Because the self and the person are adjacent specializations of the same privacy, the I and other condensations of the self are able both to pass beyond the person into the world and to sustain the person as well as the me which exhibits this in a condensed form.

An I, when contrasted with the mind and other condensations of the self, has a more central and basic role than these. It possesses them and can use them. Possessing the me, it also merges into it, and can responsibly accept accountability for what is traceable to that me. It is no single, hard, nucleal unit

behind which no one can go, a presupposition for all knowledge, a mysterious thing in itself, a final horizon, a fiction. It is
the self epitomized, able through the agency of the person to
use a body in such a way that sometimes the mind is elicited
along the way.

There is nothing in principle amiss with the theory that
every activity of the self and its various subdivisions is accompanied by some bodily activity. What is amiss is the supposition that whatever the self does has an exact counterpart in
observable parts of the body, and particularly in some such
limited parts as the cells of the brain; or that the self and its
subdivisions are occupied with detached sensations and
never with what in fact is observable both at the body and at a
distance from it, or with what governs and interrelates all particulars.

Did one insist on attending only to what is simply located
within the confines of his mind, cut off from all else, and then
with matching this with what is observed, he will be forced to
suppose that what is observed is also caught within such mental confines just so far as it is known. Consequently he will
not be able to have a knowledge of the bodies of others, supposedly matching what was happening in his mind.

3.2. A self-reference can be self-conscious.

Action is begun by the I. References to me, to you, to anything in fact, are carried out by it. When bodily expressions
are referred back toward myself, they function as substitutes
for a 'me' inevitably terminating in me. Since on arriving at
the referent, there is an inevitable passing beyond it toward
the I which is helping constitute it from within, inevitably
there is a return toward the reality which engaged in the referring. Consequently, when my thrust toward me is consciously engaged in, the meeting of it by a conscious sustaining
yields a self-consciousness. In that self-consciousness I both
attend to me and pass beyond it. This self-consciousness does

not depend on the presence of some other individual or require that I look at me from a higher or later vantage point. I can be self-conscious whether or not there is anyone about; and if I look at me from a higher or later vantage point, I will merely have a consciousness of what was present on a lower level or at an earlier time. The kind of self-consciousness that comes to the fore when I feel that I am being viewed in a hostile manner is often just an acceptance of a denigration of the me which results from an evaluation produced through the adoption of a standard presumably embodied or expressed by others. I can be genuinely self-conscious as having a lower or negative value from the position of others only if I return to the I via a me that has been subjected to a supposed evaluation. Were the return made from the position of an absolute standard, my self-consciousness would end in an absolute evaluation of me. In either way, a self-consciousness would be effectively achieved; in either way, it would be mediated by what is distinct from me.

There would be no genuine self-consciousness were an outward thrust of the I not met by a sustaining by that very same I. Were there two I's, one of which was thrusting outwards and the other of which merely sustained what was being brought to bear from without, there would be just two consciousness. Were the supposed two distinct I's to coalesce, the resultant would not even be a consciousness. The thrust and the sustaining, to be sure, are distinct acts, but unless one could have more than a single I, or unless one or both of these acts were not acts of the I, one will return toward the very I which began the thrust. That the thrust and sustaining are different acts points up the fact that I can do more than one thing at a time, without thereby becoming divided against myself, broken in two.

Sometimes while self-conscious I am aware that I am attending to myself. A self-consciousness already achieved is then overlaid by a consciousness. When that consciousness is met by a sustaining, the self-consciousness is intensified. Intensifications of this kind apparently can be repeated indefinitely, but the different levels and degrees become almost at once impossible to separate from one another. All I am sure of is that my self-consciousness varies in intensity at different times and at different places.

In an environment, territory, and milieu, distant spaces are relevant to perceiving inhabitants. These are, so far, not self-conscious, since they terminate in something beyond them and do not pivot there. Animals can do no more than this. Like men, they thrust toward what is distant, but, in part, because they do not start as far back within themselves as men can and do, they cannot know themselves. When they happen to attend to themselves, they either do so without inter-mediation, or they break up the reference into two stages, one reaching an outward terminus, the other starting there and ending at themselves. Injured, some of them make an im-mediate outward effort to deal with what is disturbing; if there is a juncture of this with what is inwardly felt, it is just lived through, not known as a me. An animal has no I to use nor to return towards. Only a man can self-consciously refer to him-self, since only he has an I and can begin from and move to-ward it.

3.3. I can speak intelligibly about myself.

Belief is to be distinguished from knowledge, perception, and inference, which it may sometimes accompany. I know when I believe and when I do not. I fear no error when I say that I believe today what I believed yesterday about the roundness of the world, the size of the sun, and the mortality of men. I know, too, that I know some things and do not know others. I am confident that I know when I have a stomachache or a backache; and that I am pleased when I quench my thirst. Such contentions have rarely been disputed. It is hard to know whether or not all of them are questioned by Wittgen-stein and his followers, since they concentrate their attention on pains and related feelings. Still, the questioning, even the rejection of these contentions, seems to be implied in what appears to be their successful assault on the theory that there could be a private language by means of which one named private sensations and presumably anything else that was occurring in one's self or mind. The most that could be held, it is said, is that one can claim to have such and such an inward experience if account is taken of various publicly available criteria, which give the necessary and sufficient conditions for the meaning and truth of the claim, or at least for its intelligibility. Being available to others, the criteria supposedly enable anyone to determine just what someone is undergoing, so far as any sense could be given to his expressions. In one step, it is both denied that it is possible to have a private knowledge or a private language about what was going on within oneself, and affirmed that one could know and speak intelligibly about another as well as that other could.

The thesis has been unnecessarily burdened—to speak gently—with such odd, unconfirmable claims that both Siamese twins can feel the same pain, or that were I to feel pain when touching another's hand, there are circumstances when it would be correct to say that I feel his pain. On this view, pains and other experiences exist or are intelligible only when given expression in public terms. The expressions are also taken to be capable of terminating in a place outside one's body, and there felt as pain. Freed from these oddities, the thesis has considerable strength. It is surely true that the application of names to isolated privately undergone experiences is arbitrary, and that there is no way of giving them any commonly understood meaning as long as they are not parts of an established, law-controlled language. But the supposition that nobody can privately know that he has a pain goes counter to the view, maintained at the same time by these thinkers, that the common use of terms is always to be respected.

It is true, of course, that 'I', 'pain', and 'me', and the like, are words in a common language, that one teaches their use to children by attending to such public expressions as moanings, outcries, and grimaces, and then trains the children to use the words as substitutes for these expressions. But it is not true that a child (or anyone else) just makes use of public substitutes when talking of its pain and inward adventures. It refers to its me. Not only is its reference to its me not assimilable to the references that others make to it in the guise of a you, but a child can speak truthfully and report accurately, intelligibly, and intelligently when it says that it has a pain. It can also know what it is privately doing when it idly and quietly attends to itself, thinks, and hopes.

The conditions of discourse are not identical with the conditions essential to the existence of a language. A discourse, to be intelligible, must make use of a language, but it does not remain within the limits of this. Sometimes when men deal with public, observable occurrences, they speak impersonally. When they refer to themselves, they always subject the words they use to new conditions. The self-reference, by making use of public words, is enriched, and the words are given a new import. That this is occurring others can know. What they cannot know, but the speaker can, is the privately undergone outcome of the juncture of the inward and outward thrusts of his I.

The position of Wittgenstein can be approximated—it could even be said, is properly conveyed—if one recognizes the distinctive role that 'I' plays in various claims and assertions. When I say "I am in pain," "I am thinking," "I believe so and so," "I was lying," "I dreamt so and so," "I feel sad," the 'I' tells others that they can count on what is being reported. This is distinct from claims which begin with "It is a fact that . . ." or "It is true that. . . ." "It is a fact that . . ." is used to report something settled, for which there is conclusive evidence to be accepted by others without further questioning. "It is true that . . ." says less, indicating only that a report can be relied on, because it recounts what one had observed or had heard; no claim is made that it is bedrock. When these phrases are dropped, one does no more than make a claim that is presumably true. If wrong, one is accountable for an error proclaimed. Had the remark been prefaced by "It is true that . . . ," one would have assumed the position of a representative man. Had one instead begun with "It is a fact that . . . ," one would have also tacitly asked others to take the report as needing no further justification or support.

When I say "I . . ." I alert another that a claim will be made. If the claim is in the form of a report, and a fact is not reported, I will have violated a trust, betrayed the confidence of my listener, unwarrantedly exaggerated, or so confused imagination with report that I will have failed to report what is beyond all questioning. When I say "It is a fact that I am thinking, feeling, etc., this or that" I go even further, for I then tell others that I am acting in these ways. I offer myself as a kind of explanation for what occurs. The meaning of what occurs is given in the explanation, in what makes sense of what would otherwise be inexplicable. When asked, "Why do you say you have a toothache," the "I feel it" refers to an absolutely final report and explains why it is so; what *I* claim here—I feel a toothache—is irreducibly true because *I* help constitute what is being claimed—a feeling of a toothache.

'I' am not beyond the world in which I am manifest, except in the sense in which an explanation is always beyond that which it explains. In referring to it I do not claim that I have an internal direct access to it—I do have a unique access, but this is via me—or know what the I is like (for it is lived rather than observed) but only that it is constitutive of what is being experienced. The fact that I cannot communicably say what is experienced without having recourse to a common language does not mean that something private and nonlinguistic is not being reported.

A report preceded by 'I' cannot be rejected without supposing that I am not a reliable, responsible speaker of English, either because I do not know the language or because I pervert it. If I am speaking properly, I am claiming, grounding, and explaining what is undeniable. "I am one hundred and fifty years old," "I never dream," "I have never lied," "I always know the answer," are all false. But they are shorthand for "I believe I am . . . ," "I believe I never . . . ," "I believe I have never . . . ," "I believe I always know. . . ." In these cases the "I believe . . ." is certain, but what is believed is not. The latter tells us what has been attributed to the I or what this sustains, not what it undergoes, certifies, and explains.

3.4. I am known to others.

As we have already seen, the you that is known by others continues in depth, enabling them to make some contact with the source of that you. When they attend to this which is a you for them, they penetrate to some degree to what sustains it from within. What they reach is not an I; the I is always beyond their grasp.

If another cannot reach someone else's I, how can he know that there is any other I but his own? It will not suffice to say that all men instance the same universals and therefore are alike, for this falls short of the individual, without which there is no I. It is not enough to say that, properly used, the terms 'I' and 'me' must terminate in an I and a me, for though this is true, the words can be spoken by parrots or be coded in machines. Nor is it enough to say that another can penetrate beyond the you he confronts and know that there is an individual who is smiling, frowning, moaning, or cringing. If these expressions are simulated by an actor or a confidence man, another may misconstrue them and their initiator. These difficulties arise because no one's reference to another can match that other's own sustaining in the way that other's own reference does. But this is far from showing that no contact can be made with the privacy of another, or that nothing can be known of it. Some contact and some knowledge of it are possible even for those who do not understand what privacy is, what the self is like, or what the I does.

If I try to deceive, I present myself for a reading as surely as I do when I am honest, the two presentations differing in what they allow another to read off readily in established ways. In reaching the you that I present, another overlaps the very same component that I do when I am self-conscious. But his contribution does not match that component. He cannot constitute the me that I constitute through the union of two moves. And, of course, he is not at their origin, where the moves are indistinguishably together. His contribution and mine meet at what is a you for him. He encounters public, relativized, diluted forms of my I, whereas my various public manifestations are both encountered and sustained by that very I. What he cannot do is to be one with my I. To do this, he would have to cease to be himself and become an entirely different being. But though he never knows what I can self-consciously know and can never unite with my sustaining in the way I can and do, he is able to know that I am, make contact with attenuations of that I, and move toward it. If he tries to achieve this knowledge in response to the words of a parrot or those which issue from a machine, he soon finds that he cannot. He is, to be sure, also stopped by autistic children, the senile, imbeciles, sleepers, men berserk or in a frenzy. But he can still make some contact with them as you's and persons.

I do not need another in order to be self-conscious. But when, as self-conscious, I make use of what I discern in another, I can, in the course of my advance into myself, keep in some accord with his reference to me. I then become coconscious with him, my consciousness ending in what is also an integral part of myself, and his consciousness ending with what he finds resisting, and even, under the pressure of my conscious acceptance of my own sustaining, with what is withdrawing from and avoiding union with his penetrative move toward it.

3.5. Self-reference has three distinguishable termini.

Instead of attending to my body, where some limited feeling might be met, I can attend to myself as readied, not yet engaged in distinctive acts, not yet with a distinguished me. I will then face myself in a diffuse form. I can also make a direct self-conscious return to myself as the locus of believing, inferring, remembering, and other nonbodily and sometimes uncommunicated activities by beginning beneath these activities and approaching them from an external position. Consciousness has these activities as publicly manifested objects of attention; self-consciousness has them in the form of sustaining counterforces to what is terminating at them.

A self-reference that externally terminates in and continues into a private outward-directed accommodating thrust is occupied primarily with feeling. Only as ending with the self or one of its epitomizations is a self-reference a genuine *self-consciousness*. Reaching to the self as engaged in some act, self-reference has the form of a *self-knowledge*. When any of these involves the use of a standard, self-reference has the form of a *self-criticism*. This last is required if there are to be justified and rectified acts of reference.

Self-referential acts of all types are sometimes said to be intuitive, i.e., immediately and, presumably, infallibly carried out. Peirce rightly objected to such a view on the grounds that one can never be sure there ever are intuitions, and that children learn about their selves mainly by finding a basis for their discovered ignorance and errors. His alternative was that self-reference was an inferential act, hazardous and perhaps mistaken. In defense of it, Peirce remarked that the acknowledgment of a self is a kind of conclusion supported by a host of premisses and is therefore more strongly entrenched than any one of them. But it is by no means evident that no single inference is ever to be trusted. No less important, there is no reason to take intuition and inference to exhaust the alternatives. The self is consciously known by the I from within, and self-referentially by the I through the mediation of the me.

Self-reference is always mediated by a me. It is, therefore, not an intuition. But it is also not an inference from one or many premisses, even if one were to take the inference to be an 'abduction', i.e., an act of forming an hypothesis on the

basis of presented data. It is a constituted outcome in which
the terminus is internally made one with what arrives at the
terminus from without.

3.6. I privately know what is publicly reachable.

The problem which concerns knowing about what is privately
attended to or undergone has to do, not with self-knowledge,
but with a consciousness of an activity which is begun from
within. Those who deny the possibility of private languages
and private knowledge have this primarily in view, treating as
futile and foolish the attempt to deal with such an activity as
though it could be surveyed like an external object, but in a
private, secret chamber. They are surely right in refusing to
reduce a consciousness of outer occurrences to the consciousness of something inner, but this is far from showing that
there is no consciousness of private activities. The problem is
solved when one engages in an act of self-reference having for
its topic, not some particular activity such as believing, but the
I attending to this. Such a self-reference begins behind the activity, passing through it twice, once when going to the outside and then, on returning, when going toward the sustainer
of the me.

I do not consciously refer to my believing or other inner activities in an act which is the double of a reference to you or to
a tree. The parallel breaks down for a quadruple reason:
Neither you nor the tree depends on my consciousness in
order to exist, but there is no believing without consciousness
of something believed. Secondly, though I can be steadily
conscious of a series of different objects, I have different con-
sciousnesses, with different natures, rhythms, and directions
when I engage in different inner activities; when I believe that
this is a tree I believe in the same way that I do when I believe
that there is a horse, but believing-that-this-is-a-tree is quite
different from believing-that-this-is-a-horse. Thirdly, when I
imagine the absence of all objects from consciousness, I con-

tinue to be conscious of an emptiness, but when I imagine the absence of all particular inner activites, I imagine a state of no consciousness at all. Finally, I refer to external objects in terms of categories, concepts, beliefs, and similar consciously used agencies which provide a setting where objects will be set, but there is no supercategory or superbelief which dictates the kind of setting where I will fit my concepts or beliefs about things. If there were, it would be a part of pure consciousness, quite distinct from the consciousness of an empty world, and from the absence of consciousness altogether. These truths do not jeopardize the possibility of knowing transcendent realities, for the double reason that there is nothing in the way of other categories being pertinent to these, and nothing in the way of the transcendent objects being present in the very settings from which one sets out to deal with them by themselves.

Though my belief is not like an external object, it can be known from the position of what it governs or with what it is involved, by tracing what had been contributed to this back to its source. Such knowledge is quite different from what I obtain through a self-conscious knowing or from a presumed internal consciousness directed at a belief. A belief is one expression of consciousness. Because this is so, it is possible to start with a belief and trace this back to the consciousness. Since belief is alternative to doubt, the consciousness in which belief is grounded is evidently specified by belief in only one of a number of alternative ways.

There is good reason to hold that there are memory traces and well-ingrained habits or strong tendencies to which a reference must be made in order to explain aberrational behavior and speech. One need not, though, refer to them for a warrant for looking to a private source (which may well be below consciousness) for the explanation. Aberrational acts appear to be the products of two components, one the conditions for normal and proper ordinary acts, the other a distortive factor having a subterranean base. If this be allowed, then one will have to distinguish conscious belief from unconscious belief, reaching the one by penetrative specifications from normal and common occurrences, and the other from oddities—or from an alien factor found imbedded in and distorting the conscious beliefs. It is not evident, though, that there is an unconscious, particularly when this is taken to be a kind of reservoir in which what had once been conscious is preserved.

It is the I that believes. Beliefs can be traced back to it within the neutral context of logic and rational discourse. The I toward which one then moves, however, is not identifiable with the I in its full concreteness; it is only a generalized aspect of this. So far as one remains distinct from that into which he seeks to penetrate, so far must he end with just an aspect. One cannot get to the I in its full concreteness except by being adopted by that I and thereby losing the ability to know it. But the aspect that is known is itself possessed by the I. In coming to know that aspect, one is aware of the I beyond it, possessing and maintaining what is being focused on.

We never know anything in its full concreteness. The point is slurred when it is held that all one can ever know are publicly available evidences of what is privately undergone by others. Such evidences are used by private individuals. On the hypothesis, the use would have to be known only in the guise of publicly available evidences, and so on without end. The regress is stopped when it is realized that I can privately know what objectively is the case, and that my knowledge entrenches on and takes account of what is maintained apart from it.

3.7. I intrude and am intruded on.

I possess what is distinct from the I. To acknowledge an object, thought, effort, act, feeling, aspiration, or even a nation, family, history, or future as being *mine*, it has to have a status of its own and be related to the I. If, instead, these were not external to the I but only limits of it, they would not be simply mine, but just my-acts, my-objects. 'Mine' terminates; 'my' attaches. What is mine is left functioning on its own, outside the point where I stop having it as my possession; 'my' expresses just the fact that I have reached toward what is distinguishable from the I. A perceiving is *my* perceiving; but the perceived is only *mine*.

There is much that is mine of which I take no notice—bodily functions, habits, letters written and arguments pursued long ago, the college I went to, the nation to which I belong, grown children, anything in fact to which I am related by a claim. Like the taxes that are mine to pay, a claim on them might be made in accord with prevailing laws, conditions, or conventions, but I can turn them into my possessions only by laying hold of them. Retracing the process by which I possessed them, I can know myself as the ground of the possession.

I can add a 'my' to whatever I possess. Attending to what I then do, and returning toward the source of my act, I can come to know myself. Similarly, when I trace what intrudes on me to its source in a power or in some external object, or both, I learn about what has reality apart from myself. Evidently, there are two outward and two inward movements with which the I is involved. I outwardly intrude, and I move to an outward source of what intrudes; I am intruded on, and I move into myself as a source of intrusions. Self-consciousness is not required in any of these, though when I move into myself as the source of intrusions, I inevitably retrace the path I follow when I am self-conscious. Self-consciousness is a single act; the return to myself as a source of intrusions instead, is a twofold one, moving out with my intrusions so as to identify them, and then returning toward their source.

3.8. I attend to myself from many different positions.

I am wherever I attend. I do not, to be sure, occupy some distant place or even move to it. I am there through a possessive act which makes it a terminus. And I am able to advance beyond such a position, both because I can go beyond the point I focus on and because I have the ability to possess through claim, interest, desire, and concern.

This assertion sounds at first to be so extravagant that a decent concern for prevailing opinion would lead one to suppress it. All of us are confident that no man produces the world; that it is not dependent on any one or all of us; that it is found to be already present with its own career, filled with objects to which we all must yield; and that most of it is unknown. Our confidence is not shaken but rather backed by the truth that each of us makes everything at which he terminates into his possession, for the act of possession is inseparable from a resisting absenting by the objects encountered.

My thoughts, feelings, hopes, and secrets also have a status outside the *my*, sometimes because they are involved with external objects, and sometimes just because they recede into the past. Held on to, they can be known in the course of an act of self-knowledge. When I face something that can be grasped only consciously, perhaps because I am unable to provide the sustaining that a self-consciousness requires, I recognize not only that it could be external to myself, but that it is in fact external just so far as I find it to be resisting my already partially successful attempt at possession.

Solipsism is based on the truth that when I know *I* have knowledge. Aware that the result cannot be transferred to another, it does not see that the object at which my possessive act terminates could be possessed by others also, with the consequence that there could well be a number of men all occupied with the same object. It also fails to see that no object is completely subjugated by or subordinated to a possessing I, thereby giving the solipsist something to acknowledge. Since what I possess remains apart from myself and my act of possessing, at the very same time that it is possessed and qualified by myself, it is just as true to say that I intrude on what is external, as it is to say that it intrudes on me. In the one way, I refer to the fact that I make a facet of what is encountered be continuous with myself; in the other way, I refer to the fact that I am being provided with content.

My, like mine, needs to be provided with content. That content may undergo change, even while it is possessed and faced in an unduplicable way. The possessing is defied by a power which gives the possessed a different career and locus from that given it through the possessive act. Normally, I take the my to extend only to what I have in mind, regardless of what else there be. But again and again I speak of 'my body', 'my family', 'my country', 'my accomplishments'. These, too, have careers apart from my possession of them. I am able to be at quite different positions, often at the same time not, of course, because I then bodily occupy different places in space or time but because I am able to engage in many different, sometimes concurrent, acts of possession.

3.9. I seek to be self-complete.

Why am I not content to just remain in myself? Why do I want to know much that is not important for my welfare? Why am I so sure that there is a self, apart from all self-consciousness? These, and related questions, have a number of interlocked answers, depending in good part on whether I attend to myself as intruding or as intruded on, and then as emphasizing completion or the self.

I am a finite being. I am not the others, but what they exclude. Their reality is lacking to me. As lacking their reality, I am finite and incomplete—finite because I do not have their reality, and incomplete because I am made by them to be what they are not. If there be just an x, y, and I, I must be not-x and not-y, and then only so far as I am excluded by them. My being not-x and not-y depends on them. Since they are outside my provenance, external to me, I am what I am by virtue of what I do not encompass. But to be in myself both not-x and not-y, I must somehow contain the x and the y, as well as the negations by means of which they are related to me. Only then can I be I.

As long as what is essential to myself remains outside myself, I will not only be incomplete, but not even be myself. To be myself, I must complete myself. Yet, if I complete myself, and this by incorporating what is negating me, I will cease to be finite. But if I remain myself, and this by distinguishing myself from all else, I will once again have external to me the very conditions which make me be what I am and, once again, will cease to be myself. If I do not contain all the conditions which make me incomplete, I cannot be myself; if I contain all the conditions which make me incomplete I become complete and there will be nothing in the universe but I. The difficulty is not insuperable.

Others intrude on me and thereby add to me. Since this which they add belongs to them, as long as I keep hold on what they intrude, they need me in order to have what belongs to them. What they intrude must be returned to them by my releasing it while I continue to hold on to it. I must purge myself so as to become just this unique being at the same time that I complete them. Conversely, I intrude myself on them through an act of possession and thereby add to myself what is available there. When I return to myself with what I have acquired, I complete myself with what continues into what remains external to myself.

A completed I, possessing all that intrudes and all that it intrudes, never exists. The attainment of it would make it at once independent of and involved with whatever else there be. A tendency in one direction is opposed by a tendency in the other. The more surely I move in the one direction, the more insistent becomes the need to turn around and go in the other. I never can and ought not give up a concern with what is other than myself, with what I have intruded, with what others intrude, or with myself.

I am self-completing. My absolute completion is only an ideal, but it governs the moves in which I engage. Although the completion I try to achieve I never attain, my completion is already present as a governing guide. I must try to saturate myself with content obtained from without, but never allow it to be in control.

3.10. I presuppose a self.

A self is single, accumulative, and persistent, forever private, beyond the reach of external observation. Allowing for the distinguishing of an I, it never makes itself available to another. But it may be entrenched upon in sympathy and, eventually, by means of a distinguished part of itself, in self-consciousness.

A person is a locus of rights which can be publicly acknowledged. It provides a backing for a you, and for the presence of a publicly reached me. An animal or a machine can be given the status of a 'legal person' with rights bestowed and supported by a state. But neither animal nor machine can sustain a you at which others might terminate. They are not true persons. They also lack selves. Even if one were to grant that they had minds, psyches, were accountable, and had other related dignities and powers, they would not even in principle have I's, be self-identical, possessive, able to both refer to and sustain me's.

I say that I *have* a self rather than that I *am* a self, for I distinguish it from the I. Even while I acknowledge it to be as singular and private as that I, I possess it and recognize it to have a status of its own. I never make it into *my* self without also making it *mine*. But I do say that I *am* a person, and not that I have a person. When I attend to my person I hold on to it; I never make it *mine* without also making it *my* person.

The I is one of a number of condensations of the self. Initially, no one of these is distinguishable from any other; initially, each is at most a nuance in an undifferentiated self. The fully matured self has each in the form of a distinguishable operation, without allowing it to be entirely cut off from or even unaffected by the others. None is a bounded-off unit, existing in contrast with the others, readied to come into the open as occasion arises. All are when they act, and have no necessary persistence or identity in the times between.

Distinguished in act, I, and other epitomizations of the self, together make a set, one item of which is primarily active and the others not. Whatever is privately grounded is eventually attributable to the self, and to the privacy of which this is a subdivision. Though the self does not act, what takes place privately can be said to originate within it because it expresses that self.

A self is not needed in order to enable a being to feel. Animals feel. Despite the fact that they do not have selves, they suffer pain and are pleased. It is possible, too, for what has no self to have a structured meaning making a difference to what is done. Machines have such 'minds'. And it is conceivable that there could be an I in the absence of a self—an angel could be credited with the one without compelling the affirmation that it has the other. But the I of a man is the I of a being with a self.

The I of a man needs a self and makes use of the possible independent functioning of other epitomizations of that self. When the I is identified as just a self-regulating moral agent, a pure ego, or a universal spirit, it may be ennobled, but only at the price of losing its status as an I, distinguished within a self, able to possess what it encounters. That self may also be expressed through a decision, acting in, with, and through the body. It may also be expressed as a mind, having thoughts apart from that body. The I can possess these various sources of private occurrences, and even the self that they all express.

3.11. I possess a self.

I am subject to a self. Were I not, I would not be. Yet I extend well beyond it. While I do not enter into my body, I can attend to what is at that body, to what is far distant from that body, and even to what is outside the world where bodies are. Evidently, I have powers the self does not have, and exercise them from a position which the self does not control.

I rightly speak of *my* self, not because I adopt it, but because I never entirely free the I from the self. As a consequence, I am able to possess a mind and this in a twofold manner—via the self which I possess and which provides a common ground, and directly as a different source of private occurrences.

Sometimes we say that a man should pay attention to his feelings, make use of his mind, and be true to himself. We never tell him to pay attention to his I, make use of it, or be true to it, not because we think that he ought not, or because we think that he will do these without our recommendations, but because attention, use, and being true to something are acts which presuppose the I, and end with the possession of that in which they terminate.

When I am true to myself, I possess my self in such a way as to promote a maximal determination of all its functionings. So far as I succeed, I am aware that I have become what I ought to be. This is not yet, of course, to have done all I ought to do, but only to have arrived at a position where I can move most effectively to that goal. It is sometimes said, though, that I will not achieve a good, satisfying sense of self until I do maximal good to others. Yet, if I am not fully myself, more likely than not, I will fail to do what should be done to them. If I am distorted or dissatisfied, I am not to be counted on to have clear goals or to promote them maximally. The self I possess, I must try to maximize for its own sake by having it engage in all its possible distinct functionings, just as surely as I must try to maximize it for the sake of others, whom I can then maximally benefit. Wisdom evidently lies in moving toward the extreme of perfecting myself for a while and then toward benefitting others, and back again, time after time, so as to do maximal justice to both myself and them.

3.12. I feel.

There are times when feelings and thoughts are present but no I is discernible. It is this fact perhaps which leads some to hold that there is no I at all. But if they are *my* feelings and thoughts, the I must not only be distinct from them, but be able to attach itself to them while possessing them. Feelings without an I are the feelings of an animal, not the feelings of a man.

Though an infant or a fetus has no distinguished I, there is an incipient and perhaps a faint I present, not clearly distinguished from other epitomizations of the self. The I of an infant or a fetus is involved with other private undergoings; it is distinguishable only as the possessive note in these. Eventually, when the I becomes distinct from other condensations of the self, it can be approached by going from what it intrudes, back toward and beyond the me toward what refers to and sustains the me.

The possessor of feelings is so dispersed as to make the statements, "I feel," or "This is my feeling," appear to be overly bold. They seem to introduce an otherwise indiscernible factor. Yet if it is *my* feeling, it necessarily presupposes an I to possess it. That I is distinguished from the self in the course of the act of possessing the felt content.

I flow into feeling so quickly and fully that it alone seems to be. My successful saturation of the feeling almost precludes a distinguishing of the I or other condensations of the self. To isolate the I, it is necessary that the feeling be maintained in contradistinction to it. Only when possessor and possessed remain distinct, each exhibiting its independent nature and role, is it possible for the self to then function as a medium through which the I can move to other private occurrences, to the me, to what is external, or to what is transcendent; only then can the I directly relate itself to other epitomizations of the self or the person.

3.13. I can become coordinate with other private foci.

The I and mind are two independent condensations of the self. There can be a stress on the one at this time and on the other at another time, without apparent rhythm or reason. We have no warrant for holding that a point of equilibrium or balance is ever reached, or that when it is, it is maintained for more than a moment. It is possible, therefore, for feeling and thought to suffuse the I, as well as conversely. The I will then be variously qualified; it will be emotional, rational, and the like. The situation has been noted by different thinkers, though most have been content to remark on just one or the other qualification—existentialists emphasizing the emotional and rationalists the conceptual.

Conceivably, this or that epitomization of the self might completely suffuse some other for an indefinite period, without there being anything amiss, were it not that the self has its own center of gravity, prompting compensatory occurrences when some one of its epitomizations achieves too great a dominance. Only for comparatively short periods are we 'lost in thought,' i.e., suffuse the I with our thinking, or remain thoughtful, i.e., have thinking suffused by the I. But there is no set time when one has to stop. Some men allow little room for feeling. Others emphasize thinking. Neither may be aware of any lack. Though they may find it difficult to make adequate provision for the presence of what had been neglected, some provision is made from time to time. So far as it is not, the men, of course, are not as they could and ought to be.

When public behavior or private misery becomes unbearable, efforts are made to achieve better condensations of the self. More often than not, the self fails to recover its balance. While a man may in fact act feebly and inappropriately, and sometimes even perversely, all the while he goes through private readjustments in favor of epitomizations that had been slighted or distorted. No genuine rectification would be possible were he identifiable with what he was manifesting himself to be, with some factor perhaps maximized at the constant expense of others. A tendency toward health needs the help of multiple condensations of the self, each supported by the others.

When psychiatrists direct attention to an unconscious, a subconscious, an id, and similar supposed centers or powers, they seem to be appealing to the self. There is considerable justification for this: A self has an integrity of its own, and provides a basis in terms of which different epitomizations of it can be assessed as more or less satisfactory. But it is futile to appeal to it. It is beyond the you to which another can refer. Appealed to by oneself, it must be mediated by the me and the I. Apart from these, it is just a subdivision of privacy, opposing limited condensations of itself by a disposition toward other determinations. Psychiatric help, in the end, comes down to a way of helping another to know how his self is in fact being expressed and how it ideally ought to be expressed.

Psychotherapy serves to point up and help remove obstacles now in the way of continuing or improving mental—or better, psychic—health. The removal can come only if an individual effort is made to overcome undesirable limitations on what his self enables him to be and do. The desires, impulses, fears, shame, and guilt that he sometimes tries to hide from himself, as well as from others, bring one epitomization of the self within the orbit of another. Analysis is needed to enable one to separate out the different factors. If successful, it ends by having all the epitomizations allowed to function independently, while they still remain within the compass of and continue to be subject to the self.

I become coordinate with other focal condensations of the self by becoming free of their intrusive presence at the same time that I cease to affect them. When I am on the same footing with them, the self is articulated in a plurality of independent ways. Multiply condensed in equally satisfying private foci, the self is thereby enriched, to be the self it ought to be. Its health requires that the different epitomizations of it function independently of one another. The disturbing feelings, which an awareness of one's guilt might introduce into the I or the mind, fortunately do not and surely need not then vanish. It is right to feel terrible when one thinks of the harm one has done.

3.14. A self and its epitomizing condensations are sources of meaning.

Meaningful items are imbedded within contexts—language, society, laws, logical systems, scientific theories. The items delimit the contexts at the same time that they counter their influence by intents expressive of the source of the items. The I and the mind are primary sources of intents; they become meaningful under conditions which are similar to those that give meaning to words, concepts, and behavior.

I and other limited, relatively determinate, active, concentrations have meanings derived from the self and meanings derived from one another. The common self enables them all to be meaningful units carrying its common meaning. That meaning is countered by the intents impressed on each from the position of the others. When any one combines with the others, it therefore constitutes a complex unit, at once a locus of meaning and intent.

The meaning of the I is determined by the self in one way and by the other condensations of the self in another. It then is not only subordinated to but delimits the meanings that the others and the self have for it. And what is true of the I is true of them. I is a source of meaning for the others as well as for the self, and in turn has a particular meaning because subject to them. All, and particularly the I, are also meaningful in relation to what is externally encountered. They do not then merely function as units interacting with what is then met, but encompass them, make them meaningful.

As a source of meaning, I am all-possessive. I do not, though, prevent what I possess from having an independent status and therefore the ability to provide the I with intents expressive of their natures. The meaning that I introduce is a constant, but what is meant varies in accord with the manner in which it operates and the nature of that on which it impinges. At the same time, the I subjects and is subject to the self, and the other epitomizations of this, with the consequence that it varies in meaning at the same time that it imposes a selfsame meaning on them, and on whatever else there be to which it attends.

The meanings that the self and its epitomizations introduce follow from their natures. The distinctive meaning of each item encountered is a function of what these impose, and the manner in which they are brought to bear. Since there are a number of distinguishable epitomizations within the compass of the self, into which and out of which one passes many times during the day, a confronted content will acquire many different meanings, sometimes in a rather short period.

The words of a public language have their own meanings; they are also inevitably subjected to additional meanings by each speaker. A public language is therefore also partly private, with words whose meanings partly reflect the nature and manner by which each man brings them within the compass of his outlook. "Spring" means something different to the poet from what it means to the gardener. It also has a meaning common to both and to others, in addition to the one that it has because it is a part of a common language with its own rules and history.

3.15. I can be located.

Since it is not public, a self lacks extension and location. Still, it makes sense to speak of it as being voluminous. Not only does the self provide a domain within whose compass the I and mind occur, but it is expressed as the living of a responsibly governed body.

The I, too, functions as a domain within which diverse occurrences take place. Though it presupposes the self and operates through it, unlike the self, it has a location though no extension. It makes no sense to ask "Whereabouts is the self?" or "Where is the self?" But it does make sense to ask "Whereabouts am I?" and "Where is the I?"—the first requiring for its answer a determination of a location within commonsense space, the other a location in the self. To answer

"Whereabouts am I?" one proceeds by locating the me and then recognizing that the I is present in it through an act of possession. To answer "Where is the I?" one acknowledges the self and identifies the I in relation to other functionings.

3.16. A self and its epitomizations are in the present.

What a self encompasses are its specific functionings. Since nothing can function in the past or in the future, what it encompasses can only be in the present. The self must therefore be both connected and disconnected from the present in which the body and the objects of the world are together. Disconnected, it has its own distinctive stretch and rhythm; connected, it is in a present with them.

An I, in relation to whatever else it possesses, whether within or outside the self or body, provides a present within which its possessions fall. The converse is also true: what the I possesses provides a present for the I. Since the I is independent of that in which its possessive acts terminate, its present is also independent of theirs; but since the I cannot be in two presents with different dates without being divided against itself, those presents must coincide. Nevertheless, they may not have the same duration. A particular act of possession can come to an end while the I continues to be present. Also, though the I acts during the present of its self, that self can exist for a longer stretch than the I does. A human being has a self before he has an I, before he is able to claim anything as 'mine', and before he is able to adopt anything and make it part of a 'my'.

Presents are of different lengths, the shorter occurring within the limits of a larger. The shorter presents are followed by others bounded off from one another. So far as a shorter present is imbedded in a larger, it loses its distinctive boundaries. Consequently, while a sequence of distinct smaller stretches related as *earlier and later* occurs outside the governance of the larger, the larger encompasses shorter sequential stretches within its own present only so far as these are merely *before and after* one another. These considerations point up the error that sets rationalistic and intuitive accounts of time in opposition. A rationalist takes time to be something shared —like everything else to which he turns his attention. An intuitionist, instead, maintains that since every part of time is a delimitation of the whole of time and does not fall under it as an instance, the whole of time is just a single, undivided domain. The two views are reconcilable, for though a man's present is a delimited area within a larger, more inclusive present, thereby making it possible for a number of private beings to be copresent for indefinite periods, it is also an intensified specialization of time, and so far a distinguished unit, lived through independently of the unit lived through by another.

A past and future are needed by a present. Without them, a present would be an eternity, not a division in time. Since what is past is precisely what is not present or future, and what is future is precisely what is not present or past, past and future are evidently related to the present by exclusion. They are also involved with the present, not only because they are the termini of its exclusions but because its career consists in their utilization. This process of utilization has been brilliantly portrayed by Whitehead. The past and future, he has shown, intermingle with different degrees of effectiveness throughout the coming to be of an indivisible present moment. That present, though, must not only have a stretch of its own, having nothing to do with any other, but be able to embrace any number of successive presents within which other entities exist. The present of my self is almost as long as my life; the present of my I is not as long, for it exists only after the self has been for a while. My mind, too, has a shorter stretch than either my self and my I; I feel, well before I can think. The present of my thinking is as long as it takes to think. As just one act of the mind, its present is only a part of the mind's; as *my* thinking, it is a possession with a shorter temporal span than the I has.

3.17. I am both free and necessitated.

Whatever occurs is necessitated, for it is the outcome of whatever is needed for it to be. It is then and there because all conditions for its presence have been fulfilled. Were one to take its
occurrence not to be caused by something external to it, one
would have to take it to be a miniature *causa sui*, a self-caused
reality of the kind that theologians have supposed to be the
prerogative of God alone. Here, too, all that is needed for an
occurrence is provided, but by itself. The cause here is constitutive, operating vertically, making unnecessary a reference
to an antecedent horizontally operating cause.

Both horizontal and vertical types of cause occur. Taken by
themselves, however, they are just conditions, distinct from
their effects, not yet sufficient to make an effect present. Another factor, a free action, is needed for an effect to be. It is an
integral part of every constitutive cause, but is external to an
antecedent cause, serving solely to relate this to an external
effect which the free action realizes.

A free action which starts at an antecedent cause makes the
effect, that the cause made possible, into a determinate, subsequent effect, occupying a new present. The free action expresses an actuality. In men it has special forms, since they
not only freely act publicly but also privately, freely deciding
what is to be done. Faced with the prospect of going right or
left and, therefore, with an indeterminate in which right and
left are not demarcated from one another as distinct units, a
free decision introduces determinations into the prospect so
as to produce an election—a distinguished right (or left) in the
foreground of a possible path to the left (or right). Starting
instead with prescriptions or commands, a man freely wills to
dictate the way he will act so as to satisfy what is required.

A free act may itself be the horizontal effect of some antecedent cause and of some prior act of freedom. One then freely
acts to this or that extent, and in this or that area, because of
what had gone before. But when freedom is an integral part of
a direct expression of a constitutive cause, or of the applica-

tion and specification which men add to an otherwise indeterminate prospect, it functions vertically. A horizontally produced, horizontally acting freedom; a horizontally produced,
vertically acting freedom; a vertically produced, horizontally
acting freedom; and a vertically produced, vertically acting
freedom are all possible. Men engage in the first when they
are productive, and in the second when they dominate over
others. When they provide factors for an external world, they
engage in the third. As representatives of mankind they engage in the fourth.

Each epitomization of the self is an effect of some antecedent cause and of a particular free act which begins at other
epitomizations, or at causes external to the self. Each, too, so
far as it is able to dominate over the other epitomizations, is
a constitutive cause of those others, making them into determinate effects of its free insistence. I freely express myself as a
constitutive cause, making my feelings and thoughts into necessitated, determinate outcomes. Each of these can then itself be freely expressed to make other necessitated outcomes.

Feelings and thoughts, understood to include memories,
expectations, and beliefs, are freely expressed. Sometimes,
they overwhelm one another and the I. The fact is usually ignored because the freedom that interests most operates on
behalf of a constitutive, responsible I. It is I who prefers, I who
choose, I who wills, the first ending in the isolation of a determinate means for some accepted goal, the second ending in
the isolation of a determinate specification within an end, and
the third ending in the determinate operation of an accepted
prescription, where goal, end, and prescription are different
types of prospects at which the I is directed. The freedom of
the I is compatible with its being necessitated to be in such and
such a state, and with its being active in other areas at the
same time that it is constitutive of preferences, choices, and
willings.

A concentration on the freely acting, constitutive I is sound
and sensible, if made on behalf of ethics. But ethics must then

be understood to have a large range, able to embrace all that for which I am responsible. Were freedom limited solely to the I's acts of preference, choice, and will, one would be forced to neglect the I's responsibility for some beliefs.

The power of the I freely to constitute whatever it reaches, makes it possible for the self to be free. So far as the I possesses that self, the self will be a determinate effect of an act of possession freely engaged in, and thereby enabled to be applied, through the agency of a freedom transmitted by the I, on other epitomizations. The freedom that the self obtains by being possessed by the I serves to make the self equally pertinent to those other epitomizations.

3.18. I exist.

It is not necessary that an existent be a substance. Corporations exist, the United States of America exists, there are existent treaties, wars, contracts, and commitments. These fill out intervals of time; they also fill out regions of space, and have causal functions, if only as conditions requiring supplementation by free actions. I exist. So do my mind and self. All have spatio-temporal-dynamic roles. A man, consequently, exists in multiple ways, at the same time that he provides a single reality which they diversely intensify.

The body of a man is charged with feeling. His I is everywhere in it through the agency of its possessiveness. That body is an irreducible, persistent, unitary accountable source of action. Merleau-Ponty has done a great service in insisting on the fact that a man is such a vital body, and that it has a distinctive set of abilities, precluding an understanding of it in Cartesian terms. But it is necessary to add that the body is also a unit in a public world, and that outside the body's control a man has a self and a person, an I and a mind, functioning in independence of one another and sometimes occupied with what is at a distance.

A body affects that on which it operates. In turn, it is subject to determinations by what it meets. In either way, its causality may be constitutive or efficient. Since a body also affects the ways in which the I and other manifestations of the self will be expressed in and through it, it has the status of an agent for them. By helping constitute it, they humanize it. This they do by expressing themselves through it. And because a man's body is partly constituted by an I and other epitomizations of a self, all of which have only limited durations, his humanized and lived body is able to come to be and to pass away.

I add specifications to my body's existence and to what is outside its reach, at the same time that I provide a constituting condition to which other expressions of the self, the body, and what is beyond that body are subject. I exist with horizontal and vertical efficacy at the same time that I am subject to private and public existents. And I am caused to exist. Exactly when, I do not know. Yet there is a time when there is no evidence of an I, and there is a time when the I is sometimes stridently insisted on. No one as yet knows all the conditions that are required for that I to arise, but among them evidently are a developed body and effective external objects. Once that I exists, it is subject to various constitutive and efficient causes, is itself able to function as a constitutive and an efficient cause, and can be a source of necessitated effects, freely produced. It never has the status of a genuine substance for, despite its independent functioning, it is never well bounded, entirely cut off from the human body or the self. Nor is it reducible to a moment in a process, or to a pattern extending over several of such moments, since it has the power to act, and to do this again and again.

I am not as self-contained or as impotent as an event. Nor do I have the ultimacy of a genuine substance. Yet there would be nothing seriously amiss in the contention that I am a substance, if all that one intended was to refer to the I's constitutive display of power. There would not even be anything amiss in the contention that I am an event, if all that one intended was to refer to the fact that I had a beginning and ending in time, and that in between I freely unified a past and a future.

3.19. I am both undivided and diversified.

I possess a body, feelings, thoughts, and self. That very same I puts its impress on whatever it terminates in, even if this exist in the external world. And though I am throughout my body, and though that body can be divided into multiple separate parts, I continue to be one, single, unaffected by such divisions. The loss of an arm would diminish me appreciably. Though the loss would not subtract from my I, it would deprive me of a part of my body that I could have enriched, which I certainly could use, and which might have served to benefit me.

Were it not that I am also diversified, that different contents are possessed and pull on me, were I not beset with many different tasks, and were I not sometimes forced back into myself so as to be able to hold on to a multiplicity of items at the same time, it might make sense to say that I am just an epistemological, linguistic, or logical unit, completely devoid of content, power, or meaning. But it is not enough to observe that I am able to terminate in a plurality of objects, for it is conceivable that those objects might tear me asunder. I am a constitutive cause, subjugating what is encountered, keeping it within the compass of the I.

Each epitomization of the self functions as a one for which others are a many. At the same time, all are under the aegis of the self. That self is always undiversified. Were it not that it is neither a logical accompaniment of knowledge nor an I, but a unitary power able to be condensed in the form of a number of independent agents, it would be indistinguishable from the Kantian unity of apperception.

Now it seems as if no one could be a single being, but at best only an aggregate of a number of insistent powers, each able to subjugate the others. If so, the self would at best be just a juncture of different independent units. The consequent would follow, were it not that the diverse epitomizations of the self leave the unity of the self undisturbed in the very act of giving it specific intensive forms. Each offers a different way in which the unity of the self is reinstated. But now it would seem that these epitomizations of the self have no unities of their own, at the same time that the self is left so barren as to make senseless a reference to it as a unity, or as anything else. These conclusions would be unavoidable were it not that the different epitomizations make the self their own in characteristic ways, and that the self has an insistent point of equilibrium which compels the different epitomizations to recede and advance in relation to one another. Were there no self, there would be no basis for the sense that some private occurrence is having an exaggerated role. Each epitomization would simply be an independent power that, by chance, was blocked or helped by others. The self does not allow one epitomization to dominate without providing a greater opportunity for the epitomization of another.

3.20. I am both primary and derivative.

An I has a nature, exists on its own terms, and provides a measure in terms of which all else can be assessed. For these reasons, it is common to speak of it as rational, existent, and precious, let the philosophers, clinging to some theory, complain and protest as much as they like. But it is also true that it is not a unit underived and self-centered, that its very presence depends on circumstances beyond its control, that there are laws and large-scaled meanings to which it is subject, that it is involved in an impersonal, extended, dynamic world, and that instead of being lauded it is often criticized and found wanting. For these reasons, it will always be dealt with by serious thinkers as a function of something else, and as that which careless men unfortunately reify.

The status of the I is in part a consequence of the kind of relations it has to other realities. The fact can be stated in a set of paradoxes: the persistent I is insubstantial, but since it is able to insist on itself, it is also substantial. The I is what circumstances determine it to be, but when it is affected by others it forever eludes their full control or grasp. Subject to laws and meanings, the I is intelligible, but the I affects everything with a unique intent. Independently existent, the I is locatable, but it is a private I that exists on its own. And, though never perfect, the I is connected with an ideal perfection.

If an I were without relation to what is external to the body, it would be related only to conditions and to the self and other epitomizations of this. But it is related to what is external. Both are governed by the same conditions. To know the conditions is to know what grounds the kinds of connections the I has with what exists independently of it.

For most purposes, no reference need be made to the conditions, it being sufficient usually to acknowledge the primacy of the lived body or of some restricted public area. Within these, a man conducts most of his affairs. But we are cosmic as well as local and singular beings, subject not only to physical, chemical, and biological laws but to universal affiliative, equalizing, implicative, distancing, and evaluative conditioning forces. The distinctions these demand do not vanish when the scope of our interests is narrowed; their full import is just not seen. Bankers manage quite well without knowing the associative, commutative, and distributive laws of arithmetic; they work with these and, in limited unreflective ways, take account of them, with considerable benefit to themselves. In a similar spirit, but with quite different rewards, common conditions may be similarly used.

We differ from one another in the ways we severally maintain ourselves, in the ways we bound ourselves off, in the ways we negate one another, in the ways we occupy extended regions, and in the purity and comprehensiveness of our unities. These ways might be so conjoined that they play equal parts. One of them could be dominant and the others recessive. Any one of them could be mediated by the others.

3.21. I am both principal and instrument.

I am insistent, bringing myself to bear on a host of objects and turning them into my possessions. I am no hard core somewhere in the recesses of the body or maintained somewhere in the self. If I were, this body of mine would be just a place within whose confines I was located, or which was irrelevant to what I was. In effect, I would be an alien soul, having nothing to do with what the body was or did. Part of that soul might be said to be attached to the body, but that part would be precisely what was unable to have independent reality.

I am responsible for what is done by my body because I am able to make it not simply the terminus of an act of possession but an instrument used and brought to bear on others. I am also an instrument of the body, since I am subject to its conditioning, turned into a specialized way in which the body's nature, needs, and appetites are united with those of the self. Because the body is itself subject to a more encompassing condition which enables that body to be in consonance and dissonance with others, I become, on behalf of that body, attracted to and repelled by what lies beyond it. The body and I, consequently, make a single complex unit.

Well before there is a conscious mind, and therefore well before there is a mind-body problem, there is an I which is distinct from, but nevertheless united with the body as its possessor. The fact raises neither practical nor theoretical difficulties, since in neither of these guises is the I a true substance, externally connected with another, supposedly closed off from it. When the I and the body are distinguished as sources of different and even oppositional needs and acts, they do not lose their interrelated roles. Instead, they carry them out within their common setting.

3.22. I am both central and peripheral.

A multitude of circumstances, not the least of which is a highly complex organized body, is a prerequisite for the presence of an I, both as a unified condensation of a self and as a possessor of both self and body.Nothing is gained by speaking of the I as though it were a limit beyond the reach of possible knowledge, for this is but to hold that it is unknowable, without making evident how that fact can be known. Were the I, instead, made central by postulation or by a grammatical or logical fiat, there would be no I that was acknowledged, but only a supposition or word set down—leaving unexplained the I which makes the supposition or expresses the word.

When things are dealt with from the position of language, logic, or scientific theory, it is not possible to arrive at anything more than variables, words, or conceived physical units imbedded in marks, sounds, or possible substantial realities. By just assuming such positions one gets no further than a punctuated context or set of rules, not yet applied. Their application requires a free imposition by an I outside them. Linguistics, logic, and science inescapably make use of an I even when they try to speak of, explain, or reach it in terms that are appropriate not to it, but to something else. To be sure, if an account is formulated in terms appropriate only to bodies as subject to impersonal universal physical laws, no I will ever be dealt with. All the while an I will be present, making it possible to refer to those laws and to give the body the status of a possession and an individualized instrument.

I radiate out within a complex privacy, a complex body, and a complex world. I can be known to be, in self-conscious acts, as the topic of other private unified epitomizations of the self and the body, as a possessor of the body, and as conditioned together with other independently functioning units. I am not just a limit at which a world of entities converges; I am a source of private acts and the object of other private acts beginning at other active epitomizations. Were it supposed that I could be reached by using the pronoun 'I', it should be possible to become acquainted with another's I, for it is no more public or private, no more available or unavailable, on the supposition, than my own. The use of an 'I' is distinctive, because it has a unique referent at which it arrives over a public route which merges into what is wholly private.

3.23. I have a relative and an absolute import.

I am relative to the self and body. Each provides a meaning for that I, which the I matches with a distinctive intent. The result is a union of meaning and intent in a unit having specific roles within a common intelligible frame of self and body. The I, in turn, intelligibly connects these.

I provide a frame within which all else can be related as units governed in a constant way. Whatever there be, at the same time, provides a frame within which I function as a unit related to other units. The I gives others their rationale, and each, and all together, terminate in the I as a unit, rationally subject to them. The outcome would be just a multiplicity of rationales, dictating the role each item has in relation to others, were there no common meaning that each sustained. In the absence of this, one would be able to know what was the case only from some arbitrarily selected standpoint, no better or worse than any other. The sole common truth that men then could have would be the outcome of their common assumption of the same standpoint, but there would be no position in terms of which they could together decide to make that assumption.

I and my body are not bare units in logical or mathematical relations. Both are irreducible and effective. That fact forces the most radical rationalist to attend to unique realities behind what is experienced, encountered, and observed. It justifies the abandonment of formal languages which substitute eternally frozen units for effective, singular powers, and the replacing of those languages by one whose grammar and sanctioned uses are sustained outside the language. Such a language cannot be expressive simply of the outlook of some community. If it were, the meanings it provides would not match what was in fact occurring, but only what was viewed from a limited position, though one shared in by a number of men.

Men in quite different communities know the same things. Despite their individual and tribal standpoints, each is able to confront the very occurrences that others do. Through the help of their limited, different languages, they can make contact with another. If our speaking a particular language meant that we had to lose all hold of the world which others speak about in their languages, translation would be impossible, since we would then not be able to know what meanings the others provide without becoming one of them, and entering into their world. We would also not be able to say that they had languages alternative to our own, since all we could know, on the hypothesis, is what fell within the range of our own language.

Mathematics and logic do not speak of the bustling world of experience. They have the anonymity and universality, however, which a satisfactory language requires if it is to speak objectively of what is the case. But they are not true languages, not even ideal languages. An ideal language allows for the major and constant affiliations and disaffiliations characteristic of the world.

3.24. I am a spatial source, terminus, and unit.

Nothing seems so evident as the simplicity of the I. It has no parts which can be set external to one another. Consequently, were I characterized in spatial terms, I would have to be said to be an extensionless point. But unless such a point could act on its own, it could not be identified with the I.

I exist and reach indefinitely outward, controlling some

things, and possessing whatever I terminate at. Just as evidently, I am locatable. I know where I now am, and others can know where I now am. Since none of us could discover that I, were it just a point, self-contained, or the limit of some bodily extension, I must be extended and also in space, even though I am not a body or part of one. To be sure, when I am located, reference is made to the place where my body is located. But I rightly then say that *I* have been located, for I am throughout that body as its possessor, without sharing in its divisibility and without losing my position as an epitomization of a private self.

I stand away from all else that is, just as surely as they stand away from that I. We are symmetrically distanced from one another, and this independently of our involvement in our bodies. Each of us is also symmetrically distanced from animals and things. Though these have no I's, they defy and resist my intrusion just as surely as I do theirs, each of us preserving an untouched density, no matter how deeply penetrative we or others may manage to be.

I provide an indefinite, distensive radiation outward to constitute a field within which everything that is encountered is set. At the same time, I am distanced from others. Since it is just as proper to approach other things from the standpoint of the I, as the reverse, both modes of speaking are evidently legitimate. The relativity that each speaking involves presupposes that I and others are already in a common space.

3.25. I am present in many presents.

I exist moment after moment, but the time in which I am is a delimitation of a larger time, undivided, all present. That time was once mathematically divided in accord with the passage of the sun, and is now measured by other impersonal clocks. From its standpoint, the time through which I exist is a specialization. From my standpoint, and even from the standpoint of any of the other items in the world, inanimate or animate, private or public, the common, undivided present time is broken up; for each of us there is only a sequence of present moments, each with a distinctive length and rhythm.

By itself an I is in an undivided present of indefinite length, in which a before and after, but no earlier and later, can be distinguished. It also is present, moment after moment, encompassed by the larger present characteristic of the self, the time encompassing all particular occurrences, and the whole of time extending beyond all occurrences, never divided and always present.

When I express myself in acts of possession and in other ways, I bring the termini at which I arrive within the present of that I. Whatever takes place at those termini will occur within some subdivision of the present time of the I, in some subdivision of a passing present common to all, and in some subdivision of the fixed present of the whole of time.

While I am in a world with other entities and continue to be contemporary with them, I also am in an undivided present of my own, of the self, of other private occurrences, of the body, of what is beyond these, and of what is common to all existents. Were there no priority of status here, one would be compelled to say that the I was both in a number of undivided presents of different lengths and in multiple shorter presents within the limits of these. But the whole of time and I, each with its characteristic undivided present, contain the smaller presents as not yet distinct. As distinguished from one another, those smaller presents are also distinct from the larger, and characterize different units and occurrences.

I transform the whole of time into an intensified, limited present, in which past and future are interwoven, even while they continue to be outside it. Dominated by the I, my body shares in its present. But since my body also limits the functioning of the I, it so far contains the present of the I as an unseparated subdivision of its own present. That body also independently specifies the whole of time, delimiting it in its own way. If the body is attended to on its own terms, from the outside, from the position of the I, or as encompassed by a common time, it will be found to have presents of various lengths and intensities. But as long as I and my body are under the governance of the same condition, they will have presents inseparable from the present whole of time, as well as presents of different lengths, separately undergone. Within the span of these, smaller present stretches are distinguishable but not distinct. Those smaller stretches become genuine distinct presents only when separately undergone.

3.26. I am subject to a universal necessitation.

I am an irreducible, powerful unit in relation to other private occurrences, able to control my body, able to make it accountable in a responsible way, and able to possess whatever I terminate in. All the while, I am linked with both antecedent and subsequent independent particulars by a necessitation. Were there no such necessitation, I would have no preconditions, nor would I provide preconditions for the presence of anything else. I might, as a consequence, have followed on and been followed by anything whatsoever.

Made pertinent to particular substances, a universal necessitation determines the limits within which these substances freely act. Made pertinent to the I, the necessitation gives it a position in a causal world. Nothing, though, is wholly deducible from what has been, since whatever occurs depends in part on the exercise of a freedom which must itself be worked through. And what is true of the I is true of actualities, though they lack the range and the ability to freely act in all the ways in which the I can.

3.27. I act freely.

Were I a substance, I would be forever apart from all else, a fact which Leibniz clearly saw and expressed in his theory of monads, each with its windows tightly closed on all else. Were I just an existent, I would instead be locatable within a larger domain but without an ability to act freely.

I freely bring about effects through controlled activities under the control of substantializing and existentializing conditions. Were there only free action, effects would follow because of a freedom which, though it might originate with that I, would escape its governance. But it is the I that converts what is possible for that I into what takes place. It is proper to speak of that I as exercising a free will, keeping the I connected with particulars in a public world, producing outcomes under the guiding control of a prospective outcome, provided that the I, the will, and the prospect be recognized to have their own distinctive roles and natures.

3.28. I am an evaluated base of evaluations.

Other items have various degrees of relevance for the I. The degree depends on the extent of the congeniality or repugnance connecting the I to them. Some things of great positive relevance are not of great value—the nourishing food I eat. Others of negative relevance have considerable value—what stands in the way of my continuance. These values reflect an objective ordering of things which takes account of their internal harmony and of their capacity to be together, considered from the standpoint of the I. Such an ordering yields a scaled world of values whose members are indifferent to one another. In that objective order, the I stands above all else, not as a source of actions or as a ground or locus of what could be conflicting intents or demands, but as a unity within which all else has a place without producing a real diversity. My single, all-encompassing unity enables me to stand above all complexities whose parts are able to oppose one another, and the wholes in which those parts are. That unity is enriched by the content in which it terminates.

I terminate in others. I also give them a place within myself where they are made to be compatibly together. They are then evaluatively encompassed in considerable independence of their objective values, just so far as I deal directly with them. I never absorb the others, and I am defied by other I's, all equally irreducible. I am not above the other I's, and I necessarily fall considerably short of perfection. But when I act with reference to whatever else there is, I function as an evaluating unity for them; so far as they encompass or govern me, and through this the I, that me and I have values subordinated to theirs.

I am able to temper my own evaluations by what is objectively the case. If I do this while attending to the way in which the valuational hierarchy is made to operate within the limits of a determination of the relevance of items to one another, I am able to make those evaluations be pertinent, not simply to what I find congenial or uncongenial, but to a compatibility or incompatibility objectively determined. The evaluations, which psychological theories set within the frame of associations, illustrate in a limited form the manner in which I and all else are objectively ordered within an objective determination of actual relevance.

3.29. I am an individual.

Freed from its traditional restriction to the self-defeating condition of finding general principles by means of which one can explain the issuance of an individual out of a complex of universals, the problem of individuation emerges as a special case of the problem of how an actuality can be understood to be an irreducible unit. It is this because its *difference* sustains its *distinctness* from all final realities, and its *distinctness* sustains its *difference* from all other actualities. When the two sustainings are in equipoise, difference and a distinctness are diffused throughout one another.

3.30. I am a being and have a being.

Beings are distinct units, equally ultimate. The being I have is no more and no less a being than any others. All are on a footing, without regard for their values, where they are, or how intelligible, and whether or not they enhance, conflict with, or are indifferent to one another.

At one and the same time I am equal with others, a limited reality, and an irreducible toward which all else is oriented. I am with them in a single universe, able to have all as coordinate, equal items. As a consequence, it is correct to say that I have a limited being, that I am but one of a multitude of beings centered about other particulars, and that I enable every actuality to have a being. When the first of these is made into a precondition of the third, and the second is ignored, one approaches Heidegger's view that without the mediation of man nothing else would have being. But many things have being apart from man. And surely no matter how I puff myself up, I am no more real than the things I use. Were this not so, it is hard to see how I could ever get a footing in the world, and how it is that a blow by a hammer or the fall of a rock is able to jeopardize my being. I do justice to that on which I act only so far as I treat this as not inferior in being to myself or any other unit. Since the awareness requires a preliminary withdrawal into a deeper privacy, it would result in a loss of the world, were it not that I still insistently continue to be in the world with others.

3.31. I am eventually overwhelmed even by what is most congenial.

As a being in a universe of beings, I stand away from all with the same efficacy with which they stand away from me. But we never reach the stage where we are entirely closed off from one another. We are different beings, each able to be a principal with respect to others. What we act on, even what we mutilate, does not surrender its being to us. But though the being anyone has cannot be taken from it by others, those others can deny it the opportunity to hold on to it as it had before. In that act they may even replace it by other actualities, subject to the very conditions which had been effective before.

When I die, I lose hold of my being. If that being were mine only at God's pleasure, one should speak of my death as due to him. My death would then not be properly treated as the outcome of what I or other things do.

The coming to be and passing away of inanimate objects and animals are to be explained as the effect of other objects. Unlike men, things and animals are unable to withdraw from and advance on what conditions them. To account for their coming to be and passing away, consequently, one looks for forces they suffer and sometimes to those they exert. Because I am unable to withstand all others, sooner or later my career, too, comes to an end. No matter how much I desire to remain in being, and no matter how congenial I find the things about, even if I am most interested in continuing to live, I will eventually be overwhelmed. If I lose interest in living, I make it easier to be overcome by other actualities. But I do not cease to be until I lose hold of the being I had possessed. Things and animals, instead, have being withdrawn from them; what had intruded is no longer countered by them. They never did possess it. Only men possess their beings, though only for short periods.

3.32. I am meaningfully related to other independent realities.

Atomism is most attentive to the fact that each actuality has a distinct being, equal to that of every other. It does not usually consider the question as to just how its units could be together, equated, or compared. To answer such questions, reference would have to be made to a common locus or referent of all the atoms. Leibniz took the second course when he supposed that his spiritual atoms, or monads, were together due to God. So far, though, his monads were all alike as monads, differing only in their degree of clarity. According to him God alone was perfectly clear, but still just a monad. How he could get outside himself and make other monads remains a mystery. A modern variant of this view is presented by logical atomism. More evidently occupied with the problem of meaning than its predecessor, it takes all items to be irreducible, independent units of meaning, subject to the common structure of a universal logic. It has no way of accounting, though, for the presence of its units, or for the relations of these to the common structure.

Earlier it was noted that the meaning I have is associated with other meanings because I am already associated with others in various degrees and ways. Now it is being noted that meaning is also coordinated with other meanings, under the aegis of an intelligible relationship. When I and others are directly governed by, internalize, and counter a common intrusive, independently grounded meaning, we also have the role of equalized units.

3.33. I occupy a position in space.

Each actuality is a self-confined reality, cut off from all others. Even a molecule has an independent reality. So far, it is not in space. It is in space only if it engages in an act of occupation, imposing its distendedness on an extended region. But were it then thoroughly spatialized, it would at most be an intensified, knotted, limited portion of space, unable to move, rest, or have a reality of its own.

Space enables an actuality to achieve a position in relation to others. Without its help, nothing would be distant or near, here or there, up or down. By occupying a region of space, each actuality becomes present in a world with other actualities, each occupying a limited region of space.

Distinct from my body, I am nevertheless indivisibly spread

throughout my body, and personalize the distance between myself and others. Spread throughout the body, I am as voluminous as it is. Concerned with whatever else there be, I extend to them, leaving them with the status of limits for that extension. The locatable limit which I provide for them, and conversely, makes evident the presence of a common space in which we are distant from one another. The imaginative removal of that space would leave us neither extended nor unextended, neither composite nor simple, neither here nor there.

3.34. I occupy a position in time.

A common time enables a number of entities to be contemporaries. Were that time the condition to which everything was wholly subject, everything would be so public that none would have a private career. None would be in a position to initiate an act. Each would exhaust itself in the process of coming to be. Actualities do come to be and pass away, but they also enjoy other roles—spatial ones, for example.

Time is only one of the ubiquitous dimensions of the universe. It does not enjoy a superiority to space or to causality. The extendedness of the one and the necessitation of the other are independently determined, and could well be without it. This truth is obvious in connection with space. It seems, though, to be precluded by causality, since this evidently takes time to unfold. But that is so, only if causality is just efficient and not constitutive.

I express my distendedness and, thereby enter into public time. I also possess a part of that time. Entering into public time on my own terms, I bound it in my own way. As a result, I have a present which is longer or shorter than that lived through by others.

I keep my identity by making changes in time reduce to the selfsame import for me. As a consequence, I remain unchanged both as a reality outside time and in it. Forced by circumstance to change the way I distinguish myself from what is all-encompassing, I may cease to possess a part of public time or may cease to make use of it. This does not necessitate that I cease to be.

3.35. I freely make use of necessity.

Some actualities are necessarily and irreversibly related. When the necessitation is charged with dynamism, each actuality is able to be a required effect of past causes, and a cause for subsequent necessitated effects. Causes and effects will then follow one another in time. Time, though, does not have the power to replace items by one another. By itself, it allows everything, moment after moment, to be and to be related as it had been before. Were necessity, therefore, wholly temporalized, the link between a cause and an effect might still continue for an indefinite period, without the first giving way to the second.

Causality connects realities, dynamically and by necessity, despite their radical independence from one another. Treated apart from time, that necessitation is readily confounded with a logical entailment. But where causality operates between realities, entailment operates between meanings. The latter can have units symmertrically and even reflexively related; the former always has realities in irreversible connections. A logical inference offers a special case of causation, since it converts an entailed, possible into an affirmed, actual conclusion. The fact has been overlooked because causality has been taken to be applicable to bodies only, or to exhibit the power of universal laws converting energy in one place into energy in another. Inference is a causal act privately carried out.

A replacement of a cause by what it necessitates requires action on the part of the cause. The result might exclude the continuation of the cause. This, of course, need not happen. I can freely act to bring about not what replaces me but something else. I can freely act many times within the limits of small- and large-scaled necessities.

When causal necessity operates between actualities, these mark its limits. To do this, they have to be where it is. Since they are distinct from it, they must be joined to it. The joining evidently requires a freely instituted act. All actualities are causally related only so far as they themselves freely participate in a necessitation; this freely attaches itself to them; some third power freely acts on both; or because of some combination of these. The freedom that men use is a more intense, personalized, and often a deliberately directed form of the freedom every actuality uses to vitalize causal necessitation. The fact is partly obscured when, on behalf of ethics, theology, or politics, freedom is taken to be the special prerogative of man. He is then set so far from all else as to make both his origin and his involvement with other items mysterious or impossible.

I freely act as other actualities do when I bring about public effects through the action of my body. But I also can decide privately and freely. If I also will, I freely make use of my body and other available means so as to bring in to the public world a possible outcome with which I am concerned.

Scotists say that one can will to think as well as to act. What they have in mind, apparently, is the fact that a man can deliberately turn away from practice or enjoyment to attend instead to what he might learn through perception, observation, inference, conceptualization, or speculation. But since he does not then make use of his body to arrive at some desired outcome, it would be more correct to say that he can *prefer* to think, rather than to feel and the like, as a better means for attaining some such goal as having knowledge. With this modification, the Scotist position is clearly stronger than that of the rival Thomists', with their supposition that will presupposes the operation of the intellect. Though we often think about what we would like to attain before we decide to attain it, the end sought may be determined causally and not be something in mind, or even be formally necessitated. The two schools carry their differences into discussions about God. Since for both, God is so simple as to permit no distinction between antecedent and consequent, one is finally forced to abandon both views, to leave room only for the claim that like any other wholly detached unit, their God would have his distinctness and difference from all else diffused through one another, with the consequence that, had he an intellect and will, the two would not be distinguished in him.

Descartes held that the human mind was finite but that the will was infinite, able as it was, undetermined by anything else, to affirm, deny, doubt, and believe the selfsame idea. His position, evidently, is a variant on both the Scotist and Thomistic, since with the latter it takes an idea to be a presupposition for a free act, but with the former denies that an idea need limit the exercise of freedom. Descartes evidently first freely chose an idea, and then subsequently freely preferred some one or other means for realizing that choice in the form of an idea actually adopted. He really had no place for a free will, since he did not allow for any productive connection between what was clear in his mind and its occurrence in the realm of extension.

3.36. I am a reality evaluationally ordered in relation to others.

Nothing has a value greater than I. I have a greater value than all others, for I order them to accord with the ways in which they satisfy me. It is also true that I am just a passing, finite being, less attractive, less coordinated, less endowed than many others; that I am not altogether well adjusted to other men, and that I would surely find myself quickly overpowered could I step outside the confines of my society and there tackle raw nature. I have a minor value from the position of all others. The great value I in fact have is then to be seen to do more or less violence to what others are apart from me.

3.37. I am a person.

A person is an individual human at whom others can terminate, with viable public rights expressing and grounded in private native ones. Laws and states are just or unjust to the extent that they support or deny the publicly viable rights. When it is said that there have been men whom the U.S. Constitution wrongly failed to credit as persons, and that corporations are dubiously deemed to be quasi persons because legally accountable for some of the things they do, "wrongly failed" and "dubious" are used properly, since the one refers to viable rights not legally supported and the other to rights which have only a legal warrant. Native rights deserve a public, viable form; endowed rights should be backed by native ones.

Persons are more or less allied. They are also meaningfully connected through a common formal structure which enables them to communicate, even while using the words of some limited, natural language; locatable within a single space where each occupies an extended region; contemporary, sharing a common past and future; supportive in various degrees to constitute a causally effective mankind; and possessing equal value as unit humans. Specializing these relations are alliances, meanings, structures, spatio-temporal-causal connections, and objective values governing different groupings.

A person exists before and apart from an I. But only when there is a self, and not before, can an I be. An I epitomizes a self, a subdivision of privacy originating later than the person. A me provides a limit for the person, allowing one to arrive at it. Once there is an actual I, all other epitomizations, whether of the person or of the self, can be possessed and used.

A person has native rights to be translated into publicly sustained ones. A viable human fetus, even if it does not have an I
or a mind, has inalienable rights because it is a person. When
that person both privately and publicly maintains and expresses the same rights others do—a result that requires maturation for a period of time after birth—it allows for the expression of an I. A fetus does not have these rights. But like
everything else, it has the right to be the reality it is, and the
right to develop a person and self. These rights belong to it
just because it is what it is, making a native claim to be and to
prosper.

It is wrong to kill a dog wantonly; it is a mitigated wrong to
kill it for a good reason. It is also wrong to kill an embryo wantonly, and a mitigated wrong to kill it for a good reason. But
it is a greater wrong to kill it than to kill a dog—because of the
kind of life it has and the promise this involves. The wrong,
though, is not as great as that which results when one kills a
human fetus come to term. The advocates of abortion on demand minimize the rights of both the embryo and the fetus
just as surely as the advocates of the absolute sanctity of life
minimize the difference between the rights of a nonviable
fetus and that of its mother.

Native rights cannot be reached from the outside. The fact
that the rights of men, embryos, fetuses, animals, and other
actualities can be violated, shows that the violation concerns
either the externally expressed conditions for the continuance
of those beings in their full integrity or the deniable rights
which publicly translate inalienable native ones. The first of
these alternatives comes to the fore in the claims actualities
make to air, food, or other preconditions for survival. The second achieves prominence when it is recognized that among
man's inalienable rights is that of being a human in a public
world together with others. This has the privileged role of giving a public frame for other native rights.

All men have the same native rights and give a public form
to them, whether or not there is an overarching controlling

public whole. Neglect of this fact forces one to suppose that there is a gap between men as having incomparable private rights, having publicly expressed rights together, and having their rights supported. Once it is recognized that men always have equal rights, and that these ground public claims, the transition from men as apart from a state to them as in a state can be seen to be a move from one way of having public rights to another where some of these rights are explicitly stated and legally sanctioned.

3.38. I have a mind.

When mathematics is freed from involvement with actualities, with their affiliations, realities, locations, and values, it exhibits an intrinsic rationale. Those who attend to mathematics in this pure form have come to be known as "platonists." They are opposed by intuitionists who grant no legitimate status to anything which cannot be constructed, step by step, out of the units used in elementary mathematics. Since these acknowledge the natural numbers as primitive, they evidently differ from the others only in the extent of their platonism. Empiricists and conventionalists are more resolute, even maintaining that any statement in mathematics could be denied, though perhaps not without considerable inconvenience. But were it just a matter of convenience, one might be willing to suffer it if one could thereby promote some end—if only that of saying something new—with the consequence that one should be able to envisage and perhaps formulate systems which break every rule and deny every claim made by the establishment. So far this has not been done. To show that it is even possible, one would have to make evident that there is no rationale to which everything is subject. Were that the case, predictions would be just guesses, deductions would be inductions, and what was self-contradictory would in fact be possible. This does not mean that every presently accepted statement in mathematics has an unlimited range, or that their denials may not have roles under various conditions.

The established logics and mathematics have to do with determinate entities which maintain their identities in multiple contexts. Other laws than those which they acknowledge, are required when one deals with the general, the vague, the changing, the incomplete, and the incompletable. The law of excluded middle does not apply to the first, contradiction to the second, identity to the third, the having well-defined premisses to the fourth, and the reaching of distinct conclusions to the fifth. Usually, though, these do apply. Even when we follow rules, patterns, and connections of our own designing; find that what we arrive at through thought is not in accord with what happens in fact; and provide arbitrary structures connecting one item with any chosen other, we often enough discover that where we had begun is ineluctably connected with something else, in accord with all these laws.

The various epitomizations of the self are intelligible units intelligibly related to whatever else there be. Each adds its own particular intent to a common meaning. The result is a meaningful unit which, like a word in a language, functions in a whole where a common meaningful structure is punctuated by distinct intents. An I is intelligibly related to other epitomizations of the self (as well as to what lies outside the self) by a primal meaning, and by various specializations of this.

A mind is used by an I. That fact is conveyed in "I have a mind." It would be odd to say, "I am a mind." That would require me to ignore the mind's distinctness from the I, the presence of other epitomizations of the self, and the fact that I can possess any of them.

Some of the items which the mind connects are also interconnected in what is external to the mind. When that interconnection is accepted at the same time that the items are, the mind structures the items as they had been objectively structured. What is then known is inseparable both from resistant, external items and a common instantiated meaning.

When one speaks, what is in the mind is expressed with the

help of the body. The meanings which the mind provides are then specialized in the grammar used, just so far as the conventionally habituated body dominates over the meaning conveyed. Complete dominance is avoidable. Were it not, one would lose hold, not only of external objects, but of the meaning incorporated in language. One would not even be able to have the knowledge that the body was having a dominant role, but would be reduced to making sounds, and that is all. Once it is recognized that the expressed mind is not necessarily under the full control of the body, there is no difficulty in seeing that it can subject to a common meaning all that it terminates in.

The fact that an I makes use of a mind does not prevent the I from being attended to by that mind, or to be referred to by means of some such term as 'I'. In the first way, the mind mediates an act of self-consciousness; in the second, it does so with the help of a distinctive term. If a private language is one whose words refer to what can be best known by the person speaking, 'I' (like 'me') is a word in a private language.

An animal can be said to have a mind, even though it has neither a self nor an I. Such a mind is not distinguishable from a private structure which can be involved with feelings. The structure itself could be built into a machine. This could be geared to say 'I' or to do something which could trigger the sounding of this. Since the 'I' it might utter or trigger would not be involved in an act of self-consciousness nor be able to function as a possessor, it will have a derivative or a dislocated sense—the first, if it be taken to be a surrogate of a mere structure or of the ways this is utilized by programs; the second, if it is presented as though it were used by the machine in the way a man uses it.

'I' is used properly only as a singular factor in an act of self-consciousness, or as a central term in a reference to what is said or done. It prescribes roles to other terms. Unlike 'this', 'here', and 'now', it neither denotes nor is used to designate except in those special cases where the discourse is about the

I—"I will now speak about the I." Its primary role is to function as a surrogate for oneself as private and irreducible, guar-
anteeing the truth of what is then said.

3.39. I am intelligible.

As long as the I is under the dominance of a common meaning, whether this be all-encompassing or of more limited
scope, the I fits within it as a unit. The I does not then exhibit
any individuality. It is the I which idealists know, a localiza-
tion of an absolute, or the I of sociologists, a limit within a social context. But, while remaining in consonance with formal
conditions governing myself and others, an I can act on its
own, attending to what is most relevant. As a consequence,
without loss to its meaning as a unit interconnected with all
others, an I can be allied with the I's of other men.

I am able to impose my meaning on whatever else I confront
and possess. As a consequence, I am able to take other items
to be affiliated in various ways and degrees within the context
of the meaning I bring to bear. Accounts of perception and
knowledge, which hold that what is acknowledged is subject
to categories or judgments, while still allowing that the items
cluster together and diverge from one another, give epistemological expression to this ontological fact.

I, with the meaning 'real', am connected with others, both
indirectly by means of a common condition and directly by
intruding that meaning. In the first way, I am one unit together with them. In the second, I provide them with an intelligible frame, a rationale. Actual affiliations and disaffiliations
add qualifications to that rationale. The qualifications are not
known apart from observation and experiment and some apprehension of a power able to associate items in ways not determined by their meaningful connection with one another. A
special case of this is involved in the use of theories. Formally
stated, a theory is just an hypothesis, a syntactical unit having

nothing to do with anything outside the reach of its formal expression. It is more than such an hypothesis just so far as it is connected with what in fact occurs, and takes account of the particular valencies that items have in relation to one another. The claim that the attachments and conflicts found in the world are just complications of a primary rationale overlooks the brute irreducible opposition to the rationale exhibited by such attachments and conflicts.

No account of the universe, Hegel saw, is satisfactory if it does not make provision for the reality of a multiplicity of independent items. He thought this could be achieved by crediting a primal meaning with the power to oppose itself. Such self-opposition stops short with meanings, but it does allow me to say that though I am meaningfully related to other realities, I am also meaningfully distinguished as a reality standing apart from all others. Neither I nor the others are thereby recognized to be and function as independent realities; all are granted only the status of units within a meaningful whole.

Denotative terms and proper names are parts of a formal language. But though subject to the same set of grammatical rules as other parts are, 'I', 'me', 'you', 'this', 'Tom Brown', and the like, have the additional status of being inseparable from realities beyond them, to which they are to take their user, once the control of language is broken. The fact makes conspicuous the limitations of a logical linguistics. As long as one remains subject to a language, it is impossible to make contact with what is outside. Remarks about 'this', 'semantics', 'commitment', 'rigid designators', 'individuals', 'unique referents' or 'values of variables' enable one to attend not to what is outside the language but to the distinctive use that certain terms have within it. No one knows that there is anything to denote, to name, to be committed to, unless he already has escaped the bounds of language and made contact with something which could be denoted, named, or committed to. Like my intelligibility, the intelligibility of what we attend to is presupposed, not constituted by the terms by which we refer to them.

3.40. I exist.

Space is countered by the I in a way not possible to inanimate things. A meaningful thing occupies a space, but a meaningful I extends its activity through it. The laws of nature, because they are meanings mediated by space have to be brought to bear on the locations in which things are. They have no pertinence to the I, except so far as this is expressed through a located body. Did I not have an experiential role, one would have to agree with Kant and take the I, so far, not to be an object of knowledge. The I though, is known by the I through the mediation of an experiencible me, and by others through intropathic acts. As private, apart from all else, it is not spatialized. But it is also, so far, not engaged in perception or involved with the body, or relevant to anything else.

The I is spatialized when subjected to space, and it is meaningfully spatialized when it functions within a rational whole. It does not then occupy a position in space. Nor is it able to move or to rest. It is still only a meaningful unit to which has been added the further meaning of being spatial with a location within a larger space. That does not make it divisible into smaller parts or separated from other items at measurable distances from it. Its spatiality is part of its meaning, a meaning which is spatially related to other meanings.

Time is indifferently sustained by things, but internalized and intensified by the I. As a result, things are subject to a single universal time, to whose pace and import they add little, while the I gives it distinctive present moments and a distinctive rhythm. That time, like space, functions independently of, is subordinate to, and subordinates the meaning imposed on all items, private and public, animate and inanimate, human and subhuman. With this is mind, time can, therefore, in some agreement with Newton, be said to be a primal reality; with Kant to be subordinate to categories; and with Bergson, to be a condition to which everything is subject.

I can attend to other items as within the time that is pertinent to all, without regard for their difference in kind. I can also attend to them directly and bring them within the time I have made into an integral part of myself. In the first way, I become contemporary with others within a common, neutral time; in the second, my own distinctive present is to the fore, with the consequence that what I encounter is brought within my present.

I exist in space, and within a causal necessitation as well, but these are not as integral to that I as time itself is. "I exist" is short primarily for "I exist in time," and this in turn is short for "I exist for a while." The time is spread out at every moment. An earlier and a later provide a setting for the present moment that both excludes and unites them. All the while, the I remains the same I, unaffected by the fact that it exists for a while, occupied with changing and different contents.

The intelligible nature of the I escapes the corroding effect of time just so far as it subordinates time. As such, it could be identified with a logical presupposition for the presence of any knowable content, provided that this is not taken to deny that the I is able to be in and live through time. Otherwise, it would not be true that I come to be and pass away, or that I know this now and that then. An I that was just a presupposed unit or the accompaniment of all perceptions would have no tasks to perform, and presumably would neither come to be nor pass away. Such an I would be quite different from the I that is in fact maintained in contradistinction from all other concentrations of the self, for this is able to possess what it terminates in, and is the source of and functions as the backing for what is arrived at in an act of knowing me.

Denied temporality, I would not by that fact either vanish or be immortal, for I would still have other roles in this world. Deprived though I would be of the opportunity to exist for a while, I would still be individual, stand away from other items, be intelligible, and have a value. And I could be referred to as the backing which is behind both a you for others and behind my own me.

A formal necessitation relates items in accord with their

natures in ways that we seek to capture in our logics and mathematics. A linear causal necessitation, instead, connects them as antecedents and consequents. When the formal necessitation subordinates the causal, the causal becomes a special case of meaning. When the reverse subordination occurs, meanings acquire roles that cannot be known by attending just to what is implied and deducible.

Causal necessitation is productive, involving a passage from an actual cause to an actual effect. A linear account of causation takes the cause to so operate that a possible effect is turned into an actual subsequent effect. If, as has already been suggested, such causation is treated as a special case of constitutive causation, its dynamism will be seen to be primarily exhibited in the interplay of the constituents of the causal situation, with the cause and effect having the status of extensionally separated termini, governed by a number of conditions which determine their relevance, independence, intelligibility, and value within the confines of an imposed extensionality.

An overemphasis on formal necessitation has led to the supposition that causation must be understood to involve the introduction of time into the formal necessitation, or the introduction of the formal necessitation into time. In these ways, though, one can get only the necessity that something occur after something else and not an effect which follows from a cause and comes about at the terminus of a process by which a possibility is converted into an actuality. The meanings which function as terms in a formal necessitation are not turned into causes and effects simply by being related as antecedents and consequents. Action is needed to bring about singularized effects. Only the general natures of these are predictable from the natures of their causes and the rationale which a universal, causal necessitation incorporates.

So far as there is just a meaning, there is no action. If a meaning is subject to causation, its import is determined by what this permits and produces. I impose meaning on other items, giving them a meaningful role within the compass of a structure that I impose. When I go on to encompass them within a causal necessitation having an origin at the I, I turn them into meaningfully connected units credited with the meaningful status of being causes and effects. The items that I connect will be in a sequential productive order, but there will be no productivity there. As in Spinoza, the causes will be understood to be just becauses, premises, or reasons for conclusions.

If all predicates are taken to remark on some limited aspect of an object, 'existence' will be found to be not a predicate at all, since it will tell us nothing specific. And if all intelligibility is credited to essences, with existence set in contrast with these, existence will rightly be termed 'absurd'. But 'existence' is neither idle nor meaningless—as the discourse of those concerned with the so-called 'absurd existents' so amply illustrates.

There is nothing absurd in something existing. It just has features not deducible from an essence. What exists is more, not less, intelligible than what does not, since it is spatial, temporal, and dynamic. There is nothing absurd in a man being here rather than there, or now rather than then. Nor does one speak unintelligibly in remarking that he is active. The 'existence' in "He exists today, here and not there," instead of being idle or unintelligible, points up the fact that the man to whom it is credited is living, is at the present time, and in a place near the speaker.

'Existence' is a totalizing transcendental term, characterizing an entire object as an occupant of some subdivision of an extension which is independent of that object. Its spatial, temporal, and causal dimensions affect different types of objects in different ways. Were objects just meaningful units, they would, so far, not exist.

When I provide a matrix within which other items can be faced as meaningful units having existential roles, I face them as so many meaningful items which have existence as a part of their meaning. But that existence, so far as it is subordinated

to the meaning I am imposing on all the items, falls short of
the existence which they have due to a power encompassing
myself and them, as well as of the existence they have in contradistinction from mine. As caught within the orbit of the
meaning I provide, the items have the status only of meanings
within which time, space, and causality have contrastive
roles.

I provide a distinctive unity within which whatever I encounter is made to submit at the same time that I am given
a value in relation to all others. Other men have values and
impose their values in a similar way. We are alike as mere unit
I's, but different in what we govern and the values we impose.
All of us are subject to the same prescriptions at the same
time that each of us imposes prescriptions of his own. Duns
Scotus's limited universals, and his most limited of forms, by
virtue of which individualization takes place within the frame
of broader, Aristotelian essences, seem to be conceived from
some such position as this. The apparent contradiction between that view, where limited meanings are mediated by limited unities, and Scotus's other doctrine, that will and power
are prior to the intellect or meaning, is overcome when it is
recognized that the powers which a meaning and a unity exert
are not native to them.

Each actuality operates in a characteristic way. Each is
strong enough to govern a multiplicity of items, but not strong
enough to enable it to stand away from them all. If it had
more power it would preclude the independent functioning
of the multiple items it embraces. If it had less, it would not
keep them together. If the power were its own, it could be
forever. Evidently it uses a power originating elsewhere.

3.41. I am a truth-condition.

To have knowledge, it is necessary to have a mind able to
structure what is other than oneself in accord with the way it is

in fact structured in a world together with others. A mind that structures in this way is trued to what occurs. If it is used by an I, that I will be trued. When that trued I expresses itself in accord with the objective natures of things related by relevance, opposition, extension, and assessment, it will know what is.

Were there no mediators of the meaning I impose on whatever there is, there would so far be no limitation to which this meaning was subject. Something would be grasped *sub specie aeternitatis*. A knowledge of laws, universals, concepts would not be pertinent to the ways in which things were in fact together.

I have knowledge, not because I have clear and distinct ideas, or because I have analyzed what I confront into components assimilable by a logic or mathematics, but because what I have in mind is in consonance with the ways in which those natures are pertinent to one another. Clear and distinct ideas, even if held to be true, just so far as and because they are clear and distinct, fall short of what occurs to the objects of those ideas; analytic components may have no objective counterparts.

Were I not to make use of the meaning within which all that is intelligible occurs, I would lose a grasp of the natures of things and the laws that rationally connect them. Were I, in imposing a mediated meaning, to make what is confronted subject to myself, I would know only what I could discern from an individual perspective. This may be biased and distortive. But were I simply to yield to a meaning, I would allow my nature to be rationally connected with others, without introducing the note of truth. Knowledge expresses in constant universal terms the nature of things as they in fact are in relation to one another, but truth connects what is in mind with external items, and depends for its presence on an I which uses the mind in such a way as to articulate items that are objectively together.

3.42. I and others are within a common space.

If what is located in space has other nonspatial roles and powers, these will be beyond space's determination. But if actualities were just located, none would be a substance, have a being, be in time or act, or have a distinctive nature or value. The occupants of different regions in space have a relevance to one another in considerable independence of their actual distances, and without reference to any other status that they might have apart from that space. I see another man across the street directly, ignoring a host of intermediates—birds, trees, cars, dogs, and other items—or push them into the background.

Different occupied regions have no status apart from space. But while part of space, they can be relevant to one another in different degrees and ways. Studies of the ways in which men cluster together and separate in various situations deal with specializations of this fact. It is also taken account of in current cosmological physics, for this acknowledges the relevance of distant masses to one another at the same time that the actual spatial distances are not abstracted from or minimized.

For Descartes there are no physical realities other than located regions of space—*res extensa*. He also took the I to be real, but denied it any spatial role. As standing apart from all else, an I, of course, has no spatial location. Still, it operates in and through the body, and reaches to external things. Nonextended it grounds a private distension which, with the help of space, enables me to be extended as a spatially present public unit via my body and my acts. The spatialization to which I am subject locates that I in terms of these, making it be continuous with the body. As operating in and through this, the I is a source of bodily acts.

When it is held that space is an 'outer sense', it is still not shown that the occupants of that space are external to the knower. If they are real, they are not yet known to be able to enter into space. They could be just limited spatial extensions.

If I provide a spatial domain in which other items are extensionally related, but mediate this by having them oriented toward that I, there will be real spatial regions related to one another, all subject to my spatialization. The last is the result that Kant sought to achieve. But since he did not allow for a space apart from an 'outer sense', he had to suppose that the objectivity was achieved by the 'outer sense' constituting the extensional connections of the items normally said to be in space.

I am always separated from every other I. No matter how intimate I am or what I possess, I make no contact with them. Forever, we remain apart and at a distance. Any 'outer sense', to be pertinent to us, would have to govern a common meaning in order to bear on our interlocked meanings.

Geography is a subject neglected by philosophers, though geometry, as its name implies, was at least initially an abstraction from actual geographical situations. Since we know no other space in daily life except one in which there are occupants and empty regions, we have no reason to believe that when one abstracts from geography, i.e., from the actual space in which items are, what is left is a real space with an inherent geometry. It is, of course, conceivable that the resultant space retains the very contours it had when occupied, but without the qualities, nuances, and densities it had before. There is no way of knowing if the conception answers to a fact, for there is no way of getting rid of all the objects in space and looking at space bare. We arrive at a geometrized space by flattening out in imagination the geography which actually prevails. Whether we take that space to have a geometry or not, in order for it to be pertinent to the natures of things and the ways in which these in fact are rationally interlinked with one another, it will have to be involved with a rationale not reducible to such a geometry.

A space in which cats and dogs confront one another is where extensional relations vary in intensity in some accord with variations in proximity. The fact can be accounted for by seeing the meaning that connects the natures of cats and dogs to mediate the space in which they are. Or, abstracting from their mutual antagonism, and considering the cats and dogs just as animals, one can know them to be spatially located items which are related in other ways as well, within a limited part of the cosmos.

When mediated by meaning, space is limited to providing locations for and extensional connections between meaningful items. I am one of those meaningful items, with a nature different from that of any other being. Locatable through the mediation of my body, that nature is extensionally related to other natures in a contoured space. Were I to intermediate an 'outer sense' by a meaning, and then used the result to constitute a frame within which other spatially related meanings were to be found, I would continue to face meanings related to one another at various distances, but what I confronted would not be grounded in objects.

The intermediated space in terms of which I confront meanings in space must either be the very space that is apart from that I, or a counterpart of which I am making use. If it be the former, I must yield to the space when I attend to the natures of others at a distance. If it be the latter, a counterpart, it must reproduce the space and the rational connections that the items have to one another apart from that I.

Only because I can both yield to and make use of space without subjectifying or distorting it, am I able to have a mediated spatial outlook within which I can confront the objective spatial conditions that govern the natures of what is confronted. I know that I have adequately yielded to the space only when I know that I have found a position from which I am both steady and compelled, intermediating a space to which I as well as others are subject. It is conceivable that the result might reflect an unprobed constancy peculiar to myself. If our distance from one another is a fact, or if what I do is duplicated by others and expressed in concordant acts, I will have to recognize the space to be neither a function of others nor of myself. To take account of the discoveries we make about the ways in which natures are separate in and function in space, it must be allowed that space has a status beyond anyone's ability to constitute, restrain, or redirect.

Space permits of delimitations of itself. The resulting delimited regions differ from one another in magnitude, location, quality, intensity, and diversity, all of which can be subject to an evaluational ordering. Because I occupy a region with an intensity expressive of a vitalizing personalized power, I can stand apart from others. I then have a different value from what I have in an order which also takes account of my substantiality, being, and nature.

From my position, what I confront has shifting values. Sometimes I find regions which are dominating and large. At other times, I find some which are dominated and small. I find that what is superior sometimes is near and sometimes is far, sometimes is like and sometimes is unlike my body. Sometimes I find myself facing the calm and empty, and sometimes what is turbulent and multiply nuanced. To achieve a steady outlook, I must yield to a more objective and universal evaluation operating under the aegis of space. But then I give up my role as the measure of values.

3.43. I and others are within a common time.

By itself time has nothing to do with relevance. Nor need a power determining relevance operate in time. But if relevance is temporalized, some items will exist for a while in some accord. Only in comparatively recent times has this consideration been focused on, and then, primarily by students of history. Vico is a lone voice almost drowned out by the rationalists who dominated his and later periods. Even today, when the historic sense has been so altered by political events and expectations, philosophers say little about the nature of a time that bears on items which are relevant to one another.

I exist in the present together with other existents, but am allied with some of them more than I am with others. As together with them, I both exclude and take account of seg-

ments of the past and of the future in which there are intensified, qualitative, temporal stretches of affiliated items. They
and I, so far, are caught up in a time without regard for the
status that we have as realities, natures, values, or genuine
substances, able to possess and to control that on which we
impinge. None of us is just a passive unit within a time that
meets resistance nowhere.

When a cyclical or dialectical course is credited to time,
nothing is changed in principle; instead, a punctuation is provided for a cosmic power which has a predetermined way of
making itself manifest. From the point of view of such a cyclical or dialectical time, I and others are denied efficacy. Yet we
fill out portions of time in independent ways and thereby
make a difference to time's course and rhythm. That filling
makes it possible for time to have distinguishable regions,
each with its own content. Since it is we who give the filling to
time, just what that filling is like cannot be known by attending only to time, whether this be taken to be substantial,
linear, circular, or dialectical.

I carve out a distinctive moment having a present stretch, a
past, and a future. Together with others, I am subject to the
whole of time. So far as I insist on the time that is peculiar to
me, what I confront is dealt with within a personalized frame.
A more adequate apprehension of others as they in fact are
relevant to one another in time requires my dealing with them
in temporal terms that are common to us all.

A temporalized being, a world of temporalized beings, and
the temporalized beings that I face provide grounds for a time
with a real past, present, and future; for an objective temporal
world; and for a world that I, with memory and expectations,
can perceive and in which I attend to other temporalized beings. Though I am in time, and make use of time as objective,
neutral, with a subjective note which I introduce, I will not
have a basis for history unless the items are relevant to others.
If they were not relevant, there would be only distinct temporal regions in a common time.

I am subject to time even when, apart from my body, I

epitomize the self and am involved with other epitomizations. It is no less true that I, as manifested in and through my body, am subject, with every other existent, to a common time. With them I fill out real subdivisions of it, excluding what is past and future at the same time that I take these into myself. I exist within my own present, and attend to other things from that position. I would so far be wholly caught within the present of a private time were it not that I use the result to provide a frame within which all other occurrences are to be located as so many subordinated, temporalized realities. Those realities are opposed to one another in regions within the time I provide. Since whatever happens to them occurs in my time, with their different presents providing intensive limitations of my own, the outcome would be a temporalized solipsism were I not also able to approach those others via the common time in which we both are, and thereby overcome making the temporal world of others pivot about my personal present.

Ideas about democracy, education, and sport have changed considerably in import over the decades. So have some ideas about mathematical items. Zero, one, and two were denied by Aristotle to be genuine numbers because they did not mark a multiplicity; they now have a status equal to that of other numbers. Faced with this observation, it still makes sense to remark that numbers always have the same logical and mathematical properties. But it should be added that they have these properties in time where they are locatable and have durations and careers. Indeed, they are so time-bound that it took generations and a new approach before men were able to isolate the core of meaning in them which was free of all temporal factors. Were there no such subjugation of meanings to time, the actual changes and definite temporal locations which characterize meanings would be adventitious. Why and how could such adventitious features attach themselves to what otherwise was fixed and eternal?

I am a temporal unit with acquired meanings. One of these meanings is the nature I maintain. That nature is mine from the beginning to the end of my life. Since I exist only in the

present, it is a nature locatable at different present moments.
These moments are related in a succession in which my identity is ingredient. Consequently, it is not necessary to suppose, with tradition, that the identity of the I is maintained
outside of time altogether; nor, with some contemporaries, to
suppose that the existence of the I in time precludes its having
a genuine identity. Both views neglect the fact that the selfsame nature is to be found at different moments of time, and
that occurrences at those times can be related through a persistent self and I. Others, of course, also persist. The world is
no kaleidoscope of events in which nothing is constant, fixed,
selfsame. But not everything, like an I, can attend to and use
temporally located meanings and thereby face different natures related to one another within its present, while they remain related in an objective, common present.

Each actuality is wholly in the present. Each is wholly present again and again. And each has an identity that qualifies
the different moments in which it wholly had been and in
which it now wholly is. The nature of each actuality is in each
of the different presents, both because it is wholly present
there, and because that is the point of origin of the agency by
means of which each actuality is able to be selfsame at different moments and over the course of time. The fact is faintly
caught in Locke's supposition that identity depends on memory, for by memory one attaches oneself in the present to oneself as at some past moment. But not only do I remain selfsame outside of time, but things are selfsame without having
any ability to remember. Though an oak has no memory, it,
too, connects a present exhibition with previous exhibitions
of itself by means of a constant nature expressed in the present. Its act falls short of the I's, for it is not able to impose an
insistent identity, on what it exhibits, uses, and possesses.
Memory awaits the I's connecting of a present with a past,
when the I also had been.

Different occurrences in time have longer and shorter careers, depending on the reach of temporalized relations. An
evaluation of the past and present occurrences in relation to

one another, as well as an evaluation of the result in comparison with the values achieved elsewhere through other unifications, is thereby made possible. Usually, the more variegated the related items and the more extended the range, the higher the value. The richer the content of each moment and the more compatible it is with all the others, the more readily is it unified with them in a variegated harmony. Nothing, so far, is taken account of but temporally related regions encompassed within unities. What the items may be apart from time or unity is ignored. But what was extensionalized by time and thereby made to have components separated from one another, and what was related in time and thereby made into separated regions, would nevertheless be evaluated, the first in relation to the second, and the second in relation to all others in an objective hierarchy of values. Within the present of the I, a similar unification occurs, resulting in the assessment of different stresses in it, thereby enabling them to constitute a single harmony. The unity that operates there has a different content, and results in an evaluation different from what is produced when a unity operates within objective time. If the I is to face other items as subject to an objective scale, it must yield its assessments to those grounded in a unity within the compass of time.

Dialectical history and other forms of the notion that the world steadily moves from worse to better, and will eventually end with what is excellent, are biased toward what is later. But time is neutral toward the units it encompasses. Though some units may be assessed as better than others, this is a consequence, not of their position in time, but of harmonies they there have and make possible. The values that items have, they have when they occur, no matter what the time. This is most evident when one considers ideas. There are ideas whose time has not yet come; there are others now flat and stale. The ideas put forward by Peirce over eighty years ago are still not altogether assimilated today; idealism and positivism live on, but without discernible movement in heart or mind. The values of these ideas differ at different times because at different times they are able to be harmonized in different degrees with others that were then available. Their values depend on what they can be unified with when they in fact occur, no matter what the time.

3.44. I and others are within a common causality.

A world of particles, alike in every respect, could be envisaged to exist within the compass of a necessitation which operates on and through all in a monotonous, uninterrupted manner, not even differentiating what is past from what is future. The present would then be a zero point, and one could just as readily move backward as forward to derive the momentum and place of other particles at any other time. Nothing answers to such a state of affairs. Causal lines are asymmetrical.

Because of the way I am present in my body, the causal situation in which that body is involved is often made so radically diverse from those in which similar and related bodies function, that the situations become inexplicable if reference is not made to the causal presence of that I. Quite apart from the considerations which require one to admit that a human living body cannot be wholly understood in terms pertinent to other types of being—no matter how closely allied chemically and biologically, and quite apart from considerations which require one to acknowledge the free actions of the self—there is a need to take account of the I in order to explain the lines of relevancy which begin at my body.

I am able to face my body, what is outside it, and both together as items involved in relevant causal situations which I constitute. But I will distort what in fact occurs if I do not make my constituting causality conform to what objectively prevails. And that I can do if I know, perceive, sense, and act in terms of the conditions which govern them as well as myself. The denial of the epistemic use of objective conditions in this and other cases forces one to suppose a way of organizing and attending to content which is so individual that no one can know what it is like or that it in fact occurs.

Actualities are opposed to one another. Each is self-contained, maintaining itself, insistent on itself, and defiant of what else there be. They enable causes and effects to stand apart from one another as oppositional units, thereby breaking up a single dynamic necessitation into subsections. As punctuating causality, the actualities are both connected and separated. The connection makes them part of one causal whole; their separation makes it possible for an effect not merely to follow from a cause but also because of it, and to be itself able to function as a cause. An actuality, of course, can continue to be, able to provide beginnings again and again for different causal lines, ending in different effects.

The beginning and ending of a causal occurrence are on a footing, warranting no preferential role for either. But I have the ability to stand away from the causal whole in which I am with others, and can then make a common causation be applicable to that to which I attend. So far as I succeed in reproducing the very causal conditions which govern myself and them, so far am I able to attend to them as the causally connected realities they have been objectively conditioned to be.

The units envisaged as being subject to universal laws are just place holders, points marked out within a single rationale, unless they are sustained and maintained apart from those laws. If the laws are taken to operate within the confines of a universal causation, the units will still be only placeholders, but in a causal order. The addition of rationality to a causally determined world limits causality to intelligibly related items. A universal determinism assumes this point of view when it accepts as basic a cosmic dynamism operating on irreducible physical units. The result is a variant on Plato's position in the *Timaeus* with its restless receptacle, rationally structured by a demiurge. An opposite stress is presented by Galileo, for whom causality is a cosmic process moving from item to item as though from premiss to conclusion. Neither approach makes provision for the action of distinct actualities. Both take the entities about which they speak to be not actualities but just terms, dynamically connected.

The components of causes or effects are like words in a language, exhibiting the outcome of the meeting of a common meaning with distinctive intents. The result is a single meaningful causal complex. An I provides no exception. It will not, of course, be acknowledged by one who allows a place only for physical components. But, as has been observed, such an account makes no provision for the presence of the possessive, perceptive, cognizing I which presents that view. Provision for an I could be made by treating it as that component of a causal complex which all the others together articulate. Were the I to have only that role, it would not exercise the power of a cause. But were it denied such a role, it would not be able to know, doubt, affirm or deny a universal determinism, or exist as a component in the causes and effects that are linked meaningfully.

Expanding or contracting the range of meanings which are encompassed in a cause or effect has no affect on the causality governing them; the causality is not thereby dispersed, solidified, increased, or diminished. Nor need the inclusion or exclusion of an I among the components of a single complex cause or effect make a difference to the causality itself, or to any conservative or creative factors that may be characteristic of it. But the I sometimes is a component of a meaningful cause or effect. There was a time when it had no place within any meaningful cause or effect, and there will be a time when it will no longer have one. But while it exists, it makes a difference to the meaning of the complex in which it functions.

It has long been held that some causes are more eminent than their effects, possessing more reality, power, dignity, or value. The idea was employed to account for the supposed creation of this defective world by an omnipotent, good God. Restricted to that imagined case, an eminent cause is evidently constitutive. It can allow for subordinate antecedent states which are followed by a consequent, persistent decay. A reverse emphasis, with its supposition that consequents are always superior to antecedents, characteristic of the modern theory of progress, is also possible. Both the declining and progressive interpretations hold that causality always moves toward one value, the first taking it to be on a lower, the second taking it to be on a higher level than what had prevailed before. But sometimes effects have their components better organized and harmonized than their causes, and sometimes the reverse occurs. Most often, no appreciable difference can be discerned.

I contribute to the value of whatever causal complex I help constitute. The greater my contribution, the greater my value in a causal world operating between causes and effects, which are not only serially related but ordered as better or worse. The values are maintained in opposition to the complex. Otherwise they would be absorbed by it, with the consequence that there would be no diversity of values. As having value, I and others play distinctive roles within causes and effects. When we assume the position of constituting causes whose operations are limited to values, others are attended to either as having values relative to us or (when our subjective biases are overcome) as having values within an objectively determined hierarchy of items, confined within the limits set by causes and effects.

3.45. I am a natural existent.

An existent is a localized portion of space, time, and causality. When it is also enabled to be relevant, coordinate, meaningful, and of value, it is part of nature. There, existents exhibit diverse biases, oppositions, intelligible natures, and controlling and harmonizing unities. There, I am locatable, dated, and active, together with other spatial, temporal, and causally significant items. I am also more. I am a self, a person, and a truth-condition. And I express myself in bodily ways, without necessarily compromising my functioning apart from that body.

Whatever is extended has parts external to parts. It would seem therefore that I, because existent, would have to be fragmented spatially, temporally, and causally. This I would be, did I just exist inside cosmic extensions. But I am an existent in whom portions of those extensions have been incorporated. Because I am such an existent, extensions do not merely overlay but are integral to me, turned into continuations of myself. I do not then constrain others as they are in fact constrained by the extensions in which they are. The constituting of objects that is due to me is made possible by them. That fact I quickly discover, for I find that they maintain themselves, act, and govern what I terminate in.

The modern temper is not disposed toward such a view. Instead, it favors the position that men formulate theories, hypotheses, and laws whose warrant lies solely in the empirical discovery that they lead to satisfactory predictions and the drawing of fruitful consequences. More and more cooperation, experimentation, and clarification, it is hoped, will take us closer and closer to the point where all serious investigators will be in agreement—and that will be the closest one could ever hope to come to anything one might be willing to call 'truth'. Changes in scientific outlook could be said to be either evolutionary or to involve quanta jumps, but whether it be one or the other, it is held, there will be no way of knowing whether or not what the scientists agree upon answers to any matter of fact. But since scientists take account of experiments and predictions, they obviously are not altogether cut off from what is objectively so. Even if one were to adopt the common view, one would still, contrary to its claims, be able to know that there were occurrences and structures not controlled by the knower. Nothing would preclude his noting how these belonged to items not previously considered and in ways not previously envisaged.

Granted that one does not know the exact specific conditions within which everything is now caught, and therefore can only grope toward that final account of the world with which science is concerned, it still remains true that the more basic, generic, constraining features of that world can be known. The fact is partially admitted in the recognition that one can know and utilize in different theories at different epochs a constant, objective, effective logic and mathematics, persistently structuring what in fact occurs.

3.46. I am a unity.

There are many unities with varying degrees of power, with different natures and modes of operation. Often items of approximately the same range and value function together. Sometimes there are complexities in which a great number of diverse items are united for considerable periods. Ours, evidently, is not a universe solely of indifferent, aggregated items. There are organisms, families, societies. Yet attempts have been made to reduce every supposed complex unity to an aggregate. Success would require the entire universe to be one vast collection of units. Why then is a stop made at various aggregated sets? Is it because of the presence or action of human interests? If so, the interests of men would be credited with the constitutive power of actually, humanistically, or privately turning a world of aggregated items into sets of them, whose items are relevant to one another. Still unaccounted for would be the fact that in some of these sets the various members are hierarchically ordered, and that, particularly in the case of animals and men, some of the sets have careers which, instead of being summations of the careers of their parts, are distinctive, dictating to some extent where the parts are to be and what they are to do.

When account is taken of the fact that other epitomizations of the self are possessed by the I, that the I possesses the body, and that it terminates in a multiplicity of items at a distance from that body, the I will itself be seen to exhibit a unity which embraces and subjugates a multiplicity of different types of entity. Though other epitomizations of the self also govern multiplicities, and do so in differing ways, they can also be envisaged as so many variants of the unity exhibited by the I, and therefore as giving the multiple items they encompass various degrees of relevance to one another.

Unlike an aesthetic or any other whole, which takes account of the ways in which items are able to supplement or subtract from one another, an aggregate encompasses items each of which has the same value as any other there. The aggregate of a cat, king, and cabbage is an aggregate of three, with members neither superior nor inferior to one another, nor to the aggregates of three cats, three kings, or three cabbages. Such an aggregation abstracts from the values that the items actually have in this world. We sometimes make similar abstractions when the particularity of items has little interest for us—when we pay fares, tolls, and taxes.

The value I have in relation to others is brought to bear on other values. The objective hierarchy of values is then crisscrossed by variegated combinations of values. As a possessor, as a responsible source of decisions and actions, and as quickening the body, I have other relevant roles, and am then sometimes antagonistic to the very entities with which I am otherwise allied. I never lose my alliance with all other men, though there are some with whom I am not intimate, and others whom I find repugnant.

The traditional view of a creating God makes him the singular, undivided source of instances of unity and being. But the items he supposedly produces can have no status apart from him unless, apart from him, they are able to maintain themselves. 'Creatures' are unities; if created, they remain attached to their creator. And only so far as that supposed creator also evaluates them are these 'creatures' in a value hierarchy. Some such view as this is at the heart of Spinoza's account of his modes. Though each mode has its distinctive degree of perfection, it does not have the status of a genuine independent reality. Spinoza here, as in so many other places, draws the bitter conclusions common assumptions demand. But he touches on only one aspect of the universe, since he does not allow for the irreducible reality, substantiality, meaningfulness, and existence of finite entities.

In an all-comprehensive evaluational hierarchy, items are not yet intelligibly connected. Thirst and hunger do not there make a difference to the value of water and food but express only animal distortions of the values these objectively have. Without in any way disturbing that hierarchy, formal lines can be provided, connecting items which are at considerable valuational distances from one another. A hierarchy of values would, so far, have its items related in accord with the demands of meaning.

I and others are terms in an intelligible relation. We are also independently meaningful, apart from the relation. As such, our positions in a value hierarchy are determined by the meanings we have. As subordinated to unities, the meanings have degrees of excellence. Leibniz's monadology is built on this idea. According to him, there is a plenum of monads, each with an intelligible place in a value hierarchy. The goodness of his supreme creative monad is here one with its supreme rationality, every other monad differing from it only in degree, within an intelligible continuum of excellencies. But meanings are not only able to subordinate unities; they are constituted independently of them.

I and others, as meaningful values, neither act nor oppose one another. We are just related in objectively prescribed ways. When I subjectively or objectively deal with others, I face them as meaningful values. I could, instead, confront brute facts and attribute values to them in some accord with my appetites, emotions, and the like, but if I did, I would deal with values under the aegis of meaning, rather than the reverse, at the same time that the meanings would be understood in a very limited way while the values were denied an objective role. As a result, erroneous judgments of value, or the understanding how all particulars could be together under the governance of a single, all-encompassing excellence, would be precluded.

Since they are unities for diverse items, must values be extensionalized, spread out in space? The idea rests on the supposition that what a unity governs are parts already dispersed in space. This does occur, but only when a unity functions within the provenance of a spatial region rather than, as in the case now considered, when a spatial region is subordinated to a unity.

Values are unities governing multiplicities. They are both locatable and extended in space, since they are where the multiplicities are. In being spatialized, the values are not altered, but they do acquire new roles. Spatialized, they are reordered, without thereby losing their relative positions in a hierarchy of excellencies. The values can also operate directly on particulars which are at different times or have different causal roles. They can also play a role in thought or judgment where they are neither extended nor extensionally related.

I am locatable. I am also present in my body. Since I am a source of bodily actions, terminating elsewhere, I am locatable, as well, where those actions begin. I can also be identified with a unity for that body, conditioning what this includes. I will then be seen to function somewhat as space itself does. Just as space, without being spatialized and thus set in another space, enables items to be spatially related, so I enable bodily parts to have spatial relations without that I thereby becoming spatialized. I then function ontologically with respect to bodily parts in the way I function epistemically when what I confront is envisaged within a spatial frame.

Locations in space are a function of the countering of space by different particulars. The distribution of these can be accounted for by attending to what happened at those and other positions at other times. But there is no accounting for the spatial distribution, if reference is made either just to space or to the items as they are apart from space. My position in space is determined by the outcome of the interplay of my distendedness with an as yet undivided space. And since, when extended in and through my body, I do not divide into spatially separate parts, I evidently there function with respect to what I then embrace rather as space does when it governs what enters into it.

I have not always existed, but when I exist, I exist in a present. Whatever value I have is presently possessed. The value itself, though it is the value of an I that exists for a while, need not have been temporalized. As a mere value, it is related to other values regardless of any date or duration. Here, as in the other cases, long-standing views about a soul come into focus. Though it is not clear whether the soul is thought to be primarily a substance, reality, rational unit, existent, or value, all who speak of it seem to want to say that it is splendid, noble, pure, the divine in miniature. What they envisage is evidently a nontemporal value exhibited in time. If the world or the body is taken to be in time already, the supposed soul will have to be said to become incarnated in a separate temporal scheme of things—a view which forces one to hold that the eternal submits to alien, restrictive conditions over which it has no control. It would be in closer consonance with what apparently is intended to say that eternal values are already temporalized, and are thereupon enabled to subject all particulars to time as well as to value. A supposed incarnation in the form of a finite man or of a soul in a particular body will then require only the determination of the moment when the eternal appears, and not an alien temporalization of it. But, since moments are distinct only so far as they are successively occupied, sooner or later actualities will have to be acknowledged. Incarnations and embodiments of souls, in the end, must take account of what, apart from them, give them an opportunity to be at particular moments of time.

Having freed oneself from the need to make sense of the mystery of an eternal value allowing itself to be subject to time, one is still faced with the fact that a temporalized value both conditions and is limited by what are thereby turned into unities temporally connected with one another, sequentially or as contemporaries. There is no need, though, to suppose that a temporalized value is anything more than an effective condition—either a universal, temporalized unity functioning without purpose, will, thought, or concern, or an I expressing its own temporalized value.

I and others are located in time. No matter what our natures or efforts, we are contemporaries, moving into the next moment together. We also intensify a temporalized value, turning it into our own presents. It is as such an intensified, temporalized value that I exist apart from all others while I am together with them under a common, comprehensive, neutral, temporalized value. To know what others are like as together with me in this way, I must deal with them in my intensified present as subject to the temporalized value that governs me as well as them.

When I cease to have a temporal position, my spatiality, causality, substantiality, reality, meaning, and value are not extinguished. They continue to play a role within my self. This does not mean I have a position in eternity, but only that, though no longer in time, I have a place in other encompassing domains. I do not acquire such a place after I have enjoyed a temporal career. I have it independently of and while I am in time, and, therefore, both as not in time and in it. If I were immortalized at the end of a particular temporal career I would be able to have the kind of immortality that men are said to cherish. But of that I cannot be assured unless I can know that, while continuing to possess a temporalized value, I am also caught up in a nontemporal domain. The only immortality of which I can now be assured is one which I now enjoy because I am involved with what is always.

The highest unity and the highest value are often identified with God. What is true of God is true of them. Since that God has been credited with at least four distinct kinds of power, so should these: a) In the ontological argument, God is held to have a power equal to his value. He is perfect, it is there said, and therefore a *causa sui*, that which causes itself. b) For those to whom God is a mind or a rational ultimate, he is also a ground or origin of ideas. c) When he is held to be a creator, he is supposed to have the power to make some or all of the ideas he entertains acquire another status, where they can interplay with one another. d) When, finally, he is thought to sustain the universe, he is credited with a constitutive power for an effect which, though distinct from him, is kept in existence by his operative presence. The first of these deals with God by himself. It has trouble in telling us how the effect of the *causa sui* differs from its cause. The second places within God all the meanings that result when particulars counter the common meaning with their different intents. It has difficulty in understanding how there could be such a plurality in him. The third allows the ideas or values that God entertains to have another role, but where, or how, or what it cannot say. God cannot set meanings or ideas apart from himself unless he provides a residence for them in a matter, or something similar. But such a supposed support itself needs to be freed from him and needs a support of its own; otherwise it would not be maintained apart from him. The fourth takes God to have causal power with reference to the universe. But this he can have only so far as the universe that he supposedly constitutes is thereby endowed with its sequential causality. But a constitutive cause need not produce a sequential causal world. The world could conceivably be unchanging; it might perish as soon as it was produced; it could be an arena for the play of pure chance. More important, it cannot be understood from the position of just one power. In any case, the universe which God supposedly produced is necessarily inferior to him, for if he duplicated himself he would, by that very act, either have self-contradictorily limited himself by another who was just as powerful as himself, or he would be identical with this and therefore would not in fact have produced anything. A creating God necessarily brings about what is inferior to himself and must, therefore, be an eminent cause of what he creates. If,. then, God and the highest value were identical, value would cause itself, be the origin of ideas, be a creator, or be a constitutive cause. But it need be none of these.

Value can be subject to causality. When so subject, it could conceivably be made into a cause of what is superior to it, if the process of causation itself is creative, productive, fecund. But there is no warrant for supposing that this mode of causation, or the reverse, prevails everywhere and always. Causation is not forced to take account of the place that causes or effects have in an objective hierarchy of value.

Different I's have different causal roles. Sometimes they function together, sometimes in opposition, and sometimes sequentially. As a source of the particular causal dynamism which begins at it, the value of an I is a cause of other values. Morality and ethics are grounded in that fact, attending as they do to the values that men, as units of value, produce. Though men usually order things in terms of their ability to contribute to the satisfaction of human wants and desires, they are also able and sometimes do take account of the ways in which higher or lower values come about, regardless of human need or interest. Most often the judgments reflect men's estimates of what they take to be desirable human acts, such as the feeding of the young or the care of the feeble. But sometimes objective impersonal judgments are made of the ways in which evaluative unities replace others that have a wider or narrower range, and a better or worse control over their encompassed multiplicities.

3.47. An I is the measured measure of all things.

The reverberations of Protagoras's challenging claim, "Man is the measure of all things," have not altogether died down. Because it expresses a partial truth, the claim has neither vanished nor flourished.

Unlike an aggregate which has members that are indifferent to one another, and unlike physical things whose unities govern only what is physical, living beings and particularly men, provide unitary conditions for whatever they confront. Men's feelings, consciousness, thought, and claims, in addition, bring what is encountered within themselves. Each apprehends others by means of the same unity by which he governs his parts, but operates on them in different ways and with different results.

Every I is subject to a primal value, and assumes the position of a primal value with reference to others. Every I, as a consequence, becomes the measure of whatever it confronts, treating it as a value connected with others by affiliation, opposition, implication, and distancing extensions. That measure can be so subjectivized that the result reflects nothing more than the way in which a single I attends to what interests it. Protagoras's claim has been understood to maintain that, and nothing more. Whether this is what he intended or not, it is still true that every I is also together with other items, all subject to a common valuational ordering.

An I has a status apart from the body, able to involve itself with other epitomizations of the self and with what lies outside the body. The fact would drive one into a Cartesian dualism, with its separate spiritual I and extended body, were it not for the fact that the I imposes the same unity on other epitomizations of the self, on the body and what it confronts, in different ways and with different results. Were the I not capable of attending to others via the very same condition which governs both them and the I together, it would have only the kind of value that results from the impress of itself on what it encounters. Because it can attend to a common governing unity in the course of its apprehension of what is beyond it, it is able to encompass what it confronts as already objectively ordered. To the extent that it succeeds in doing this, to that extent it unifies what it confronts in accord with the way this is unified by a primal value.

3.48. An I is a one for a many.

The claim that I know and can know nothing more than some suppositions momentarily sustained by experiment and experience is supposed to do justice to the relation of ideas to what is the case, and to allow for an objective measure of what I know. Since it does not say anything about what might finally be the case, it can really claim no more than what I have in mind is different from what holds in fact. Since to be different from one another, they must be together, what I have in mind and what is external to it must be subject to a single unity. We have much to learn, but what we learn (as well as what we misconstrue) instances a generic truth condition. This we acknowledge when we say that we have learned or misconstrued, or even that we are in doubt as to whether or not we know anything that is true.

There is more than one effective condition. Each functions independently of the others. Each, too, mediates and thereby qualifies the activities of the rest. Since there cannot be a many, whether of things, ideas, or conditions, except so far as the items are together and therefore subject to an encompassing unity, the many conditions must be under the aegis of a one which enables them to make a single set. We would be at the beginning of an infinite regress now, looking for a one which would encompass the many, and then for another one which had the one and the many together, and so on endlessly, were it not that each actuality is a unity enabling the conditions to be a many. No infinite regress is involved, for the ones already are realities apart from the many for which they provide unities.

I am able to be a one for whatever conditions me because I am distinct from and, as such, contrast with them. In addition, I make private use of the conditions, thereby acting in still another way as a one with respect to them. I am also, as we have already seen, an individual, a person, a truth-condition, an existent, and a measured measure, due to my ability to internalize the conditions to which I am subject and of which I make use in attempting to grasp other entities as objectively together.

With others, I am subject to conditions. By myself, I attend to others via those conditions. In myself, I unite all of them. I stand apart from all as their locus. I make use of them as standards. And I give them a role in my self, my body, and my acts.

Each internalized condition is the object of a primitive emotion. This is directed in a distinctive way toward what is objective, effective, all-encompassing, and final. Reverence, awe, hope, openness, and humility are instances. It is more correct to say that I am caught up in them than that they are aroused in me. I also have other, more individually produced emotions. But the primitive emotions relate what I internally am to what made this possible. The more individually produced emotions, instead, express in different ways and degrees the nature of the involvement of the I with the other epitomizations of the self, and with the body as well. As a result, the privately grounded emotions both overlay and are caught up in the emotions of reverence, awe, hope, openness, and humility. Aroused most effectively and directed most accurately when one immerses oneself in religion, art, ethics, speculation, and mysticism, each of the individually produced emotions, sooner or later, involves one in the more primitive, thereby making possible a termination in what finally governs all of us.

Machines are insensitive. They are, therefore, not responsive either to injuries or to benefits. Nor are they able to adjust themselves so as to promote their survival and enhancement. Unlike animals, they have no environments and, of course, cannot interplay with them. And, unlike men, they are not able to withdraw into a privacy. Only men can start from the position of an I. And the more surely they hold their I's in radical contrast with their bodies, the more surely are they able to thrust themselves forward into a distinctively human milieu, as well as toward the conditions that govern all there is.

Both those who take the mind or soul to be a distinct substance, and those who suppose that each man is wholly alone, groping in the dark with suppositions, hopes, and beliefs, fixate man at a point which is midway between where he is habitually involved with his body and daily tasks, and where

he is involved with final realities. Both positions are extrava-
gantly metaphysical, the result of a sudden leap to a position
where no man would be able to communicate with anyone
else. The one that I am is related to many items in the self
and person, in the body, beyond the body, and outside all
actualities.

3.49. A fictional I has a created individuality.

"Give me my robe, put on my crown. I have immortal longings in me," says Shakespeare's Cleopatra. There is, of course,
no actual Cleopatra who sustains the 'me', 'my' and 'I' used
there. There is no Cleopatran real me to whom a robe can be
given, no real Cleopatran I who has immortal longings. The
me and I here are effective, plausible fictions. Somehow they
must be constituted and possessed of roles that are distinct
from but not yet altogether alien to those characteristic of
nonfictional me's and I's.

The me and I to which Shakespeare has his Cleopatra refer
must be like my own in one way and unlike it in another. Were
the fictional and real me and I totally unalike, there would be a
need to suspend unbelief when sharing in the vicissitudes of a
drama. Were they totally alike, there would be no difference
between the portrayed Cleopatra and a real person.

Like my me, a portrayed me must be taken to be sustained
from a side other than that from which it is approached by
means of 'me', and 'my'. And there must be an I for that me,
beyond and continuous with it. But Shakespeare's Cleopatra
has no genuine I or me. His Cleopatra is not real enough to
have either. Our understanding of her or of any other fiction,
however, does not stop with an acknowledgment or an acceptance of it. Inevitably we are pulled into an involvement
with powers outside the fiction, to end with a sense of a tragic
or benign ultimate reality. The deeper the emotions produced
in the course of an appreciation of a fiction, the more surely is
there a contact made with that reality. As a consequence, the

fiction is lived with as a special expression of something which is more basic and permanent than either creator or spectator. The reader provides a unity for all the terms. At the end of his reading he has become the solidified presence of all that had been presented, sustaining the entire fictional being. The I of the fictional being is also sustained but as having the role of a sustainer for what the being supposedly said and did.

In living discourse, various expressions are adopted and utilized by different participants. Only an observer is able to assume the position of the discourse itself and take account of both sides neutrally. When he does, he approximates the position that one assumes when reading either a report or a work of fiction.

A report is made up of statements, each of which orients the various terms in a single actuality or occurrence, or in some limited set of these. In a work of fiction, and most evidently in a poem, the various terms, statements, and discourse are united by the appreciative reader by means of an emotionally toned act, thereby making himself the locus of a figure of speech, and particularly of metaphors. But instead of referring what he thereby unites, he holds it in abeyance, supplementing each unification with others until the whole is completed. Over the course of the work, helped by its development and its consequent nuanced effects on his emotions, he brings the entire work together as a single unit pertinent to what is ultimately real, and to individuals or groups so far as they epitomize this. While the work makes him into a single emotionally affected unity directed at the only reality that could objectively ground what he unified, the metaphors and other figures of speech utilized in it serve primarily to specialize and intensify his emotions, thereby making the final reference more vivid and pertinent to him. Figures of speech give emphasis to the fact that what is referred to has a depth of its own, to be reached with the help of the emotion that is thereby elicited.

In the course of his reading, a reader faces an emptiness

which begins at the differences, pauses, skips, omissions, and other gaps, and continues on into an unspecified, indeterminate reality beyond. The reading, with its gradual solidification of what is said into a single emotional whole, enables him to discover that the emptiness he first confronted opens into a final reality beyond all specific occurrences. Something similar occurs in the course of an appreciation of any art, each being read in a distinctive manner. The test of a good reading is the degree of penetration into an ultimate reality that it finally promotes.

These observations force into sharp focus Freud's positivistic bias. He supposed that to be physically ill was to deviate from the conventional patterns of daily life. Cure was achieved by making explicit the cause of the deviance, and the eventual elimination of this, to leave one functioning as commonplace men do. The man who said "My brother married my father" was to be brought to the position where he would say "My mother married my father," and act accordingly. That solution supposes there is nothing correctly expressed in the deviance. Yet it is precisely the deviance that is being insisted on. Attempts to eliminate it entirely are bound to be resisted, and to increase the likelihood that there never will be a true cure. Deviance is better understood to involve an emphasis on an essential factor in an objective state of affairs, supplementing and being united with—not underlying or canceling—a more familiar factor.

The suspect statement conforms to conventional grammar. It unites with what is accepted, to constitute a single expression: "My brother, mother, and father are intimately related." The understanding of this requires a supplementation by another statement which remarks on something disturbing, perplexing, regrettable, the two being emotionally held together at a depth by the speaker on the one side, and by the occurrence on the other.

To these observations, it is certainly proper to remark that the speaker is being examined not because his speech is deviant but because he tried to shoot his brother, beat his mother, or bite his father, or perhaps all three, and that he is being analyzed in order to help find the cause for this, and to eliminate it. His speech is just a source of clues. These considerations do not change the problem or its solution; they just set it in a new place. Instead of attending to deviant speech, one will now attend to deviant action, try to find its cause, and then see how this could be eliminated, to leave the patient acting as others do. But what was wrong with the patient was his exaggeration of one side of a complex occurrence, thereby overwhelming and obscuring a supplementary, more conventional way of acting. One should not deny the legitimacy of a supplement; rather, a better form of the supplement should be found, and this united with the conventional in such a way as to allow each its provenance, as well as the union of the two at a deeper, more intensive level. The patient will then be seen to provide an emotional unity for diverse ways of acting.

Artists are deviants for the Freudian. But it would be more correct to say that a Freudian is himself a deviant since he denies an objective role to the referent of unconventional expressions and acts. Where the later positivists take those expressions to reveal a personal confusion, the Freudian takes them to reveal a delusion. Both are content to remain with what is obtrusively present, and to deny objective reference to any speech or act which deals with what is beyond this.

The ordinary man is not entirely without the insight characteristic of the poet, the dramatist, the storyteller. He can dramatize; he can exaggerate; he has his ironies. He is aware that there is more to the world than what is on the surface. To be sure, his usages are banal, and his inventions feeble. He is often unaware of what he suppresses and of what lies beneath his own surface expressions, speech, and acts. All the while he keeps focused on the fact that there is something more than the conventional, the established, the surface of things. What he must be taught is to give an appropriate role to each of the factors that he emotionally unites. He needs to learn how to make better metaphors and better unions, to engage in more complex and better nuanced activities in which each component is both distinguished from and is enriched by the others, thereby becoming better able to express the nature of all. From this perspective, dreams provide vivid ways of quickly experimenting with possible combinations in the attempt to find those which best express what had not been properly expressed before.

The present view provides some support for Bradley's contention that judgments are hypotheticals with a categorical base—if some important distinctions are made. He took the base to be a single, all-encompassing absolute, but this it is only for an appreciated artistic work. Ordinary reports have a categorical base in detached items. Metaphorical expressions in daily discourse have one in delimited sections of a final base. Later, Bradley spoke of "finite centers," but it is not clear whether he meant to refer to detached or to delimited items. Proper names address and thereby merge with the detached; metaphors address and merge with a delimited base; primary feelings address and merge with an unlimited base. All three are addressings, backed by men caught up in emotions with different intensities.

Philosophic statements also are hypotheticals with a categorical base. Unlike others, though, they speak about any actuality or any finality. When we restrict ourselves to what is familiar, more limited bases suffice. These ground the claim of a traditional community, a stable society or a state. A logic, a mathematics, and a religion also make use of categorical bases, but rarely to speak about actualities. A fictional I can eventually lead us to their bases, with the help of folklore, or a teaching, or when it functions as a component in a controlled created work which is emotionally effective.

PART TWO

We and the Others

CHAPTER 4

We

4.1. 'I' and 'we' have different referents.

THERE ARE times when it is desirable to speak anonymously, excluding references to oneself, perhaps to state an impersonal position, to represent others, or just to avoid having a statement credited. Recourse is had to a 'we'. In many cases, it is not clear just what is meant. Writers of editorials often use 'we' impersonally. "We, the people," in the Preamble of the United States Constitution presumably encompasses the authors. "We are brave men" may or may not be meant to include the speaker. Convention, other terms, and circumstances must be taken into account in order to determine exactly the meaning of 'we' that is intended. Usually, 'we' must be accompanied by auxiliary aids so as to enable one to know that its referent is of a particular kind, the auxiliaries telling where and how the 'we' is to function.

'We' can have neutrality denied to it when held on to by some of those to whom it applies, or by one who projects it as an area within which others are to be or act. Whether this is done or not, it differs in role and status from 'I'. 'I' refers to what is not diversified; 'we' refers to what could be diversified by that to which it is referred.

4.2. A we is simple, factual, or complex.

Whether used anonymously, intended to include oneself, or left indeterminate, 'we' may have any one of three referents: it may refer to a *simple we*, a condition for a number of men; to a *factual we*, an interlinkage of men; or to a *complex we*, a combination of the simple and the factual. The first is an encompassing domain. If connected with other domains, under some more embracing condition, it functions as a base in terms of which the others are approached. The second concerns men as actually together, affecting one another directly. The third, a product of these two, is distinct from both, and able to interact with other complexes.

The we referred to in "We, the people . . ." where it is not *projective*, a statement awaiting acceptance by those who agree to what follows, is simple. As used at the beginning of the Preamble of the United States Constitution, it was, when written, nothing more than part of a draft, awaiting acceptance by the different legislatures. 'We' there was projective, not necessarily applicable to any of the men who helped in the writing of the Constitution. It did, of course, apply to them, but like contracts drawn up by lawyers, the 'we' did not require an application to its author. Once the Constitution was in effect, of course, the 'we' had a different import. It then was complex. Any member of the United States who thereafter said "We, the people" was necessarily one of those to whom the 'we' applied.

A simple we may sum or condense what individuals are or express. Authoritative figures, rulers, representatives, and spokesmen use 'we' to refer in both these ways, sometimes expressing what summarizes a number of men, and sometimes expressing what can be attributed to no one. The 'we' at both times may have the role of a grammatical subject.

The 'we' in "We are a family" usually refers to a simple we. It conditions the members of the family and these, in turn, resist and qualify it in many ways. They may do so individually, or they may do so as interconnected. A mother and a child may interplay with the we, referred to in "We are a family," in different or similar ways. Whether they act as distinct individuals or as a pair, they stand apart from the we. They may be bound together by love or hate, but their we is on a footing with the 'we's' of other families and other groups. Each of the we's, when joined to individuals or sets of them helps form a complex functioning family.

4.3. A simple we provides a condition which, with interrelated men, constitutes a complex we.

An individual may express himself and thereby enable an aspect of himself to be merged with the aspects of other individuals. From this standpoint, the result seems to be an abstraction from them all. But it is no abstraction, if by that one means what has no nature or functions, for the result is a simple we. This, however, would not be able to stand apart from all the men, were it not sustained independently of them. It can constrain the very men which make it possible only because it is forcefully imposed on them or is yielded to. At either time, it specializes more general, common, constraining conditions.

When a man says "This is what we, our family, does," his family is not necessarily affected by what he says. It surely does not depend on his reference to it. All individual members of it have nonfamilial roles and relations. They are stronger or weaker, workers, citizens, soldiers, criminals, officials, bankers, teachers. As family members they are subject to the simple we of the family; they are also interrelated apart from that we, and interplay with it. If the simple we had no power, it would not constrain them or interact with them. They are subject to it because it exhibits some of the actual force or persuasiveness of a broader condition. Men usually are conditioned by and interplay with specializations of that condition, specializations which they themselves produce. Sometimes, though, the specializations are due to others, and are forcefully imposed.

Without people, a state would be nonexistent, while a people without a state would not be explicitly organized and would not interact with political units. As a simple we, a state has relations to other simple we's at the same time that it constrains and is qualified by the very men who interplay with it. Interlocked with a people, it is a significant historical complex we, having the spread of an actual people and a structure of a simple we. Were it a simple we, it could not declare war, make treaties, have a constitution or a history. These require individuals for whom a simple we is a condition, and with which they interplay.

"We are on strike" refers to a complex we. Though it is a product, presupposing an interplay of a factual with a simple we, it is known first. What is known first in experience is not first ontologically; what is ontologically first, awaits discovery with the help of evidence which is found to be interwoven with what is empirically encountered.

The way a simple we conditions its members, the ways in which they respond to it, and the complex that then ensues may all be quite changed by the roles that the complex has in relation to others—and conversely. Nevertheless, a we has to play a role as a condition and must be a component in a complex we before the complex can function as a unit in relation to others. As involved with other complexes, it is to be distinguished from its members, from itself as conditioning them, and from the complex as merely constituted by the condition and the men.

A dictator speaks anonymously, using a 'we' to refer to a condition which is to govern others. An editorial writer lacks his power, contenting himself with conveying a condition which a number of individuals might conceivably sustain even while they think about other matters. Both are interested in a simple we, to be accepted as a condition by others, without alteration. When an editorial writer fails to have his 'we' refer to a we that is maintained apart from himself, he expresses some opinion anonymously, but does not ground it in a genuine condition. When a dictator fails to free himself from his decree, and thereby fails to have it caught up in a public patterning, he expresses a hope. Both he and the writer will use 'we' only projectively, awaiting the presence of a simple we which conditions and interacts with a factual we and thereby, with its aid, constitutes a complex we.

A nominalist grants a we no other status but that of a generalized, individual, depersonalized simple subject, derived from and parasitical on actual individuals. There is a type of anarchism which takes a similar approach to the simple we, treating it as a fiction which is nevertheless able to get in the way of men's rights and acts. The fact that the simple we has an integrity of its own allows one to extract a truth from both positions. Despite the anarchist, there are simple we's with careers of their own, even while (as the anarchist sees) they are diversely utilized by different individuals. A simple we (as the nominalist sees) may sum up aspects of individuals even while (despite the nominalist), it is able to function as a common condition for them all. In an anarchistic world, effective simple we's are shorn of their power. In a nominalistic, they never had power. A nominalist is a metaphysical anarchist giving no role to institutions like the state; an anarchist is a utopian nominalist who finds common constraints to be both oppressive and unreal.

By itself, a simple we is a single, conditioning unit able to offer any one of a number of ways in which individuals can be together. Even if these alter it radically, it continues to constrain them. When it interplays with men, severally and together, the complex it helps constitute has a nature and career which may be quite different from either the simple we or the men.

Without change, a simple we can interplay with different individuals at different times, with different combinations of them, and as combined in various ways. It may have a constantly or intermittently enlarged or contracted range. At the same time, its members may be conditioned by other simple we's. Men who are now working together as a team may find themselves on different sides of a political struggle.

A simple we is a condition for men to be together as you's, as I's and you's, and as you's and me's. Supplemented by means of predicates, practices, descriptions, and conventions, which determine how it is to function, a simple we may demand that its members be affiliated; that they be on a footing; that they be intelligibly related; that they be set within a common extended area; or that they be evaluated. When one speaks of a family as an institution, of the justice of a legal system, of the nature of the state, of the presence of pockets of influence, or of a prevailing outlook, one refers to simple we's separated off from other prescriptions and from the very men those we's in fact govern.

A we may apply to what has none of the features that it itself has. The application will then be brutal, imposing a condition on what may be irrelevant or antagonistic. When a political system assigns roles regardless of men's natures, capacities, desires, or interest, it approximates this kind of application. As a consequence, a 'we', which may have been expressed on behalf of the demands of a political system, will be made to include those who have been forced under its governance. The more successful the governance, the more likely will the men be altered, severally and together. If, instead, a we applies to men so far as they have features that are congenial to it, even though these may be only incidental to the ways in which the men are by themselves or in fact interrelated, the we will not be radically changed. A we most effectively conditions those who match its demands with appropriate, insistent expressions. That political system which gives men roles going counter to the ways in which they are in fact interrelated, sooner or later, finds itself defied by them.

There are at least five different, independently functioning simple we's: a *social*, an *equitable*, an *organizational*, a *distributive*, and an *assessive*. Some, particularly the distributive, have a number of subtypes worth distinguishing. All interplay with men who are independently interrelated. The result is a number of complex we's. A complete account of these complexes would show how each type of simple we interplays with men interrelated in a number of primary ways. It will be sufficient, though, to show how only some of the simple we's interact with the main types of interrelated men, since the rest can be easily derived.

4.4. A complex, affiliative we is conditioned by a simple social we.

So far as a we is simple, it has the status of a condition. It is then like a rule or habit whose nature and range is exhibited when it organizes, qualifies, or controls men. Unlike a rule or a habit, though, it can prescribe a way in which men are to associate with one another. It is then a simple, *social* we. When a simple social we conditions men, it adds a new determination to them, and they more or less accommodate it and thereupon maintain themselves accordingly. The power of the we may not be very great compared to the power which in fact binds the men together, but it is never entirely absent.

Though a simple we is never wholly impotent, just an arena where something indifferent occurs, it also rarely makes a very great difference to what is within its provenance. Always with enough power to be an effective constituent of a complex we, it never has enough to make the men it conditions be completely paralyzed. The men are interrelated independently of the simple we. If affected, when they interplay with the simple we they constitute a complex *affiliative* we. The constituents of this, the simple we and the men, are modified by the result they make possible. The most evident of these complex affiliative we's are social—families, clubs, teams, tribes, societies. The men in them are governed by social simple we's even while they are interrelated apart from these. As so interrelated, they may be affiliated in ways which may or may not be in consonance with the ways in which the social we associates them.

The effectiveness of a simple social we varies in accord with the degree to which it succeeds in governing interrelated men. The resulting complex affiliative we is one in which individuals maintain themselves with various degrees of vigor at the same time that they are subject to the simple we. Their interrelation as independent men is qualified as surely as the conditioning social we is defied, to make the result a new, not altogether predictable complex. Apart from that complex the men were interrelated by means of a common outlook, tradition, convention, myth, practice, common standards, as well as by conditions applicable to all actualities. That is why they are together able to counter the social we effectively and, with it, help produce a complex we.

Seven types of complex affiliative we, all governed by a simple social we, are worth distinguishing:

a) Apart from any we, men may be together with one another congruently or oppositionally. They may be bound by love, hate, habits of cooperation and opposition, work, privileges, location, power, importance, history—all these separately or mixed in various combinations. Whatever the reasons and the mixture, the men are then relevant to one another in a single set. As so interrelated, they may then be subject to a social we whose primary demands are that what it encompasses be joined and separated on the basis of sex, age, size, strength, and so on. The men will inevitably resist the imposed determination, not because they have thought about it or have set themselves in opposition to it, but simply because they are effectively interrelated in other ways.

The affiliations of interrelated men take place apart from a conditioning by a simple we. That is why they are able to resist that we. That is why some of them are able to move outside its scope. Even when restricted to just those who will be governed by a social we, men form a factual affiliative we, functioning independently of and interacting with the social we.

A social we has a nature of its own, and could be produced and empowered without regard for what is subject to it. Affiliated men, in contrast, not only form a single set without necessarily having regard for that we but may then be so strongly tied together that the social we does not seriously affect them. Sometimes, though, men may work together in such a way as to give added support to the we which conditions them. Usually the interrelationship of the men is somewhat modified at the same time that the conditioning social we is qualified. The result is a not altogether predictable complex.

The families to which sociologists attend in their field studies are different from the localized duty and task combinations which anthropologists focus on, as well as from the actual families that interact with one another and other effective complexes. The first interest themselves in families made up of interactive individuals, a factual affiliative we; the second interest themselves in conditioning, simple, social we's. The third is the product of these two.

When it is said that "We Americans began a great experiment in educating millions free of charge," reference is made to a complex we which has the status of a past historic unit. The simple we that now governs us is only partly like the simple we which helped constitute the complex that was produced years ago. Our affiliations as interrelated men today are also only partly like the affiliations which united our predecessors. The present complex we, which results from the union of the social we and of ourselves as affiliated apart from any we, is related to past and future complex we's in which no one of us was, is, or may be a member.

Dependent as it is on the manner in which a conditioning social we and affiliated men interplay, an affiliative complex we may change in nature and functioning moment after moment while these remain unchanged. A weak social we would leave the men without a definite persistent structure, able to bound and constrain them, while weakly affiliated men may not be able to help a conditioning social we, which associates them in a different way, to constitute a stable affiliative complex. Since a social we may be more effective at one moment than at another, men can be more or less affected by the we than they had been, and may even be made to assume new roles. But even when there is no change in the condition or the manner in which men are affiliated, there can be constantly new ways in which the men are able to function together. The outcome of the interplay of the two in any case yields a complex which has its own characteristics, career, and role.

b) The residents of a city, when speaking of a team which has its headquarters there, often say 'we'. Yet no member of that team may be a native or even a resident of the city. The residents may not even watch the team or approve of it. The we is *projective*, if they are ready to bring themselves under it, perhaps when the team has had considerable success.

Though players who are suspended speak sometimes of a team as 'we', they are related to it in a way quite distinct from that which characterizes the other members. But they may allow it to condition them. It would not, therefore, be amiss to say that they are subject to the same social nonprojective we, but that they just interact with this in different ways.

Around adolescence, there is a tendency for the young to see themselves and sometimes to speak and to act as though they were separated individuals, unfortunately residing in the same place for a while with others with whom they think they have nothing in common. Nevertheless, while maintaining themselves in opposition, and perhaps being opposed by the others in turn, they are in fact interrelated, even affiliated with them. They are part of the same family or community, as surely as they would be were they congenial and supportive. Even when they ignore the social we that governs the others, it continues to encompass and constrain them. If that we has considerable power, it will force their opposition into the background. Weak, it will still make a difference to the effectiveness of their opposition. For them to be able to withstand it, they must come under it as independent individuals who are interrelated as equals with the rest—perhaps as persons with rights, or as having interests, minds, attitudes, or activities of their own.

"You and I make a good combination," and "We make a

good combination" are not interchangeable. The 'you' and 'I'
refer to two individuals, without regard for the way they may
be governed, while the 'we' is ambiguous, referring either to a
common social we or to the complex which this helps constitute. 'You and I' tells about the members of the 'we'; 'we' refers to a common condition which applies to unspecified individuals or to the complex which results from the juncture of a
simple we and interrelated men. The gap between them is
bridged by "We, you and I, make a good combination." Equal
men, members of a pair, are then understood to be subject to
a common social we.

Driving along the highway, men are not only associated
together as drivers facing common dangers and opportunities, but are also together as separate men, exercising the
same right to be on the highway. If they suddenly find themselves interrelated in new ways because of some accident, a
traffic delay, or a police siren, they do not abandon their independent status but bracket it, ignore it for a moment, or, while
continuing to be independent function under the aegis of
some other conditioning we. In saying, "We're delayed," one
of them may refer to all as being together in a new way or as
continuing to be interrelated as they had been but under a
different condition. The resulting complex, in either case,
may be quite different from what it had been before. It is not
possible to say just what is intended without further information. "The policeman is holding all of us up" refers to all as
conditioned; "We, the only ones in expensive cars, are being
let through," instead, refers to a complex in which independent men are subject to a common social condition with which
they constitute a distinctive, effective, affiliative, complex we.

Equality is the outcome of a conditioning by a power which
overrides the uniqueness and functioning of individuals.
When the equalized men interplay with a social we, its associative powers are limited and the equality of the men qualified. The result is a complex in which men are associated and
more or less equal.

c) A simple we is met by individuals interrelated in any one of several ways. The we and the interrelated set of individuals limit one another's effects in the complex that they together constitute. But when individuals are formally interrelated, they make less of a difference to the functioning of the social we than when they are in other kinds of interrelationships. This is one of the reasons, no doubt, why it is so readily assumed that formal relations are indifferent to the individuals they connect.

Men are interrelated formally by size, mass, age. They may also have formal relations to one another which terminate in nonquantitative features, such as their shape and color. When tennis players are paired, their formal relations are combined with an affiliative conditioning social we, the pairing, which requires them to supplement and support one another. Sometimes individual players well-matched in strength, experience, and ability, when subject to such a requirement, fail to play well together. The pairing meshes poorly with their formal interrelation, with the consequence that the complex we produced—the pair playing together—performs poorly. Each player may blame the other. Yet neither may be at fault. The particular formal relationship they have may not have been able to constitute, with the pairing, the kind of complex which could compete successfully. Since formal interrelations are duplicable, one is inclined to suppose either that similarly interrelated individuals would bring about the same results—which evidently is not the case—or that the differences are due to the players being interrelated in nonformal ways—which violates the supposition that they are now being viewed as just formally interrelated. Both alternatives are avoided with the recognition that individuals, even when interrelated only formally, make a difference to the resulting affiliative complex.

Though a simple social we takes no account of the individuals related, it interacts with them and therefore necessarily helps constitute a complex we which differs in nature and career from case to case. Whatever the result that is produced when such a simple we operates on formally interrelated men, it will differ from that produced when that very same we operates on men interrelated in affiliated, coordinated, or other ways.

If, regardless of their competence, men are forced to retire from work on reaching some designated age, they are taken to be formally related as of the same age at the same time that they are made subject to a condition which associates them in the single class of men who must retire. The formal relation and the classification are independently determined. Another formal relation, having no regard for age at all, could have been considered; or they could all have been subject to some other condition. A just and reasonable warrant for retiring all workers at a certain age requires that the condition imposed on them be pertinent to their work or age.

Conditions are often legitimately invoked to govern individuals who are in a certain formal relation—children at a certain age are identified as having to go to school; youths of such a height, weight, and age are subject to a draft. If those conditions do not specialize others already governing, the conditions will arbitrarily cluster the children or the youths. If the conditions operate on those who are interrelated in ways to which the conditions are irrelevant, the application of the conditions will be arbitrary.

d) Spatial relations are not indifferent to individuals. When these occupy places in space, they also acquire neighbors and are faced with opportunities, obstacles, and dangers. They occupy the places in distinctive ways, thereby making a difference to what they present to others at different distances. Men are members of a family even when far away from the rest. They remain citizens of their country even while living abroad. Their distances from the rest may be a matter of considerable concern; some quite remote may feel allied, while others very near may be indifferent or opposed. Subject to a social we, all are part of a complex, where they function in new ways. Whether close by or far apart, they may then be just as effectively governed, though their distances may make a considerable difference to the functioning of the complex that is then produced. The same family bond, stretched over parents and children at a great distance from one another, yields a complex whose tonality and activities are often very different from what they are when the parents and children are within calling distance.

It seems odd at first to say that a family stretches over a distance, particularly if one thinks of a family as a conditioning simple we making no reference to space. But it is not the conditioning we that stretches over a distance; it is the complex which results from the union of the condition and distanced individuals. Even if all the members of a family were in the same room, holding hands, they would still be spatially separate. Together with a conditioning social we, they constitute a spatialized complex affiliative we.

Like a tribe or society, or any other complex, a family is a contoured, changing region of space at various portions of which different individuals are locatable. An identification of these as though they had nothing to do with one another involves a tacit neglect not only of the complex in which they are in fact functioning but of them as interrelated apart from the complex and its condition. Though the men independently occupy different places, they are inevitably related spatially, and together are subject to and interplay with a simple social we. The resultant complex has its own nature and career. When this conclusion is ignored—as is done when it is said that there is an objective, indifferent, geometrical space occupied by entities which are not affected by it, nor it by them—unsolvable problems are created.

An objective, geometrical space is never encountered. The occupants of space act with and against others, sometimes with and sometimes without regard for the distances between them. We may have to shout to get the attention of a friend across the street; or we may greet him, making contact with him directly, and paying no attention to insects, cars, stones, and people closer and in between. Each occupant of a space helps give a place a distinctive, limited configuration. Together with others, each constitutes a set of spatially interrelated items, all acting within a single region which they severally occupy. Were there no men, and were nothing psychological or living allowed to make a difference, the space could still be occupied and contoured by things.

Though spatial proximity may have little to do with the ability of men to mesh with one another, they do live, work, and play primarily with those close by. A social we operates on men comparatively near; their joint reply to its common constraint turns this into a specialized condition pertinent primarily to them, to make them into a single spatially related set of affiliated men, able to interact with other complexes elsewhere.

e) Each actuality is temporally connected with others. It is contemporary with some; it is related to what is past; and it is related to a future. Each occupies a present moment which it contours in its own way, and each may continue to be contemporary with others, moment after moment.

Most of the items in the world have little import for any chosen one. Chronicles seem to celebrate that fact, placing apparently indifferent items side by side, or one after the other. But even when a chronicle does not focus on what is important or relevant, it connects only some of the occurrences which take place at a particular time. The ones it fastens on presumably are thought to be major or crucial. If it just set down items indifferently, a chronicle would join what occurred in the home, barn, river, palace, and on the battlefield if only they had the same date. A chronicle would then be hard to distinguish from a randomized report. In any case, unlike chronicles, histories apply socialized we's to temporalized items.

There is a cosmic contemporaneity. There are also many localized ones. Concerned only with what light signals can report, relativistic physics finds no use for the former. But this is presupposed, since apart from the signals and the dating, all occurrences have spans of comparable but differing temporal lengths. Both in the cosmos and within limited, local systems, some physical entities, and other kinds as well, are contemporaries. Despite their private rhythms, they pass into the next moment together. All are temporally related to certain others that have taken place in the past, and will be related to a limited number of others which follow.

Whatever occupies time is in a present, united with other items before and after it. It stands apart from the whole of time in a present it has made its own, distinct from the presents of other items. Future time is identical with what is at once possible and relevant to what is present. There are no actual divisions in it. When we say that one tree will bear fruit next year and a contemporary will not, we distinguish subdivisions of the possibility of fruit by relating them to distinguishable present occurrences. Apart from such distinguishings, future and possibility are indeterminate, the one lacking moments, the other instances. The day after tomorrow is not yet distinct from tomorrow, any more than possible apples are from possible pears, or possibly many apples from possibly few. If we imaginatively take a stand with tomorrow, the day after tomorrow will be imagined to be future to it, but then it will not be distinguished from the day after it. If we consider only apples, we have already introduced a determination distinguishing them from pears, and can then go on to face the as yet undifferentiated possibility many-or-few, and so on, indefinitely.

Traditions relate contemporaries with one another to and by means of a common past, and help determine the ways men will act together. Because of their common tradition, a number of men keep the same holidays, carry out similar practices, and face a common future. The kinds of interrelationship that they once had to one another is altered by the traditions they accept. The contemporaries are directly related to a common future by programs, laws of inheritance, and promises. These are parts of social we's pointed toward distinctive futures. By carrying out the programs, laws, or promises, others are provided with delayed satisfactions. Usually one pays for their waiting and trust.

The realization of a conditioning, common social we requires distinct acts by the differently involved men. The role that the condition will have in the resulting complex may be anticipated, but the role will lack determinations until the condition is in fact present and interplays with temporally interrelated men. A full, adequate knowledge of the result cannot be had in advance.

f) There is a cosmic dynamism which affects whatever there be. This, men try to express in cosmic laws, understood to be specialized by and channeled through a multitude of different agents. The result is a multiplicity of situations in which limited numbers of actualities are causally interrelated. The causes and effects in those situations may have so little to do with men's natures and values that the linkage of the causes and effects might be held to be a miracle, or to be due to chance or unpredictable spontaneities. References to miracles, though, take us from the world of intelligibles to the inscrutable acts of an unknown God. And though chance and spontaneity could be credited to a cosmic dynamism capable of producing results beyond the predictable reach of any laws, their presence in limited situations need not involve an abrogation or defiance of causality, but may serve just to vitalize it in limited unpredictable ways.

An effect follows because a process of causation, beginning at the cause, introduces a productive dynamism, enabling the effect as possible, future, and indeterminate to become actualized, present, and determinate. If the dynamism of causality, moving from an actual cause to an actual effect, be ignored, one approximates the position that Hume assumed when he supposed both that antecedent (causes) and subsequent (effects) were independent of one another, and that we think that there is causality only because we habitually associate certain antecedents with certain successors. Once it is seen that a reliable habitual association is both an effect and a subjectivized version of the connection between causes and effects that in fact occurs, the initial objective state of affairs can be recovered. There, an actual affiliation between an antecedent and consequent interlocks with a dynamic conditioning necessitation to produce a complex causal situation in which the antecedent functions as a cause producing the actual effect that ensues. What Hume did not allow for was the causal process which actualizes an effect that otherwise would be just a possibility.

Whitehead took all actual occasions to exist only for the span of a single moment, and that no longer than the stretch appropriate to the smallest particle. So far, he was an extreme Humean. But where Hume took account of subjective habits by which his units are affiliatively related, Whitehead posited impotent objective patterns and, therefore, allowed for no affiliations at all, apart from those which God makes possible or which are produced in the course of an entity's coming to be. None of Whitehead's actual occasions is causally connected with others, subjectively or objectively. At best, each just takes internal account of what had been and, with the help of God, that friend of distraught metaphysicians, functions in some accord with the possibilities he supposedly makes available to it.

By synchronizing their strokes, a rowing crew effectively propels a boat. The coxswain, on behalf of them all, presents a common condition dictating their speed and sometimes their direction. His beat allies them. As a result, the rowers form a single complex, an effective crew at some particular position on the river, to be followed by another complex, that crew at another better position. Were the crew not causally active, the beat would be a condition they might verbally or imaginatively repeat. Did they not to form a crew, they might still cause their boat to move, but not as well. It is because they are conjoint causes of the boat's movement and are conditioned by a common associative we implicit in the beat called out by their coxwain, that they are able to be a single, effective crew, moment after moment.

g) There are good men and bad; handsome men and ugly ones; those who help and those who hinder; efficient and inefficient ones. Their different natures, activities, and abilities place them in different positions within objective orders, whether or not these be recognized by them or by anyone else. We may misjudge them, giving them too high or too low a rank, as we discover when we come to know them better and thereupon yield to the fact that they had an objective order which our estimates failed to match. Apart from our judging, they have values related to one another as higher and lower.

"We'll win this case," a lawyer says to his client. If he or his client allows their differences in achievement or self-discipline to interfere with the way they work together, they will together fail to be part of a needed complex which is to effectively interact with others. A social we, which has little effect on the status of what it governs, helps constitute a complex with a different nature and career from that which results when it effectively constrains. Even when the values of men in this or similar cases greatly reduce the effectiveness of a conditioning social we, it still is appropriate to speak of the complex as an affiliated set of items, different in constitution from one where some other type of we dominates over the same values.

4.5. An equitable single we is an equalizing condition.

An *equitable* we takes all within its provenance to be equal for it. It not only operates apart from any decisions or acts of men, but their decisions and acts are often assessed in terms of their accord and disaccord with what it prescribes. In each situation, the condition provides a principle of impartiality. Since the equitable we operates on individuals already interrelated in a way that may have nothing to do with their equality or inequality, the result of its involvement with them may well be a complex we in which the men are more or less related as they had been before, or in an entirely new way.

Only in rather special cases does the application of a principle of impartiality end with individuals accorded an equal standing. Since justice demands that equals be treated as equals, and unequals be treated as unequals, it is more likely to be achieved when impartiality is not the governing principle, or when its operation is restricted and modified, particularly if the individuals already have well-established bonds. When men are formally related by age, affiliated by background, graded by education, and the like, an impartial treatment of them will normally end with some of them achieving preferential treatment. A blindfolded weighing of goods will help produce what is just only when the result is effectively applied to equals.

A number of cases similar to those previously examined, but all subject to an equitable conditioning we, are worth distinguishing:

a) 'We' entrains a presumption of impartiality. Supplementing it with 'the people', and the like, provides indications where it is to be applied. Auxiliaries such as 'in this family', 'the property owners', 'the hospital patients', though usually intended to have the 'we' apply in a differentiated way, begin with it as applying to all of them impartially.

Men are usually affiliatively interrelated in many ways. They may be friends, relatives, enemies, co-workers. Interplaying with a condition which demands impartiality, they may help form a complex in which their different roles are underscored, undermined, or altered. When it is said that equals are to be treated equally, and unequals in accord with their relevant inequalities, it still is undetermined which of these occurs. The ways in which the men are affiliated will affect the ways in which a principle of impartiality will operate on them.

I speak of myself and my colleagues as together subject to an equitable we and, with this, forming a single complex. But we are also differentiated in rank and sometimes in task. So far as we are governed by an equitable we, our different ranks and tasks are ignored or overcome. To the degree that the equitable we is ineffective, the complex, despite its being constituted with the help of that we, will exhibit multiple effective inequalities. As interrelated by rank and tasks, my colleagues and I prevent the production of a complex in which we act simply as impartially together, having such and such roles. If

we are to be affiliated under the governance of an equitable
we, this must minimize the ways in which our roles are maintained and interrelated.

b) A Hobbesian natural man, if an enemy to all, is not solitary, entirely alone. If he were solitary, he would be cut off
from them, unable either to oppose or to agree with them. A
genuinely solitary man is an atom, a monad, unrelated to any
other units. Whether friendly or antagonistic, all men are
coordinate, directly related as equal units; associated by sex,
strength, task, and age; involved in multiple formal, biological, and perhaps kinship relationships; related spatially, temporally, and causally; and have different places in objective,
evaluational hierarchies. A condition imposed on them all has
a nature and role distinct from them, operating in independence of the manner in which they are interrelated.

Men are coordinate, independent beings. They are equal as
persons because of the presence of a limited equitable condition with which they interplay. It affects them and they affect
it in turn. As a result, the manner in which the men function
together reflects the fact that they are at once coordinated
and equalized. If the coordination is stronger than the we,
the men will be related as equals because of the way they confront one another. If, instead, the we is stronger, the men will
be equal primarily because they are subject to it. The complexes, resulting from the interaction of coordinated men and
those very men as equitably conditioned, have natures and
careers not determinable from a knowledge of either, or from
a conceptual combination of both. One must attend to the
complexes that ensue to see just which is in fact dominant,
and what that dominance helps make possible.

An equitable we is a condition whose application places all
within its scope on the same basis. Affected by the manner in
which they are directly coordinated with one another, it qualifies that coordination, as well as the different individuals. As
a consequence, indifferent men will sometimes be found constrained to be and remain equal. Sometimes, too, they will be
found to so insist on themselves or on their independence that

a common equalizing condition can hardly be discerned. As a consequence, the resulting complex may have them together primarily because of the condition, primarily because of the way they take account of one another, or primarily because of some mixture of the two. Only the first, where an equitable condition is in control, gives some assurance that those who are now equal will continue to be so. Only the second, where men are in fact coordinated, gives some assurance that they will have equal roles in an effective, complex interacting with others. Only the third, where an equitable we is interlocked with coordinated men, gives some assurance that the complex will be both equitable governed and effective.

c) Men are formally interrelated in many ways. The quantifiable and qualitative aspects of one man have formal relations to similar aspects of others. Their work, celebrations, rituals, and dances exhibit formal patterns. Much of what they do falls under rules, though these are often not known or articulated. There is an enormous difference between the ways in which they are in fact connected in some group, and the way they are required to be connected by some established common custom.

Grammar brings 'we' within the compass of rules applicable to a number. Discourse uses it in a rule-governing way. So far, 'we' is like every other word. All are rule-governed and rule-governing, the first because they are part of a language, and the second because they prescribe how some items are to be related to others. And what is true of words is true of combinations of them. We speak in accord with established conventions having formal characters. What we say serves to relate things and sometimes ourselves and other men in abstract, formally expressible ways. The rational is embodied in the rules which a language illustrates and in the ways in which words and expressions serve to select and collect certain items rather than others.

Discourse uses language to turn men into directly related beings. Whatever rules a language exhibits and which a discourse uses are involved both with the words interchanged and with the discoursing men. The fact is not jeopardized when the men fail to attend to, or when they violate the rules of their language, expressed either in the grammar or in the use of words and sentences. Whether or not they abide by the rules, these still govern the language.

'We' impartially applies to oneself and a number of others already directly and formally interrelated to constitute with them a complex in which the impartiality may be dominant or recessive. Defied or not, the 'we' applies to individuals as having intelligibly defined positions. Without making reference to the formal relation that directly connects them, the 'we' may apply to all. Were this not possible, if there were no equitable we which conditioned and interplayed with intelligibly related individuals, no one could properly say something like, "We, the elders," where the 'we' refers to men who are interrelated intelligibly.

d) The occupants of space are involved with one another gravitationally, by interest, and in other ways. When viewed solely as occupants of positions in space, they are distributed in no apparent order. Despite their differences in insistence, and the ways in which they cluster, separate, and function, it is therefore not difficult to envisage them as making up just an aggregate of units, apparently governed by no common condition. They are in fact constrained by the common space. But if they are then subject to an impartial we, they will be dealt with without regard for whatever spatial connections they may then have.

Though 'we' has no necessary bearing on what is in space, it can be used to refer to an equitable we which conditions men as together at different spatial positions. Its application requires that it range over a region and, in disregard of the distances that the occupants have to one another, condition them as just so many units. "We, in this room" refers to men who are at different places within a common spatial region, without regard for their distances from one another. The distances, nevertheless, may make a considerable difference to the resultant complex. Some who are included within its compass may be too far away to be able to benefit from an impartial acceptance of them, so that their inclusion leaves them somewhat as they had been before. In order to have them effectively on a footing with the rest, the same condition would have to be applied to them differently from the way it is applied to those close by.

In compensation for the lack of differentiation characteristic of an equitable we, there is usually a differentiation in the way it is imposed on those within its range. One of the problems that confronts judges, and others who are required to apply a law, here comes conspicuously to the fore. Presumably, laws are to be imposed indifferently on all who fall under their provisions. But if no attention is paid to the difference that distance makes, those who are too far away to know of a newly created law will be punished, though they act in unavoidable ignorance of it.

Equality among spatially located men is produced if an equitable we is brought to bear on those who are able to be on a footing, despite their distances from one another. There is, though, nothing in the we, nor in the ways in which the men are related, that tells how the we is to be applied. The variations in the application of an equitable we that the achievement of an actual equality in a complex requires are not derivable from any principle or theory. The fact does not reveal the equitable we to be unnecessary or to be without power. Without it, there would be interrelated occupants of space which were not together as equals in a complex we; did it not have power, it would not be able to affect those occupants, so as to help constitute such a complex we.

e) "We, the people" may encompass contemporaries and posterity; "we, of this dynasty" encompasses contemporaries, predecessors, and perhaps successors; "we, today" refers only to contemporaries; "we who began this great experiment" refers to the past, the speaker imaginatively including himself among them; "we who will vote next year" refers to the future, with the speaker, once again, imaginatively including himself. Though the 'we' has no temporal import in these various cases, the we to which it refers encompasses temporally related individuals. The application of the we does not annihilate the sequential order in which items occur but, instead, depends on that order for its items.

History, memory, and tradition make available what has passed away, not in its full concreteness as it was when it was present, but as occupying a temporal position in relation to other temporally placed occurrences. Since what is past is no longer active, and since what is in the future is not yet actual, a we which encompasses these together with what is present will not have them all on an equal basis, unless it operates on them as units merely at some temporal position or other, regardless of their sequential order. That order, though, is so resistant that it allows only a minimal efficacy to any impartial governance of its items.

Temporal complexes within which there are past, future, and contemporary individuals give little play to common conditions. If those individuals are to have equal roles and status within the complexes, it is necessary to impose a common equitable we on them differentially. This is what is done when legislation ranges impartially over those who are still to come as well as over those who are now present. Nothing is gained by supposing that the legislation constitutes a complex with just present individuals, except in those special cases where these alone are being expressly considered. Normally, it offers a general condition ranging over a stretch of time, without provision being made for its application to those who will come later. But what is yet to come is not without import for what is present. It now functions as a possibility relevant to it, limiting the range of its causal actions and dictating the kinds of things that can be rationally proposed.

Though legislation actually applies to those not yet born only when they in fact have become present, it is not altogether accurate to say that its application to them is deferred until they are actually present. They may, as in the future, be now intended by the legislation and may in fact now be identified as being present at some later date. As occurring at the later

date, they will become the very entities to which the legislation applies as it had applied to those now present. It is
applied to them differentially now so that, when they in fact
are present, it will affect them in the same way that it now affects those who are actually present. The posterity included
within the implicit equitable we of legislation can be part of an
actual complex, only if this has an actual temporal duration,
embracing men earlier and later.

f) Causes and effects are connected by dynamic processes
of causation which begin with the one and end at the other.
The processes convert possible into actual effects. Were there
no such processes, a cause would be just a rational antecedent
for a logically derivable conclusion. Still, it is possible to subject an actual causal situation to a we which ranges over the
causes and effects without reference to the process that in fact
connects them and thereby makes them be causes and effects.
Problems and resolutions similar to those met when dealing
with the application of an equitable we to temporally related
items will then arise here as well, due to the necessary temporal difference between the causes and effects. There will be
additional problems, since causes and effects are not merely at
different times but are linked with one another. Relevant to
what had been earlier, an effect is actualized through activity
originating with its antecedent cause. It is therefore not just
what is temporally later, even if it be an instance of what always comes after some other.

Causes and effects are not merely sequentially related, they
are paired. Abstraction from the pairing would leave one with
units in a temporal order which had been denied causal roles.
An attitude of impartiality respects the difference between
causes and effects, at the same time that it allows for the equality of causes and effects as distinct causal units.

The members of a basketball team constantly shift in role
from cause to effect. When one of them says 'we' he refers to
an equitable we which ranges over them all. If that we applies
to them as causally connected in pairs or triplets, they will be
combined in a number of subsets of causes and effects. Within

the compass of the equitable we, those subsets will be just alongside one another. In actual play, the ways in which the causal relations are in fact carried out will not only place the men in various positions within the larger context of a game but will make a difference to the operative import of the we of the team.

An equitable we that applies to all causal combinations of a playing team interlocks with them to constitute a complex in which those combinations diversely affect one another. Only in principle, not in fact, will the team be made up of completely equalized, causal units. But if these are equitably conditioned, the team can still be properly referred to by an equitable 'we'. Though the referent of that 'we' may have little effect on the way the men interact, its presence allows the outcome to be credited to the team as though it were a single complex we in which all had an equal role.

g) Men are to be differently rewarded and punished, depending on what they are accountable for, with the consequence that their places in an objective or other evaluational order may be altered considerably. But before this is done, the men, as deserving to be dealt with impartially, must be faced as on a footing, even when they differ considerably in value. Unequal treatment of unequals presupposes an equal consideration of them all. An equitable we will be applied to them without regard for their relative status as good, strong, useful, intelligent, or industrious. Despite their different values, all can be confronted in a common way. The values that the men have in the resulting complex is the unpredictable effect of their interplay with an equitable we.

Men are relatively better and worse, and this in two ways: as apart from a common condition which applies to them severally, and as jointly interplaying with the condition. When dealt with impartially, their independent evaluational order is usually ignored, and their relative standings changed. The change would be avoided were they not affected by the equitable we.

There is no distribution of goods according to merit without an ordering of men and goods in accordance with their values. If that distribution is preceded by an impartial consideration of the values of the different men, the distribution will usually relate these in a new way. By being dealt with impartially, they will be changed, if only to a minimal degree, so as to enable them to be objects of a distribution according to their merits. The impartial treatment is consistent with an unequal distribution of goods. That fact is implicitly recognized in the allocation of different rewards and punishments to men who are impartially dealt with.

4.6. An organizational we prescribes positions for interrelated individuals.

A state cannot originate through the actions of isolated men. Only interrelated ones, even if fearful of or armed against one another, could be men together. Only they could agree with one another. It is not possible, consequently, to save a 'contract theory' of the origin of a state by abjuring all claim to historical acuracy, and treating it as though it were only a theoretical possibility. Since it supposes that individuals could come to an agreement, it already supposes that those men are sufficiently united to make it possible for them to be together through an agreement, and in other ways as well. A state, moreover, cannot arise just by having some or all men yield their rights to some one of them, or to an impersonal system; it must have power enough to constrain and interplay with the men. The condition neither does nor can originate by some act on the part of those who are being subjected to it. A mere assignment of power or rights will not assure that the power or rights will be utilized, or that they will be utilized with reference to the very men who assigned that power or those rights. At the very least, for a state to arise, provision must be made for a constraining by a common condition.

To stop with the consideration of a state's power apart from its effect on interrelated men is to reach the point where just one of two necessary factors is acknowledged. A functioning state is the unpredictable outcome of the interplay of common constraining conditions and interrelated men. The state's supposedly dominant power is inevitably countered by the interrelated men, thereby producing a single complex, whose nature is a function of the two.

A state makes use of an organizational, conditioning we. This may mark out positions of various kinds, but the outcome will be idle unless those positions are occupied. The we itself does not separate out individual roles. Even when spelled out in programs and diagrams, it is just single and undivided.

"We, the farmers," "We, the settlers," and "We, the milk producers" may all have the same range. Different features may be exhibited by the same men in different positions or in differing types of relationship. Other men, outside the provenance of the organizational we, may be more compatible with some individuals encompassed by it. The ways of those others may be more alike than some others within its range. Individuals in interrelationship are independent of any we under which they might be organized, both because they are independently interrelated, and because they possess features independently of what the we requires. The complex that results will nevertheless be confined to the individuals encompassed by that we.

"We, the people," refers to a we ranging over the members of a particular society, nation, or state; it ignores the way in which those members function. Applied, the we interplays with men already interrelated by custom, language, tradition, and long established practices. It organizes them as so interrelated, to produce a complex in which both the interrelationship and thereby the individuals and the we are given new meanings and careers, sometimes quite like and sometimes quite different from those that they had before. The selfsame we interlocked with differently interrelated individuals yields different complexes:

a) Men form clusters, affiliating themselves with one another in supportive and oppositional ways, while remaining indifferent to many others. A society is a particular combination of such clusters; a nation is another; a state a third. No theory is antecedently plausible if it ignores the fact that the men in these have traditionalized and habitualized lives, making a difference to their common condition, and conversely.

An organizational we provides a rule according to which various positions, roles, functions, duties and privileges are assigned. The scope of that we can be quite limited. Two men can be subject to an organizational we as surely as a larger number. Also, the roles ascribed could conceivably duplicate the very ones which the men were carrying out apart from the we. Even then, the we makes a difference, since it involves an identification of those who are pertinent to the condition. That we's assignment will be appealed to in hard cases, and may be forcefully imposed in others.

Knowledge of the demands of an organizational we makes one alert to the independent functioning of interrelated individuals and the need at times to counter their activities by new restraints. Child labor is now known to be uneconomic; the spirit of the times, too, is against it. But it is good to have the prohibition stated so that one can know what to do in borderline situations, and to have a check against the unreflecting and sometimes aberrational practices of a few. Interrelated individuals, no matter how tightly bound by custom, are always free enough to act in novel ways. It is one of the marks of a utopia to ignore this truth and to take an organizational we to govern men fully. If an organizational we could so govern, the individuals would first have to be abstracted from the interrelationship that they have to one another and then be treated as though they were identifiable with their roles.

In order to find out what men ought to do in order that justice prevail, it is not enough to attend to what they might be like in some imagined state of nature, and then to suppose that some invisible hand leads them to the position where they make provision for a rectification of or a compensation for their initial inequalities. One must attend, instead, to the way they are in fact interrelated, and what such interrelation does to the common organizing condition. If one seeks a justice which requires that men be equally treated so far as they are equal, and therefore so far as they are subject to conditions which disregard their differences in race, religion, background, gender, strength, color, and the like, it is necessary to attend to the results brought about through the interaction of an organizational we with men as they are in fact interrelated. If the result is found to be biased for or against some men it will be necessary to change the organization, its effectiveness, the way the men are interrelated, or the power of that interrelationship. The first type of change has interested philosophers almost exclusively; practical politicians show a preference for it in particular legislative decisions. The enforcement of laws is primarily occupied with the second. Sociologists, instead, attend primarily to the ways the men are interrelated. Though reformers and educators are interested in knowing how the interrelationship is to be altered, mankind, for the most part, has been content to leave to history and bitter experience the effectiveness of an interrelationship, particularly in its interplay with an organizational we.

b) Implicit in contract theories of the origin of the state is the supposition that all men are equal in one way and unequal in another. The contract is thought of as formalizing the sacrifice which men make of their possible or actual advantages in order to turn their equality from an ineffective or endangered dignity into one that is constantly maintained publicly. As has already been observed, it supposes that the men are sufficiently equal to be able to make a contract. Each is given one vote, and this counts exactly as much as any other. Were the men just units, unrelated to one another, they would not have such equal rights, since they would then be incomparable.

Even when a contract fails to designate individuals, it may take a number of them to be equal, at the same time that it assigns roles having different efficacies and utilities. Ignoring the relation that in fact connects the men, the contract introduces a relation of equality. Had they been equal apart from it, the contract would make them equal for it. The two equalities are not necessarily alike or compatible, for the one requires that the men be equals as together, while the other requires that they be equals for the purposes of the contract. The one depends on their mutual goodwill, habit, tradition, training, desire; the other on a prescription which is perhaps backed by a force behind the contract.

Opponents to all use of force would have to object to it even when it is designed to bring about equality. Defenders of law and order must endorse the use of the force, if it is the only or the best way for assuring stability and uniform treatment of all. The conditions which dictate the way men are to act will still be countered by the limited actions of some who pay no attention to, and thereby undermine a concern for them.

The pressures of a civil society where men behave even-handedly toward one another are countered by legal or other formalizable demands which, while they may merely give expression to what all desire, abstract from the common practices and men's moral and social regard for one another. When the two are united in a single complex, the result bears the marks of both. There, the men act partly because of what they are being required to do by an organizational we, and partly because of what they are being required to do by tradition and entrenched habits.

An organizational we can extend to all mankind; it can be limited to the members of a nation or a society; it can encompass just two individuals—partners, a married couple, a buyer and a seller. In all, the same two types of constituent come into play, each affected by the other. The functioning of individuals within the resulting complex cannot therefore be credited entirely either to their subjection to a common force or to their direct dealings with one another. And since the men are not only equalized but, while subject to a single organizing control are interrelated in other ways as well, they evidently belong to a number of different complexes at the same time, with the very same organizational we exhibiting different degrees of efficacy.

Affiliations challenge an organization in one way, equalizations do so in an other. Other interrelations introduce still other challenges. Because the men who are ruled by an organizational we counter it in as many ways as they are interrelated apart from it, no account of its functioning will be complete until all their challenges are considered and their success determined. Since the governance of one type of interrelation by a limited condition is independent of others, it is proper to examine them separately. Though this observation is also pertinent to other types of we, it is most important to note it now, so as to counteract both the common tendency to minimize the resistant power of equalized men and the accompanying supposition that a contract, or any other controlling condition, alone accounts for the ways men function together.

c) An organizational we can govern men who are formally interrelated. Even when the organization repeats the very relations that hold apart from it, the two relations differ, for the one is maintained directly by the men, while the other depends on the men being subject to the demands that the organization imposes. But no organization ever wholly covers all the formal relations men have to one another.

The more interesting formal interrelations connect men as having different economic standings, degrees of power, roles, and tasks. It is the intermeshing of these different interrelations which turns the men into a functioning, intelligible, interlocked group. Since an organization usually makes no reference to the way men are in fact formally interrelated, the organization may fail to deal with them effectively. Since the organizational we and the interrelated men nevertheless do affect one another, the resultant complex's nature and functioning may differ considerably from both. Every organizational we, no matter how effectively applied, qualifies and is qualified by the established ways the men are united apart from it.

There are three kinds of nominalism, all opposed to this analysis and conclusion: One denies that there are any organizational we's; a second denies that such we's have power; while a third denies that men are interrelated. The first is unable to find common controlling conditions; the second has no men gathered together through the agency of these; and the third has no single set of men to whom such we's might apply. All would like to acknowledge just a number of men, but this they cannot do unless the men are at least subject to common conditions specialized in the form of a conjunction. Once that is allowed, there is no reason for denying the effective role of a governing we.

A shrewd nominalism maintains that a we and the interrelationships of men are both abstractions. This they surely are when torn from the complex that the we and the interrelationships together constitute. But each has a nature and a power before it is part of a complex. Nominalism is unable to explain that complex or the presence and functioning of its constituents. It is a halfway house, taking only certain items to be irreducible and alone effective. Were it both persistent and consistent, it would accept as irreducible the entire totality of things and suppose that everything short of this was an abstraction. Its concern for individuals would then turn into a concern for radically separated units. One consequence is that the nominalist's world would vanish, leaving him with nothing to know. The fact that individuals have power and careers should not be allowed to stand in the way of the recognition of powers and careers possessed by organizational we's and by the complexes which are constituted by the organizational we's and the interrelated individuals.

d) Men occupy positions in space and maintain themselves there. They are spatially extended as well as spatially distant from one another. Any number of them can be within the range of a we stretching over a region. This, if it is made to apply to them as at different places, will have no necessary regard for the actual space separating them. A post office, a railroad, a geography, provide different we's for such spatially located individuals, often taking some account of the distances they are from one another. Those organizational we's may locate the men in different zones, taking some to be intermediaries and others terminal. The individuals will then be both spatially located and spatially distant in the resultant complex.

An organizational we may take all locations to be of equal or different import. The actual distances separating located individuals, though, usually make them have different bearings on one another. By and large, the more remote, the less significance does one thing have for another. When the distances make a considerable difference to the individuals, the organizational we may make provision for just that fact. Whether it does so or not, the organizational we will be countered and modified by the ways in which the men are in fact spatially interrelated.

Baseball, football, hockey, and other teams are made up of players who have both well-defined tasks and are assigned locations within a common space. Though the assignments take account of the fact that the men are there at various distances from one another, some of which are clearly prescribed, the assignments allow for considerable variation in the actual distances that the men are from one another. A first baseman is at first base and not at third, but constantly changes his distance from his base. Though his location and the measured distance of his base from the other bases is prescribed, there is still room for him in which to maneuver.

An organization's distribution and governance are illustrated and spelled out in ways it does not determine. Though men may act within set limits, at differentiated locations, and within prescribed distances, they can therefore help bring about unpredictable combinations of themselves and unpredictable interactions with other organized wholes. A strategic plan may assign them to various locations, but it is the distances those men are from one another which determines whether or not, and how, the strategy can be employed. If it can, it may be so altered by the ways in which the men are in fact spread out in space at a given time, and by their specific performances in relation to other organized bodies of men, that the plan is no longer discernible in the actual course of events. Had one begun with the plan, one would have found it so altered when it was brought to bear on the men, as they in fact are spatially related, that special moves will be required, not specified in the strategy. An organizational we applying to spatially located men is usually so altered by them that it helps produce a complex where that we is somewhat obscured and only partly effective.

e) A we usually encompasses contemporaries, but it may range over those who are past and those who are future. If it is organizational, it will usually, though not always, prescribe different roles for those who exist at different times. The assignment is inevitably faced by the fact that what is past and what is future have different natures from what is present. What is past is determinate but impotent; what is future is indeterminate but capable of guiding; while present actualities are partly determinate and partly indeterminate, making use of what they can obtain from the past so as realize future possibilities.

An organizational we imposed on temporally ordered men, even if it assigns the same roles to all, has a temporal direction. It makes provision for differences among men differently dated, but without attending to the actual time that at once separates and connects them. Those who come later can have their tasks ascribed—whether similar to or different from what is assigned to others—when tasks are being ascribed to those who precede them. Account, of course, must be taken of the fact that the temporal positions are irreversibly ordered. Since an imposed sequence is countered by a succession of men carrying out their assignments at different dates, an organizational we, if it is to apply to such temporally distinguished men, must deal with them as so ordered. Because the successive application enables the men who come later to attain a status and capacity for action comparable to what was characteristic of those who had preceded them, assignments all made at one time become assignments assumed at different dates.

A we may encompass men who are sharply divided by generations. It might assign the same status to all the members of a family, tribe, or nation, but still distinguish them according to their differences in age as presumably involving differences in abilities and accountability. The men, while in fact copresent, will then be temporally ordered by this common we. Copresent men of the same generation, in contrast, might be assigned different tasks which they are to take up in a designated order. These, and other programs, when applied to the men as they in fact exist over time, will be effective in different degrees. Unable to change what had been, they will qualify and be qualified by what is, and will define what the men prospectively are without being able to guarantee that they will eventually function in accord with those programs.

Temporally connected to constitute an ordered set of individuals in a single extended present, men make a difference to one another's activities. Interacting with the we, they limit and are limited by this in an ongoing complex. That complex differs in nature, content, and career from both the organizational we and the interrelated men. Could the men be programmed individually or together so that different functions are carried out by them at different times, the men, through their actions, will both modify the program and change themselves. A similar result ensues when, instead of men, we have just physical particles encompassed by an organization which carries out an impersonal law of nature. The particles and the organization here, too, make a difference to one another, yielding unpredictable consequences, though not conspicuously nor to a high degree. The resulting complex and its career cannot be known simply by attending to either constituent. No imagination of what both would be like as together will necessarily anticipate the result that is produced when condition and conditioned interplay. There is no need, therefore, to suppose, with Peirce, that there is chance loose in the world; the unpredictability is explicable as the outcome of the ways in which conditions and conditioned affect one another. That the outcome of the interplay of the two is a new item is tacitly acknowledged when we sequentially feed a program in accord with the time involved in a machine's functioning, in using a machine in consonance with the stipulations of a program, and in determining the way in which a program is to be brought into interplay with an ongoing machine.

f) A causal situation differs from one merely temporal, not only in requiring a different program, but in having that program countered in a distinctive way. A purely temporal program may be made to accord with dates when these are treated as just positions in time. But while nothing is at once a cause and effect of the same object—for a process of causation takes time—a program may identify individuals as having the roles both of causes and effects of one another.

A machine's program marks out pivotal points where causes and effects are to be distinguished. It does not produce the causes or effects, though it does range over them. That program is an organization which can be applied only if there is a world where causes and effects occur. Arranging the beginnings and endings of various causal processes in sequential and supplementary orders, it leaves to the users of a machine the supplying of energy by which it is possible to pass from specified causes to specified effects.

An organizational we ranges over men as having causal roles for one another. The program which it prescribes marks out their pivotal roles. If the we had no influence on the men, there would be no limited causal situation that was isolated. If it alone had influence, the causal operation would be constituted by it and would have no necessary sequential order. The two together, the organizational we and the causally interrelated individuals, constitute a complex we, causally interacting with other complexes.

Each man may take himself to be under an organizational we which ranges over himself and others in causal roles. He and the others will then have the triple status of being comprehended by that we, subjected to it, and united with it.

Apart from the we, the men directly interact; united with the we, they form a complex organization. If the we is brought to bear on the men as involved in causal roles, what is prescribed may not be matched by the ways in which those men are inter-related. But matched or not, the roles will be given a new im-port.

g) Individuals fall into various valuational hierarchies in accord with the features they have in relation to one another. The hierarchies may be objective, governing without regard for men's judgments and interests, or subjective, having to do with features which have been focused on for some purpose. Whatever the hierarchy, it can be brought under the scope of a we. If that we is organizational, it will mark out various po-sitions. It may, but need not, remark on the kind of values that must be exhibited by those who are to be at those positions. When it applies to men as having values, those values will have to be distinguished from the ones specified by the or-ganizational we. In the resulting complex, the we will be qual-ified by and qualify the values the men in fact have.

Physical things are on too low a level of value to make it possible for them to belong to a we. It is more difficult to assess the use of a 'we' which includes one's pets. But the more surely animals are part of a household, the more likely it is that they will be taken to be subject to the very value scale that governs the other members. The extension seems to have little warrant beyond that of having the sanction of sentiment.

A centrally controlled economic system may spell out the various positions which different types of producers, con-sumers, and distributors are to have to one another. Applied to men as related in noneconomic ways, it will be irrelevant and ineffective. Applied to them as already economically or-dered, and even in the positions which the economic system designates, it will bring them within the scope of the system, where they will still maintain the relations they have to one another as interactive, differently positioned individuals. The men, as in other noneconomic relations, may then be affected —and conversely. The converse is denied legitimacy by economic determinists; they think that the complex which the application of an economic system produces overwhelms the relations men might have apart from it. But the political pressures which must be imposed on those who do not function in consonance with the economic system make evident that there are individuals who are not entirely controlled by it. Those men not only function as irreducibles in contradistinction from every we and every type of interrelationship, but their interrelationships make a difference to the manner in which they are able to participate in the economic system.

4.7. A distributive we distinguishes locations.

It is perhaps evident now that there are a number of independent ways in which men are interrelated, possessing features which may not be pertinent to the we that ranges over all of them. I will assume, therefore, that it is no longer necessary, when considering further types of we's, to examine every one of the kinds of interrelated men that are encompassed by those we's. Two types of interrelationship, though, have special import for a *distributive* we ranging over different spatial locations: In one, a) men are primarily interrelated in nonspatial ways; in the other, b) they are spatially distanced from one another.

a) 'We' usually refers to men who are at different spatial locations. It does not make that reference explicit, except when it is intended to range over units independently of any other way of their being together. Since the 'we' may not bear on their distances, and since for it one location may be as good as any other, the 'we' will either take all the units to be alike for it, or will tacitly introduce some differentiation—'remote', 'near', 'at hand', etc. The 'we' of a quorum is restricted to a particular place within which it may range over the individuals as just being present together. So does the 'we' of a census. This, in addition, may ignore the purpose for which the individuals are being considered together. The 'we' of a colonial power, in contrast, emphasizes the locations of the colonials, with some grasp of the fact that they are differentiated by virtue of their distances from an accepted center, even at the times when discriminations entailed by a differentiation between center and other places is officially denied.

When men are subject to a distributive we, they are dealt with as located. As also affiliated, with features which reflect that fact, they are together in a complex whose nature and career are determined by the way in which they and the distributive we interplay. The locations of those affiliated men are incidental to their affiliations, even though location may originally have been a precondition, and may have an effect on the ways in which affiliations are carried out. As the men's affiliations change, so may their locations, with some of them becoming so remote from the rest as to make them no longer be under the governance of that we. What the we treats as a unit, too, may be so affiliated with others as to make all in effect be a single spatial object, even though each member occupies his own particular place. But as long as the men remain distinct, their affiliations with one another will challenge the import of any we which takes them to be together in terms of their locations alone.

The locations that men in fact have could be quite irrelevant to the kind of affiliations they have—corresponding chess players—or they may be affected by it—a friendship which is strained by distances. Did the actual spatial locations that men occupy, apart from any we, make a difference to the kinds of features they also may have, the result would be a special case of b), the second application of the distributive we.

b) While men are in different parts of space, they may be subject to a common distributive we. This, though it may be formed with an awareness of their actual distribution, will not duplicate that. A we has designated locations inseparably together. In actual space, locations are distanced from one another. Though one might remark on those distances when spelling out the nature of the we, one will still not have dealt with the space which actually stretches between the locations where the men are.

The occupation of a position turns the position into a continuation of the occupant. Were this not done, there would be two spaces in the very same place, one provided by the occupant and the other by the whole of space. By making limited portions of space integral to themselves, men do not tear them out of the whole of space, any more than their being located in space precludes them from occupying places in it.

A distributive we takes account of men in filled-out regions of space, but not of the ways in which those regions are connected, or of the status of the men apart from their occupation of those regions. It may tacitly take all to be at the same time; it may read into different locations their distances from some common point; it may be pertinent to their magnitudes. The individuals, without regard for what the we requires, may qualify and overlay their occupation of spatial positions with other factors. They may, then, so minimize the fact of their occupation that the inclusion of them within the scope of a distributive we will serve merely to mark them off from one another without bearing on what they in fact are. "You, over there" may be translated into "We, over here" by the men who have been pointed out through the use of the 'you'. The identification of them as belonging together because they are in a given place may be rejected as not relevant. Men might ignore or rebel against the encompassment of themselves within a we to which they momentarily yielded in their translation of the 'you' that had been addressed to them.

The encompassment of men as merely spatially located may be affected by them as inescapably related to one another in space. "We, on this queue" encompasses a limited number within a limited spatial region. There, each occupies a position of his own. A we applies to all the members of the queue, but the complex that results from its application is a function of the way in which the separate locations over which the we ranges are interlocked with the located individuals as making up the queue.

While keeping the same order in a queue, men may place themselves at distinctive distances from one another, depending on the country in which the queue is formed. In England, the distance between any two will be considerable; in the United States it will be less; and in other countries much less. "We, on this queue" consequently can tell us nothing about the distances that the men maintain from one another, any more than it can tell us of the roles that their spatial positions have for them as distinct, self-maintained individuals.

4.8. There are three types of temporally distributive we's.

A temporal we ranges over men marked out as possessing temporal features. Since the men may be considered only so far as they are just copresent, sequentially ordered, or copresent and in a sequence, they will so far be brought within the compass of different we's. Each we may have the same range, apply to the very same individuals, but will be pertinent to them as having different temporal relations. A 'we' may refer to a family whose members are just copresent, have different ages, or are copresent over a period to time.

"We today" refers to a *synchronizing* we, marking out men who are copresent. "We of this dynasty" refers to a *sequentializing* we, marking out men who are in a temporal order. 'We of this nation' refers to a *processive* we, marking out men who are copresent moment after moment.

4.9. A synchronizing we ranges over copresents.

a) Men are copresent as in the same common present. b) They are copresent, too, as just occupying places in the same space. c) And they are copresent as actualities. Implicit in the latter two modes of copresence is the fact that they are at the same time.

a) Men are contemporaries even when not encompassed by a we, for they are interrelated within a single present moment of cosmic time. Each, also, delimits, intensifies, and incorporates that present in its own way. A synchronizing we is pertinent to them, not because they are related in a cosmic present, or in some subdivision of this, or because they have specialized that common present, but solely because they are units for it. Since the synchronizing we takes no account of the ways in which the individuals are within a common present, it makes no provision for the fact that this present is affected by its past and is involved with its future. Because that common present is outside the provenance of the we, the rhythm and direction of that present and the way it affects copresent individuals will so far not be known or considered. No one can, from the position of a synchronizing we, anticipate or satisfy the challenges which interconnected, copresent men inevitably offer it when it ranges over them. And because that we takes no account of the specialized forms which a common present has in each of the copresent individuals, it must also fail to take account of the ways in which the men confront one another, and the distinctive import that the present has in each.

The fact that the present complex which men constitute with a synchronizing we is a not predictable product is neglected when it is supposed that a synchronizing we applies not to men but only to the present in which they are. If it did, there would not be a genuine we for the men but only a common condition applied to delimited portions of a common present. That condition, moreover, would be challenged by the interrelated men over which it ranged, and would, so far, be affected by the fact that they were interrelated in a way not provided for in the condition. If it be denied that men could ever be copresent, the we, one would have to conclude, would be idle, pertinent to no one, indistinguishable in fact from the bare possibility that men could be synchronized.

b) A synchronizing we might be applied to individuals occupying regions in space. They must, though, also have a
temporal status if the we is to be pertinent, for such a we can
encompass them only if they are able to provide features over
which it can range. If the men are present primarily as spatial
units, and only incidentally temporal—the view of the classi-
cal determinists with their mechanical laws which operate indifferently backward and forward over spatial occupants—a
synchronizing we will still be able to apply to them, though
what one will be able to say of them will have little to do with
what those men are as together. "We today," applied to men
as occupying distinct places, is radically qualified by the ways
in which they are spatially related as well as by the ways they
make their occupied spaces integral to themselves.

Temporal copresence is as root a fact as spatial copresence.
A synchronizing we, that ranges over men as merely spatially
located, ignores that truth. Dualistic theories of knowledge,
which assume that what is perceived is somewhere in space
but at a remote time, adopt something like this point of view,
denying that what is perceived in space is copresent with the
perceiver. Limited to men brought together under a synchronizing we, the view does not allow that men who are confronted at a place distant from the perceiver coexist with him.
No one, on such an account, would be able to say 'we' of any
but temporally sequential individuals.

The application of a synchronizing we to men as primarily
occupying delimited portions of a common space is neither infrequent nor useless. Pairings and many other correlations
may deal with men who are just together in space. But both
because spatial occupancies and relations make a difference to
the ways in which the men function individually and as members of a correlation, and because the temporal copresence
that they in fact have apart from a reference to them also
makes a difference to the ways they are and act separately and
together, the complex that results from the application of a
synchronizing we on spatially copresent individuals will have
quite a different nature and career from that characteristic

either of the synchronizing we or of the interrelated men.

c) Equally real, men tend to appropriate whatever impinges on them, so as to preclude an alteration in their natures or possessions. Every feature—temporal, spatial, valuational, and the others which are due to common effective conditions—is subordinated by them to a self-maintaining. When one of the men includes himself and others within a synchronizing we, he ranges over himself and them as copresent in a stretch of time. That we, though, will be of little or no significance for the coordinated men unless it is brought to bear on them in such a way that their status as present is enabled to become dominant. Yet no we is so powerful that it can entirely overcome the functioning of actual men. All that can be done by a synchronizing we is to subject men to a confining copresence. If the we is conceptualized, it will provide a means for understanding the men as together in a present moment. But if the we is objectively effective, if it actually interplays with interrelated men, it will produce a complex with them.

A synchronizing we does not itself relate men as contemporaries. Contemporaneity requires an objective present which remains undivided even while delimited and specialized by individuals. This does not mean that the we is without cohesive force, or that it is not qualified by the men. A synchronizing we ranges over men, but not without joining them and being affected by them. Otherwise it would be not *of* but only *for* them.

"We today, with our rights . . ." refers to a we which ranges over men who, with that we, make up an effective complex. The power of that we is not due to the men's ceding some of their own power to it. They are subject to it and subjected by it, whether they cede anything or not. Nor does it make any difference whether or not the we and the interrelated men are characterizable in the same way, or if one is characterizable in one way and the other in another. Both are altered in constituting the complex.

d) A synchronizing we may range over men who are affiliated with one another. Its influence checks and is checked by the ways in which the men continue to be affiliated and what that affiliation means to them. Since the affiliation binds the men together in a way that the other modes of interrelationship do not, it offers a sharp contrast to any condition which, like a synchronizing we, effectively allies them without regard for the manner in which they are in fact interrelated and what this means to them individually. As at once synchronized and interrelated, men are effectively governed and unpredictably interconnected in a complex. If one speaks of them as 'we' one then refers either to the altered we which then governs them, or to the complex.

4.10. A sequential we orders men temporally.

A sequential we may apply to men who are a) contemporaries, b) earlier and later in time, or c) in some other interrelationship. In the first and third, the we requires that the men be interrelated in a new way. The second, instead, orders them in a sequence at the same time that they are sequentially interrelated.

a) A sequential we relates men who are not only before and after one another, as they could be on a queue, but as earlier and later. If those men are in fact contemporaries, there is no assurance that they will continue to be so at some subsequent time. Such a sequential we is quite different from one which moves over time to relate earlier with later members and which, therefore, can never fully be at any one moment. A sequential we, fully present and specifying positions to be occupied at different times, is used when considering contemporaries dealt with in the light of their different times of arrival or in terms of a series of tasks to be carried out one after the other. In the first way, contemporaries may be ordered in terms of the dates at which they were born or had begun some journey—or more generally, in terms of the different points in the past from which they arrived in the present. In the second, they are dealt with as contemporaries whose actions are to follow one another in time. In both ways the men can be spoken to and spoken of together.

For a sequential we to apply to contemporaries, it must be applied on men who are together within a single present. Since they are not in sequence, the sequential we must await the passage of time in order to be able to have them be items over which to range. One makes use of such a we when he speaks of what he and his children will do when the children are grown, how he will work in tandem with a partner, what positions he and others will occupy one after the other.

When the participants in a contractual arrangement speak of themselves as having come to an agreement, they make use of a synchronous we. If they go on to refer to themselves as having to engage in acts which are to follow one another in time, they will refer to themselves as encompassed by a sequential we. No explicit notice may be taken of the fact that one kind of we has given way to another. The shift becomes evident once attention is paid to the fact that an agreement involves symmetrical relations, while a series of acts involves asymmetrical ones. The explicit expression would run something like, "we have agreed that we will act in such and such an order." The second 'we' in this expression has a sequential referent encompassing men who were governed synchronously by the referent of the first 'we'. It treats them prospectively or, acknowledging them to be men in agreement, views some of them relatively to the actual speaker, and perhaps others. The first alternative emphasizes an open future, occupied by actual men to whom one refers as actual at some later time; the second, instead, lays out a program to be carried out subsequently. The one treats time as though it were an indifferent agent enabling the men to be available for what is ready to include them; the other takes all to be available now, but with some of them involved with possibilities to be realized. The second allows for more novelty, since it makes provision for the dynamic conversion of the possibilities into actualities.

b) A sequential we may explicitly range over men who are at different times. There is here no confronting of contemporaries. It is the we of prospective parents, the we of the ruler whose commands and decrees he expects to have carried out at some later time. That we may encompass no present individual, with the possible exception of the speaker. The men to come depend on actions by those present; as possibilities for those present men, they are part of a future. Like those in the past, they lack concreteness; unlike those in the past, they are not determinate. When the sequential we ranges over such men, it cannot have them on a footing with the speaker, except by taking him to lack concreteness, or by taking something in the past or future to give them a concreteness equal to his. But references to ancestors can be carried out only imaginatively, not in fact. Though references to later generations also can be carried out only imaginatively they could of course also be carried out in fact later.

If the only actualities that there could be were momentary units, there could be no sequential we. To be sure one might envisage a pattern which overarched the succession of units and took all that came within its scope to make up a single group. But this would not be a we. Not only would there be no individual who had taken himself to be together with others under a condition but there would be no applying of the condition to them all, sequentially or otherwise. It would just be exhibited over a stretch of time. There is no we unless someone takes himself and others to be together, and no resultant sequential complex unless the we applies to individuals as they in fact exist at different moments of time.

Only if what has been is united with what will be, and together affect and are affected by a we, will a complex we result. A special case of this, carried out even with reference to animals, is provided by Skinner's theory of operant conditioning. Moves on the part of a subject are rewarded by giving it a satisfying product at the end. Putting aside the question of how a pure behaviorism could justifiably speak of 'rewards', or even of 'satisfactions', the view supposes that 'rewards', which come at the end of a movement, somehow become effective in promoting a beginning of another movement like the first. This is not possible, unless an end is able to affect a beginning. Since time does not run backward, if an end is to affect a beginning, there must be a single condition which makes beginning and end relevant to one another in such a way as to permit of the conversion of a desired 'rewarded' end into a desirable prospect which is inseparable from a new beginning. Skinner's behaviorism requires an animal to provide a condition which functions like a governing sequential we.

c) A sequential we may range over individuals who are associated, are coordinately real, have formal connections, differ in value, and are related causally in space and in time. It then provides a sequence for items which are not sequentially arranged, or refers to features of them which are to be actualized at later moments. It evidently has to await the passage of time or the sequential actions of individuals before it is able to help constitute a complex.

When a man, who conceives himself to be subject to a sequential we, attends to the others who are in some other arrangement, he is forced to apply the we to them, moment after moment. He thereby takes advantage of the passage of time or of the conversion of those others into units appropriate to the we that is to be applied to them. In both ways an initial arrangement is replaced by a sequence of items. All the while, the initial arrangement may continue to be operative. The replacement occurs only if there is a production of temporal features relevant to the we, enabling this to apply to them at different moments. Those temporal features are not produced by the we.

Whether a we is sequential or not, it is normally applied sequentially, since it usually takes some time for it to be brought to bear on a number of individuals. When the we is non-sequential, it is altered in being so applied, unless what is insisted on is answered by something in the sequentially reached items. When the we is sequential, a similar alteration occurs in the application of the we. It is not just the timing of an application that determines how individuals are encompassed; what encompasses them plays a role. When the timing of an application is not in accord with the timing required by the we, the we is misapplied. Because its application awaits the passage of time or the action of individuals, the misapplication, in effect, is the replacement of one sequential we by some other we.

The application of a sequential we makes a triple difference: It cuts off the items over which it ranges from others with which they are in fact united; it gives a role to what otherwise could be just in the background; and it encompasses what time and other agencies make available to it. It becomes most successful through the help of time and the conversion of future possibilities into subsequent present occurrences.

Alert to the fact that a we—particularly one that ranges over a considerable number of men—will take time to apply, one might conceive of a sequential we which bears on men just so far as they are sequentially reached. Those men will, like objects of an intention, exist only as and when arrived at, having no other status but that of terminating the application of the we. So far as that was true, there would be no accounting for their presence. Once it is granted that men have some reality of their own, a sequential we, no matter how neatly geared to the presence of the men, is challenged by them as interrelated apart from that we.

4.11. A processive we has a twofold spread.

That men should be copresent for an indefinite time is a matter of indifference to a synchronous we. Though a sequential we may provide a number of positions to be occupied over time, the men who will occupy those positions are not considered. This is not the usual form a temporal we assumes. A processive we provides positions for copresents, but is applied to them as in successive moments of time.

A synchronous we can at most mark out a beginning and an ending; a sequential we marks off a particular temporal strand. Together, they can embrace a number of men who are interrelated long enough to undergo changes in their interrelationship and in themselves, or who can succeed in bringing about something attributable to them together. A processive we shares features with both. But it is not the product of the other two, any more than these are abstractions from it. Each we has its own distinctive use and power.

Discourse would not be possible were men not under the provenance of processive we. Indeed, discourse is best carried on when each takes himself not only to be a member of such a we but identifies his 'we' with the 'we' of the others. Each then takes himself to interplay with a processive we ranging over speakers as well as listeners, listeners as well as speakers. The fact that they might be members of the same we, of course, does not assure that they will be fully in accord, but only that they can speak and listen to one another. The we has sufficient power to keep the men within the bounds of a common language, utilizing as it does the vocabulary and grammar of well-established institutions. But it does not have power enough to make the men continue to be subject to it, and usually does not have enough to overcome other ways in which the men might continue to be together under the governance of some other we. Men might, as diplomats do, talk with one another at the same time that they function as members of different, more effective, oppositional we's. But even when men speak in perfect accord, they act in some opposition to a common, processive we, for this is pertinent to them as units while they in fact are interrelated in a number of vital and possibly nontemporal ways. Two cases are worth examining: a) Where men are interrelated over a period of time, and there provide the units which meet the demands of a common processive we, and b) where they are interrelated in ways that are not pertinent to those demands.

a) Men can be subject to a number of we's at the same time. One of these may be processive, another synchronous, a third sequential. Some we's, too, may encompass other we's as de-limited regions. The men in a community are processively one, at the same time that they form smaller groups where they are affiliated, and interrelated in other ways as well. The processive we that rules their discourse is confined within other we's reflecting the fact that they are members of the same nation, work group, spatial region, or club.

'We' usually includes the speaker as an I, and brings the others up to the level of some expression of that I. But 'we' is not a precondition for a we. A we could but need not be re-ferred to by means of a 'we', and when it applies to men, it may be countered by them in the guise of interrelated me's, I's, me's and I's, me's and you's, or you's and you's, regard-less of the demands of that we.

Men may processively function together in the very way that a processive we demands. If they do, they will exist through time and not merely be in an assigned temporal or-der. In the course of their existence together over time, they will dictate to the we when it in fact can function as a proces-sive condition for them. A similar determination of the appli-cation of a we may occur when the men are just sequentially ordered.

A processive we invites a number to remain together, but applies only to those who in fact do so. "We will do the job" begins with a number who may in fact not continue to be part of the we as it completes its application over time. The indi-viduals, who may even have been explicitly named, are then either governed by a synchronous we, or are encompassed as possible subjects which never attain the state of being actu-al subjects for it. The opposite stress, on just such and such men being within the compass of a processive we, requires changes in the rhythm of the application of the we just so far as the men do not keep in perfect accord with one another. If a speaker fails to keep apace with others, though he will not thereby destroy the processive we to which he may have referred, he will no longer be a member of it. The we might still continue and function as it had initially when he was part of it. The fact points up the objectivity and power of the we. Because it does not depend on its being referred to by means of 'we', it does not depend for its existence or functioning on the presence of one who says or thinks of himself as together with others.

b) When men are interrelated by affiliation, as copresents, formally, spatially, causally, or as values, a processive we is not able to range over them unless and so far as they also have the status of contemporaries functioning over a period of time. This may require an emphasis on what are only minor features of the men, or it may require the intrusion of factors which are not part of them. The first occurs when the men, as interrelated in one of the foregoing ways, also happen to be temporally ordered; the latter occurs when they are not ordered at all but are dealt with as though they were, either by someone insisting on applying a processive we to them or by giving it power.

What is not temporally ordered may be dealt with temporally by one who makes a processive we effective with respect to items forced within its compass. One might decide to deal with a limited group of arbitrarily chosen men as though they belonged together over time; or a community may make some limited group of men function processively for a while as a family, warriors, or hunters. Were the men primarily interrelated nonprocessively, the processive we would not apply to them except by accident, through the help of acts which transform them, or by its bearing on minor aspects of them.

Unless one is able to change men so that their functioning together over a time is in accord with the demands of the processive we, they will continue to be and act independently and perhaps in opposition to it. The complex that results from the imposition of a processive we on those men will have a steady nature only if the we is brought to bear on them again and again in new ways. If it is a we which has the support of a community, the men will be subject to social constraints whose effectiveness will vary from individual to individual, to yield a complex in which all fit more or less in the same way.

4.12. A transactional we sets the limits of a causal situation.

Kant took causality to be a necessitation which added a categorical condition to the sequential unfolding of cosmic time. Such an account fails to acknowledge causal transactions between limited numbers of items. It does not recognize that causation converts a possible into an actual effect. Kant's view, though, does point up the fact that there is a causality which is constitutive. A transactional we is a special case of it. But unlike a Kantian category, it applies to what is already interrelated apart from it, both in a) causal, and b) noncausal ways.

a) There are situations where some men are causes and other men are effects. In other situations, men constantly shift from cause to effect, somewhat as they do when they change from speaker to listener and back again. In both situations, the men are interrelated causally. If causation took up no time at all, the second type would reduce to a combination of instances of the first. But it always takes time for an effect to be realized and to assume the role of a cause, even toward the very items which had had the role of causes for it. There are also situations in which those who, while they are being acted on, also act, and toward the very men who are acting on them. A man may restrain, redirect, contribute to the very action that is being directed at him. He may be an effect of a transaction in which he was one of the causes, and he may be affected in one way while acting as a cause in another.

A transactional we offers a condition applying to men who are interrelated independently of that we. It may be applied to men causally related in ways which differ from that which the we requires. In any case, the we will depend on the men to produce the causally effective transactions over which it is to range. Its constitutive power is restricted to the determination of what can be cause and what can be effect; it has no ability to bring about an effect at some time after the origination of a particular dynamic process.

Even when a transactional we, and activities carried out by men independently of this, have analogous structures, they will, on being brought together, make a difference to one another. The one sets the limits at which causes and effects are to be, and does this apart from any causal process; the other is a dynamic ongoing in which cause and effect are termini whose import is determined by the nature of the activity by which the effect comes to be. On interplaying, they affect each other to constitute a complex having a nature and career different from either.

Apart from a transactional we or a similar effective condition, a causal situation would be just an arbitrary segment of a larger dynamic world. The familiar supposition that a we has no power is here tantamount to the denial that there are genuine causal conditions which can make a difference to the functioning of interrelated men. A transactional we is a constitutive cause. Depending on an ongoing, over which it has no control, to provide the passage that is needed if there are to be real causes and effects, it acts somewhat in the way in which Kant supposed that freedom did—by intruding on what is and continues to function apart from it.

When a causal situation interplays with a transactional we, an actual, limited causal transaction occurs. There, the we is spelled out over a time, and causally related men function within its limits. The resultant complex has a causal role of its own in relation to other complexes, some of which, like it, are the unpredictable outcome of the interplay of a transactional we with causally interrelated men.

Biographers are inclined to attend to causally interrelated

men, with an emphasis on one or a few as central. Jurispru-
dence, political theory, the study of constitutions, tribal structures, and social organizations, focus instead on transactional
we's. In contrast, historians, particularly those occupied with
the careers of nations and states, tend to concentrate on the
careers of complexes. All minimize or ignore the role of other
factors. The biographers nevertheless assume them in setting
boundaries and in the treatment of different families; the legal
and social thinkers assume them in their understanding and
application of the we; and the historians assume them when
they divide off epochs and episodes to pay attention to the
men who happen to be living at a chosen time.

b) A transactional we can be imposed on men who are
interrelated in noncausal ways—as affiliated, equals, intelligibles, extended in space or time, or as values. It will not
apply to those men, however, unless they are able to exhibit
features which are pertinent to that we. This requirement is
overlooked when, with Spinoza, causation is taken to be identical with a logical necessitation linking intelligibles. Not only
is there then no room made for actual transactions, but antecedents or premisses are unwarrantedly identified with
causes, and consequents or conclusions with effects.

If causal features are recessive, a transactional we requires
them to be brought forward. If they are not available, they
must be produced. Noncausal features can come within the
compass of that we only incidentally, by accompanying features which are germane to that we. The actualities which
possess them will still, of course, have their own integrity and
be interrelated apart from the we or the focusing on other features. And any complex that is produced will have its own
nature, powers, career, and causal role.

The traditions of work and language which are characteristic of a nation account for the ways in which it interplays with
habituated men, but not for the ways in which the nation distinguishes itself from the world about. When the men take up
approved positions with respect to what is outside the bounds

of their nation, they do so partly because the nation enabled them to act in these ways.

Until interrelated men interplay with a transactional we, the we will be just a condition not yet applied. It will be like the decrees of a league of nations whose specified causes and effects play no role in what the nations do to one another, or on the various ways in which those nations are in fact interrelated. Apart from such a league, nations are of course governed by various common transactional we's, just so far as they trade, communicate, or share a heritage. Only a completely isolated nation could escape governance by a transactional we of this kind.

A transactional we is a condition, objectively possessed and exercised. It has power enough to set some men off from others, and power enough to make a difference to their interrelations. Men may, of course, be supposed to be together in ways which may answer to no matter of fact. They may be classified and characterized arbitrarily in a transactional we. But then the application of the we will give the men, as they in fact are, quite new roles. Though there may be no difference in scope or even effectiveness between humanly imposed conditions and those which operate apart from men, usually, though, the conditions which men impose are more radically affected by the interrelated men than objective conditions are. The application of a transactional we may result in considerable alterations in it, and in only minor changes in the way men are interrelated.

A transactional we is just a program of operations if it is merely imagined and left unapplied. Applied, it operates on men who may be primarily interrelated in noncausal ways. Objectively conditioning, it provides an agency for relating the men as causes and effects. If the men are already interrelated in noncausal ways, the objectively operating we will emphasize what are minor or suppressed features of the interrelation. All the while, it will be challenged by the noncausal interrelations that the men have to one another.

4.13. An assessive we ranks what it governs.

Men think of themselves as forming quite limited groups. The 'we' they use is usually restricted to those of the same background, color, wealth, privilege, location, power, gender. The individuals in these limited groups are more or less equated and are set in considerable contrast with the members of other groups who are often tacitly taken to be on a different level of value. But once a group has been marked off from others, it sometimes becomes evident that its we, initially treated as a value common to the members, is in fact differentiated, crediting the men over which it ranges with different values, sometimes in considerable dissonance with the values that the men in fact have.

Were a common condition alone the ground of the values that men have, it would be applied to them as interrelated in nonevaluational ways. Were it without power, it would be able to apply to them only so far as it was effectively imposed on them. The imposition might then conflict with whatever values those men may in fact have and with the ways in which they are interrelated, evaluationally or otherwise. Were values solely subjective, an evaluation would grant judgments, attitudes, and assessments an application to actual men, perhaps for considerable periods. But since it would, on the hypothesis, terminate in what was without value, it would apply to what was irrelevant to it. When an assessive we is countered by men who are in nonevaluative interrelationships, the men will either have to be altered so that they have values to which the we can apply, or the values that they have, but which are recessive, will have to be made the topic of the we and, with its help, make a difference to the way in which the men function in the resultant context.

4.14. A simple we may be both governed and related.

When applied, a we helps constitute a complex. It may then be subject to other conditions, in a way similar to that which its members exhibit toward one another and toward it. On a new level, there will be a repetition of the kinds of situations that have already been examined. One would be caught in an infinite series of conditions were it not that there are final conditions to which everything is subject.

Final conditions have bearing on every actuality, organic or simple, and on every subordinate condition. The indivisible particles which physics seeks to know are the subject of final conditions as surely as are more complex items. Though some actualities operate with respect to their parts in the ways in which conditions operate on them, all are irreducible subjects of conditions. Some of the conditions governing the wholes also directly govern the parts. Some conditions, however, govern only certain types of entities, and have no further bearing on what those entities embrace. The citizenship of men is dependent on their being under the governance of a state. Though the men behave in ways which affect the location of the particles within them, those particles are not subject to the conditions laid down by the state.

Conditioning is not transitive. Some of the limited specifications of ultimate conditions directly govern some actualities and, only indirectly through these, their parts. The conditions governing a we may also function in this way. A treaty not only allies a we, in the form of a nation, with another but, through the mediation of these we's, affects the encompassed men.

A we obtains part of its power from the set of limited conditions of which it is a member. It appropriates some of the effects of the others on it in the act of maintaining itself. At the same time, more general conditions, governing it and the others, make their presence felt. The result is a doubly empowered simple we, maintained within an interrelated whole of conditions, themselves affected by ultimate conditions

governing all. An understanding even of such a comparatively innocent and apparently personally instituted we, as that
which governs a pair working together, has a power and a
nature reflecting the way in which it is maintained apart from
other limited conditions, as well as the way it is governed by
more basic and comprehensive conditions. The manner in
which the we is maintained apart from other limited conditions with which it is interrelated, as well as the ways it counters and is modified by those that govern it, determines the
influence that the we has on what it in turn encompasses.

Reflections such as these depend for their final justification
on an understanding of the nature of ultimate conditions and
the way these operate. For the present, it is sufficient to observe that these conditions give a we power enough to make a
difference to what men do severally and together, and enable
the we to be effectively interrelated with other limited conditions. A we has properties and a career of its own; it is also
interrelated with other we's and sometimes with I's, you's,
me's, and combinations of these.

4.15. A simple we is a partial analogue of an I.

The individuals who interplay with a simple we may be interrelated solely as I's, as I's and you's, as me's, as you's and
you's, or as you's and me's. The we itself may be related to
some other we's, each encompassing a different set of interrelated men. In all cases, the we is unlike an I, for it has no interi-
ority, no self which it epitomizes and represents, and no other
epitomizations of which it could make use. Like an I, though,
it provides a position from which other units can be approached. Not reducible to a blurred way of having a number
of distinctive individuals together, it has a nature and power
of its own. And it can be held accountable.

By submitting to the very we it makes possible, an I enables
that we to stretch over it and other unities. A complex in
which the conditioning we interplays with those units is

thereby produced. That complex is powerful and effective, able to interact with other complexes. Unlike the I, the power that it has is the power it exhibits—which is to say, it is what it does.

An individual's declaration to fight another connects them. The two, even with the declaration, do not yet constitute a complex, though actions thereafter may be prompted and guided by the declaration. The declaration is therefore quite different from a declaration of war. Declarations of war are made by men on behalf of a we which functions as a unit in relation to other units on the same plane. Before and after that declaration, the individuals interplay with one another, sometimes in disregard of the declaration of war. Only so far as they are constrained by a common we, do interrelated men form a single, bounded insistent, claiming nation at war.

4.16. Us is a partial analogue of me.

An us is a we externally referred to by members of that we. Sustained by the very individuals who sustain the we, the us functions neither as an object nor as a subject. Instead, it has the role of a translucent medium for the men who, from a position outside all of them, attend to themselves as together. When a number of men try to understand what they are in the eyes of others, they do not produce a common self-consciousness but merely view their we in terms provided by others. Nor does an us provide boundaries for, or form a complex with interrelated men. It is a complex of condition and men which is dealt with from the outside. The referent of 'us' is not altogether separable from we.

Other groups cannot know us in any other guise but that of a complex interplaying with them. Since they cannot provide a pivot by means of which we can look at ourselves as an us, we cannot come back to ourselves, via them, and cannot possibly be enriched by something obtained from them. We do, of course, learn that other people have a different impression of us from what we have of ourselves. We remark on how they misconstrue us, and sometimes we try to change our ways so as to be differently dealt with or thought of by them. We do not then act as a single judged we or us. Yet, since complexes can be approached from the outside, it seems reasonable to suppose that they might function in the very way a me does. Might not a family recognize that others treat it with disdain, and might its members not approach that family from the position of those others? They could and they do, but as a complex which is actually being constituted from within by those members. The us that the members recognize is but themselves interrelated under a condition; it is just a complex we approached from without.

A complex may react to charges leveled against it. It may be affected by the way other complexes act. It could be coldly examined. But it cannot be self-conscious. A representative for it might function in terms of the judgments that others make about it. Again and again, the members of it may say that "They are speaking about us." In its interplay with other complexes, it may sometimes be primarily passive and sometimes primarily active. If passive, it will so far be identical with the terminus of an external reference. It will then function not like a me but like the surface of a you.

"Give it to me" has me in the role of a recipient, sustained by an I who can attend to that receiving me. "Give it to us" has an us in the role of a recipient, but that us is not sustained by the members, nor do they attend to if as receiving. Instead, in the act of receiving, the members exhibit themselves to be constituents of a we which accepts what is given. Because there is a me that can receive, the me can be publicly known by giver and recipient. Because there is no us that can receive, when something is given, the us must immediately give way to a pluralized you for you and to a we for us. From the outside, a me is known only in the guise of a you by you; it is a me only for an I. From the outside, us is known only in the guise of a pluralized you by you; it is just a we for its members.

There are times, though, when the analogy between us and

me does seem to hold. "Look at us, weak and defenseless," might require an outside reference to us together. "Think of us, with our long and honorable history" seems even more sharply to be referring to an us that its members sustain. Both contrast with "Look at us, dirty and bedraggled" and with "Think of us, just women and children," where the referent of 'us' dissolves into the individuals within the confines of a we. But in all, 'us' refers to a complex formed by interrelated individuals and a common conditioning we, dealt with from an outside position. "The treaty humiliated us," nevertheless, seems not to use 'us' in the same way that "Do not ignore us, the alerted citizens" does. The first seems to refer to a terminal us backed by a complex we, while the second seems to refer to a terminal us which is backed by the we of bounded, interrelated individuals. But it is not easy to determine just what is intended in these cases. The fact supports the thesis that us is an analogue, though not an exact one, of me.

4.17. There are conditions which apply to every we.

A we is related to other we's. The relations presuppose powers enabling them to be together. As has already been seen, these are of various kinds—associative, coordinative, structuralizing, extensional, and evaluational. As confined to a limited number of men, such conditioning powers have a limited range, and are usually modified on being applied. The individuals over which they range continue to be subject to the more general conditions.

I am a member of one family as a son and of another as a father. I am a colleague, a citizen, a taxpayer, a westerner. In each of these guises I may be primarily subject to an associating condition; in one of them I may be primarily subject to evaluations at the same time that in another I may be primarily subject to a coordination or some other condition. At the same time, I am one of many actualities in the universe, subject to conditions governing all. When it is said that I should be true to myself, it is not yet clear whether reference is being made to myself as a self, an I, or a me; as a member of this or that we; as a member of some larger group; or to myself as a unit in the cosmos. It is not clear if I am expected to recognize all the conditions to which I am subject, whether dominant or recessive, and if I am to take account of the manner in which I did and could counter these, separately or together with others. When all are taken into account, the maxim takes the form "Be true to yourself in all dimensions, private and public." Unfortunately, the demands and satisfactions of one condition sometimes conflict with those of another. As a consequence, the maxim has to be altered once again to require that maximum justice be done to all the conditions. This still does not make evident which is to be favored and which muted in a particular situation, or if equal weight is to be given to all, even though they then limit one another's range or effectiveness. The ideal, unrealizable in fact and unenvisageable in detail, is to have each demand fully satisfied, and all harmonized without loss.

One can do no better than to begin with what abilities one has, and utilize these maximally before going on to consider other demands. Since that answer may lead to the neglect of areas which have not yet had a role and which might deserve attention more than those which had been explored, that answer must be enlarged to include the demand that one must try to enhance all else. Humanized, that expanded answer has the form of an amalgam of the greatest men in art, science, philosophy, religion, politics, adventure, sport, education, home, and other areas where great achievement requires great character. Evidently, the result to be attained is an inclusive complex we in which every man, enjoying the peace of fulfillment, epitomizes and helps realize an ideal universal we maximally. To be as splendid as it is possible for a man to be, each must be fulfilled together with all the others.

CHAPTER 5

They and the Others

5.1. They sustain the others.

'They' refers to a group of which one is not a part. 'The others' refers to such a group set in contradistinction to oneself or one's own group. The referent of 'the others' is made determinate and sustained by the referent of the 'they'. The others presupposes a they but, unlike a they, the others has no status or power of its own. By itself, it is just the terminus of a negating relation, relative to an I or a we.

The others also has a more impersonal unrelativized status, deserving separate consideration. But, since that status is not entirely independent of the personal and relativized, it awaits an understanding of this before it can be properly dealt with. The personal relativized status of the others is covered in 5.2–12; the impersonal is in 5.13–32.

5.2. The others terminate negations.

Concerned as they are with formalized units and relations, logicians have had little occasion to consider different types of negation. But even within the austere confines of an abstract system one can, with considerable gain in understanding, differentiate $-(p)$, $(-p)$, and $-p$, where the first yields p by a negation, the second precludes this, and the third leaves the question open. If one of the three must be chosen to represent the others, it should be the third, where the negative is understood to be the terminus of an act.

'The others' is a relative term. Its referent has a different import when reached from one position from what it has when reached from another. Even in those special cases where they comprise the same individuals and function in the same ways, the others for myself are never the others for you. The others for myself are what I face as not myself. The others for you are what you face as not yourself. We both negate the others, but our negations begin at different points and are imposed with different strengths. The others for you may be more congenial to you than the others that I face are congenial to me. As our purposes, locations, and knowledge change, the others will have new weights for each of us.

A they is not affected by the negations which terminate at it. The negations, though, give the they a new role, of which its members may be unaware. Conversely, the men negating the they may themselves be negated by the members of the they, of whom they may know nothing. The two negatings are independent, and may differ in force as well as in nature.

A negation which terminates in the others may follow on a prior acceptance. It may be followed by, and perhaps even be accompanied by, an acceptance. And it may precede a knowledge of the others. After a man has become acquainted with a number of men, he may wish to insist on a negation of them. Confident of himself, aggressive, demanding, dismissive, he may, without having taken note of anyone else, allow his negation to alight where it can. Having made as evident as possible that the others are set apart, he may follow with a new way of making a union with them.

The same men may be negated from many different positions and in many different ways. In different cases, the negations differ in strength and in meaning. It is one thing to negate others as just somewhere else or as involved in something else, and another thing to negate them as undesirables, repugnant, or alien.

5.3. There are two types of others: the distributive and collective.

'The others' may be an abbreviated way of naming a number of distinct individuals. It may also be used to refer to them as together. If the first, the referents are like you's in being acknowledged to have a status apart from the reference to them, but unlike you's in not being backed by something more substantial. In the second way, the collective, the others is taken to form a single group, not yet differentiated, even though that group may be, and may even be known to be made up of such and such men. "I'll pay no attention to the others" dismisses a number en bloc, whether or not they are individually known.

The collective others may be acknowledged on the way to an acknowledgment of a distributive. Two acts of negating are then employed one after the other, sometimes so closely that it is hard to distinguish them. Still, an othered complex of individuals is quite different from othered individuals. Sometimes it is possible to note a considerable difference in the negations, particularly when one assumes quite different attitudes toward the collective and distributive others. It is possible to reject individuals violently while only mildly opposing them collectively; it is possible to oppose a collective while being sympathetic with its members. Diplomats are inclined toward the first; those who travel abroad are often inclined toward the second. The way one faces either makes a difference to the way in which one approaches the other. It is also possible to negate a collective at the same time that one unites with the individuals within its confines. Conversely, it is possible to negate individuals at the same time that one joins their group. One may not like the type of group they form and may want to have them in another; one may like that type of group but not the membership.

A negation directed toward collective others terminates in a unit. That unit is so far like a single individual, the unitary object of a negating. Unlike an individual, though, it lacks the power to reciprocate. But the individuals encompassed by the collective may effectively negate those who negate it.

A negating is instituted and carried out by individuals. It can be credited to a collective—a nation, we say, repudiates a treaty or an alliance. But though the nation may have the status of a unit origin of a negating, the negating itself is the work of its representatives or members; it is a we which may suffer a negating but is unable to negate. Of course, if a nation is identified with a complex of condition and interrelated individuals, it can be credited with a power to negate, and could itself be negated.

5.4. A they is the others as anonymous and oppositional.

Though there are no others except for one who negates, there can be a they apart from all negating. 'They' refers to what has a standing of its own, pointing to an as yet unspecified region, occupied independently of any reference made to it. The they is anonymous, indefinite, and not located; it functions on its own, but it cannot be reached except through the agency of a negating. If a they is not identified, the negating will not be known to have found a terminus, or that terminus will be lost in giving the they a standing apart from the negating. But once the they has been identified, it can be joined or repelled, can be faced by individuals or collections of them, can be acknowledged without regard for any of the individuals within its compass, or can be taken to encompass certain men and not others.

I may credit a they, whether this be collective or distributive, with the status of a standard or a judge. It then becomes a pivot in terms of which I can become self-conscious, or it can be taken to support a condition to which I more or less submit. Since it cannot provide content or even a genuine objective position in terms of which a return to myself can be made, a self-consciousness which pivots about a they credits an im-

agined attitude to a group of men. When, instead, a they offers a support for a condition, it may be taken to pass judgment like a Greek chorus, at the service of what is anonymous
but objectively right. "What will they think?" is a question
which no one perhaps ever avoids asking and which, to some
degree, is always left unanswered.

When they and the others are distinguished, the they may
be given boundaries. These are usually vague and not clearly
remarked. The others may then be taken to include all else,
perhaps even animals or things. The situation can also be reversed, and the others more or less identified, leaving the
they to cover all the rest. The others which the they presupposes, in these cases, necessarily stands in contradistinction
from the others with which the they had been contrasted.

A they can mediate between ourselves and the very others
which we directly face. Fashion arbiters, politicians, minis-
ters, and popular moralists often view the others in terms of
the judgments thought to be incorporated in such a mediating
they. For the arbiters and sometimes for the politicians, in contrast with the other two, the judgment is not taken to have a
transcendent justification. The they to whom the judgment is
credited is nevertheless given a special standing as compris-
ing the best or right people, those with a correct outlook or
acute sensibility.

A they has a preferential standing in contrast with the
others. It need not, though, be taken to be superior to oneself
or to one's group. To look at animals as the others is to look at
them as strange. To look at them as a they, is to be attentive,
alert to them as actual, able to stand away from and even to
oppose us. When I defend the remark "I don't care what they
say," by showing the inadequacy of the judgments made
about myself, perhaps by appealing to some objective standard, I still take the they to have an importance, despite its
vagueness and anonymity, that the others do not have.

A negation which ends with the others never gets beyond
having the others terminate it; but a they can negate what
negates it. Where one's othering is thrust outward to termi-

nate in what is negated, the facing of a they involves the acceptance of oneself as a possible subject for a negating. The acknowledgment of a they adds the prospect that one may be negated in turn.

A negator sets himself apart both from that at which his negation terminates and from himself as an origin of that negation. Strictly speaking, it will not be correct to say that he is other than the others, but only that he is other than they, for the others do not sustain a negating and, therefore, cannot be in a symmetrical relation to him. Since other-than is a symmetrical relation, it needs a they as one of its terms. If other-than is to terminate in the others, it will have to be a consequence of the release of a terminus from a negating, thereby enabling that terminus to be rooted in a they and, thereupon, able to have the original negator as the terminus of its negating.

Since a negating is not necessarily countered by a they and since, when it is so countered, the negating need not have the same force it had before, the relation other-than is evidently not the product of reciprocal negatings. It needs only the presence of the negator in the role of the reciprocal of the they. The greater the power and depth that is allowed to the they, the deeper is the reach of the relation. Only if the they is also a we or an I, can it be just the terminus of the relation other-than, whose other terminus is a we or an I.

There is a relation of other-than holding between various individuals as well as between various collections of them. That relation does not depend on an initial othering, a separation from the terminus of this, and a consequent opposition to the source of the othering. The failure to institute a relation of other-than by transforming others into a they, consequently, does not jeopardize the relation of other-than that holds in fact. The latter is there whether or not an entity takes account of any other.

The other-than which relates individuals or groups to one another is different from that which relates individuals and groups to conditions. Only the former allows for a they. When the two kinds of other-than are not distinguished, there is a tendency to speak of conditions as though they were the expression of Gods or other individuals. Conditions, though, unlike individuals and groups, are both negated and beyond the reach of a negating. They are negated as merely conditioning; they are beyond the reach of a negating so far as they are empowered by their sources. Whereas in the case of individuals and groups, power is possessed and exercised by what is not negated, conditions possess and exercise power while they are being negated.

5.5. What is beyond the others can be known.

We know of a they and of effective conditions when engaged in a negating. The knowledge is acquired by finding a) that the negation is forced to come to an end; b) that we are met by acts which the negated cannot provide; and c) that we are part of an interactive situation.

a) A negating ends in content negated. That content terminates the negating but does not provide it with a terminus. As together with the negating, the content is just a limit *of* this, even while that content is maintained apart from the negating as a limit *for* it. One becomes aware of that fact in encountering resistance to the progress of a negating, for one then faces content, beyond the terminus, still to be negated. The resistance beyond the negating, which brings it to an end, has a depth to it into which one penetrates to some extent, meeting greater and greater opposition. Because it terminates at the forefront of what is defying the power of negation to terminate in it, a negating is therefore always successful but never wholly so.

b) While a negation is being expressed, acts may originate at the negated or beyond it. A they or an individual is acknowledged when it is seen that the acts neither follow from the nature of the negated nor exhibit powers possible to the negated. A condition is acknowledged when the acts incorporate a power that is common and governing.

c) Apart from all conditioning, actualities interact with one another. They affect one another with a vigor and dynamism greater than that possible to mere negatives. When the actualities interact they are interconnected and, so far, are compatible, even while continuing to be other than one another. Also, each, and all of them together, interact with common conditions, qualifying these and being subject to them at the same time. Actualities are interrelated and also interplay with their common conditions independently of any negating.

The old questions: is it possible to perceive an external world; is it possible to know that there are other men; is it possible to know more than particulars; are answered by attending to special forms of the triple way in which negatings are transcended by a they, by individuals, and by conditions. We know that we are perceiving an external world by learning that what is perceived is countered by a force stopping a movement in depth. We know that there are other men and even what they are like because we find ourselves acted on in ways which are the independent reciprocals of what we are doing. We know that there are more than particulars because we suffer conditions which forcefully control us. We do not know what men are in private, but we can, in sympathy and through symbols penetrate them beyond any preassignable point, beyond all perceivings and negatings. Inference is needed, not to assure the presence or status of what is beyond what we negate, but to enable us to understand what is being thrust toward.

I assert myself when I open my eyes in the morning. My assertiveness is met by a diversity of objects. The acknowledgment of them as negated by me is one with the acceptance of them as having a standing apart from me, as having their own grounding and functioning. Were that in which I terminate a mirror image or some desirable or congenial object, it would still be faced as that which, despite my negating, is grounded elsewhere. By negating what is encountered, whether this be particular objects, combinations of them, or conditions governing myself and others, I do not affect how these will act and affect me.

5.6. A negating may have a contrastive terminus.

A negating ends at what does not itself stand apart unless it has a power of its own or is sustained by what has such power. This may be most compatible, even desirable. If so, the negating will provide a first stage for efforts to become united with it, thereby enabling us to benefit it, to benefit from it, to adopt it, or to use it.

One knows what is present and, therefore, just how one should deal with it, by attending to it as something other. It is possible also to begin with the acceptance of something as congenial or desirable, and then set it aside, negate it in order to examine or understand it. The first begins with oneself as active, and ends with reflection. The second begins with experience or an undergoing, and ends with what then might be examined or understood. Evidently, the first falls within the compass of the second.

A negating need not be produced consciously. It may express the very nature of a man as he asserts himself, ex-ists, occupies a position from which everything else is to be reached through a negating. The negating may also be consciously or deliberately instituted, express a persistent or transient attitude or feeling, or be directed at some specified particular. It may end in some quality, in an essence or nature, or at an individual, though short of it in its full concreteness as lived through from within. It may be directed at a complex, at a conditioning we, at integrated individuals, or at universally applicable conditions. In all, it ends with what is set in contrast primarily with the negator, and sometimes secondarily with other items.

A contrastive negating ends with content which is set apart.

The outcome may be due to the negating having only a minimal role, so as to allow what is confronted to stand out and,
thereupon, be able to be unaltered while joined with the
negator. Or it may be the outcome of a conversion of one item
into another, accepted as already standing apart. The first is
the negating that occurs at the terminus of an idle survey; the
second, at the end of explorations and examinations. When
the force of a negating is resisted, with a consequent facing of
a they rather than the others, another negating becomes evident, expressed through the agency of the negated terminus.
The two negations would of course be just diverse in nature,
duration, and effectiveness, were there no single condition
which encompasses their termini and what expresses itself
through these.

5.7. A negating may have an attributed terminus.

A negating is an act thrust outward. What it terminates at may
be held onto by what lies outside the reach of the negating.
The terminus of a negation will then be both inseparable from
the negating and from what accommodates this. It will then
have acquired the status of an *attribution*. Predication, charac-
terization, symbolization, and penetration are special cases of
this, the first two being bounded off from that to which they
are attributed, while the second two continue further into it.
None stops at a terminus and follows this up with another act
which credits that terminus to something else. The terminus
is arrived at with a force which continues into what is beyond
it.
   Attribution arrives at a surface continuous with what is at a
greater depth. It stops, not with a separated white or white-
ness, but with a white-of; not with a confronted place, but
with an occupied region; not with the character of soldier, but
with a soldierly set of items. White, place, soldier are concepts
or abstractions; white-of, occupied region, and soldierly are at
once termini of negatings and outside the negatings, limiting

the negatings through the agency of forceful expressions by what is outside them.

Reciprocally produced attributions are kept together by a condition which maintains them apart from one another. At the same time, I or we, and they, as sources of the independent attributive negations, are enabled to be together. Were there no common condition governing the reciprocals, they would belong to separate realities and, so far, would have no relation to one another; were there no common condition governing the sources, they would be sunk within themselves.

Attribution need not be deliberate. Rarely do we have the time to reflect on, to question, or even to attend to what we are attributing. Nor need attributions be conscious. A negating can originate with a they and end with us as the others of that they.

Apart from all thought or consciousness, both we and they can adopt the attributions which are forced on us. It is common, though, to take attribution to be an epistemic act. Men are thought to entertain private thoughts which are projected outward toward what may not be present at all, may not be knowable, or may somehow allow one to say that what was being attributed was true of something. The view requires one to hold that animals engage in no attributions or that, if they do, they also hazardously project their private thoughts or feelings outwardly, without an assurance that there is anything on which these might alight. What should one then say about plants and inanimate things? There is no warrant for supposing that they are conscious or have feelings or thoughts. Either they attribute nothing, or attribution is ontological, whether or not it is epistemological as well.

Why suppose that a negating, even if it be ontological and terminates in objective content, makes the slightest difference to what is there? Does not the most insistent negating leave everything as it was before, unchanged, acting as it always did? An affirmative answer would require a grounding in the supposition that there is an objective world with self-enclosed items, and that a negating must stop short of them. It does, of course, stop short of the full reality of what is there. But if it did not lay hold of any of the reality, the negating would not terminate but merely come to an end. It would be constitutive of its content, making it into just an intentional object.

Were there only one reality, there would be no negating. But then there would be no one to know it. Or he who knew it would be that reality. He would then be indistinguishable from the entire universe and, of course, would never be in error. Either there is a plurality, and the items in it are necessarily connected by negations, or there is just one unknown reality. If there are a number of entities in the universe, whether conscious or not, they must be related by the relation other-than. Whether this be taken to be the product of a juncture of opposing negatings, or the opposing negations are treated as abstractions from this, the negatings will reach at least as far as any other connection does. The conclusion will leave one with a feeling of something amiss as long as the negated content is treated as though it were divided off and then repossessed by entity to which it belonged. But just as it is unnecessary to suppose that the weight that is consciously attributed to a man is either projected outward from a mind or is somehow torn away from him only to be given back to him in a judgment, so it is unnecessary to suppose that a negating is a purely mental act or that it breaks an item into pieces. Your weight is oriented in you in one way and toward me in another; I know it when I face it as part of you, maintained apart from me. Similarly, my negating ends with content that is at once relative to that negating and is part of what is beyond the negating.

5.8. What is negated may be completive.

Content negated is free of the negating just so far as it is integral to a reality beyond the terminus of the negating act. Though I am not able to do anything with the negated content unless I am able to have it on my own terms, I am sometimes able to lay hold of the possessor of what I terminate at, and thereby am able to reach content unavailable to me through the negating. I do this by eating, through work, and in art. And I can also join with a they to constitute a single we, and thereby share in a common nature with the others. But I need not go so far. Instead, and even as a preliminary act, I am able not only to terminate in what is other than myself but to claim it. My negating becomes a means by which I continue into what is beyond, and the negated content is accepted as that which belongs to me. I then not only arrive at the terminus of an initial thrust outward, and thereby end with a negated content, but do not stop insisting.

I could simply face the content as a terminus which is part of an independent reality. If I did, I would be deprived of it by that reality, and lose what I claim is mine. It might be good for me to give up what is claimed by me. It might be better for others, or for all of us together, if I do not claim it. But as claimed, it is completive of me, what I must make part of myself to be myself in myself fully. If it is inappropriate in its present guise, it will have to be transformed in being possessed and internalized.

Negated content terminates a negating at the same time that it is part of some other reality. As at the end of the negating, it is faced as a lack, that which is present for a claim but not yet present to the claimant in a required way. In bringing the negating to an end, the content is not yet distinguished from the reality of which it is a part, having the status only of a that-which-is-lacking, something to be possessed by the individual who provides the negating.

A man lays native claim to what is needed for his completion. As a consequence, unless he could join with it or make it part of himself, he will face what both makes and keeps him incomplete. His claims connect him to what is lacking; could it be possessed, it would complete him by becoming part of him, the source of the negating. Assignments and obligations start from the other end, with what is to be realized. They define him as incomplete, just so far as he is apart from them. But no matter at which end one begins, power must be used to make the end be that which in fact completes.

Because the others are grounded in an independent they, the others can never be fully possessed. I lay claim to them as what I need but never can have. They are completive in principle, but not in fact. And when I attend to them, severally or collectively, I see that I am what they require for their completion. If I could satisfy their claims on me I would become what they required. Conversely, if they could satisfy the claims I make on them, they would become what I require. But though each of us can make some use of what is available, each continues to remain apart and therefore to lack what must be had if it is to be complete.

Though I am never able to complete myself, I am able to benefit from the accomplishments and support of others. Success requires that we function both as distinct units and as interrelated. If I and all others could act in perfect consonance, we would strengthen one another and share in what we together make possible. Such an ideal joint achievement offers a measure in terms of which our actions and interactions can be judged, redirected, and improved.

They has an unlimited range, able to encompass everything not myself. They make evident that my lacks are great and cannot be made good. As a consequence, I tend to emphasize not my claims but theirs, and to see myself falling far short of what I should be. And when I translate what they are into what I suppose they believe, think, or judge, I see myself as insignificant.

5.9. A negating may terminate at a distance.

To take a stand here is to negate another here, making it into a there for this here. The others are there. Sometimes, though, we speak of them as being here, related with us to a common there. But even then, while they are here with us, they are in that here away from us; they are there relative to our here, within a common here.

Because what is negated is at another here, its acknowledgment involves the at least tacit acknowledgment of this here as a there for it. The two are related; a negation going from one to the other is matched by a negation going in the opposite direction. To maintain this, of course, is to take the negatings to have real termini. Such a view goes counter to some accepted ways of looking at negating. One is supposed to reach content before it is negated and just change its status. When negating is given the role of a relation, it is then taken to connect items in abstraction from some supposed positive relation connecting them. The relational complex, (p)–(q) is made to ride on the surface of pRq. But negation is an instance of R.

The present view also goes counter to the usual ways of viewing occupied space as a sheer extendedness, a homogeneous continuum in which nothing opposes anything else, containing no heres and theres. On such a view, here and there are just abstracted termini set in opposition to one another. But though mere space contains no here or there, occupied space does. While remaining single and undivided, it has many distinguished locations, one of which is here where I am, a region of space which I for the moment occupy and bound. Relative to that, every other distinguishable part of space, occupied or not, is there.

Wherever anything is, is a here. Everywhere distant from this has the status of a there for it. Each occupied region is here in relation to many theres; each is a there because of its relation to that here. Neither the here nor the there can be credited to an occupying object for three reasons: Firstly, here and there mark off the spatial regions and not occupying objects; secondly, nothing at all may be there, and yet the there is as effectively negated by an occupant here as it would be were something occupying it; and thirdly, what is here is, from the position of some other here, also there. The occupation of a region of space holds the region apart without tearing it away from the rest of space, maintaining it in opposition to other distinguished regions.

References to a there must always stop short of its occupant, since the act of occupying makes that region of space into a here. Since the occupying of each region suffices to make it into the here of its occupant, the here is not relative to another. And because each actuality occupies space independently of the others, an oppositionality occurs not only between what is here and what is there but among the different heres, each integral to a distinct occupant.

Each region is here for many different theres. Each is there for many different heres. Each is occupied as a here maintained in opposition to heres distant from it in space. Each is distanced from other regions of space as a here relative to a there, and as a there relative to a here, at the same time that it is an unrelativized here possessed by its occupant.

The others are there in relation to my here. I am not related to them as there, except so far as those others are the surface of a they that in fact occupies a region of space. When I say "They are there," I refer to them as being in a here in the same way that I am here.

A spatial distance is doubly negating, terminating in different spatial positions. One of these at least is occupied, while the rest are occupiable. An occupant of any position possesses it as its here, for which every other distinguished region is a there, at the same time that it makes a there available for the heres of every other. I, here, am there in opposition to the they of those others. They, in turn, are there, relative to me, each member having the status of an occupant maintaining itself at a distinctive here relative to theres spatially distant from it.

5.10. A negating may have a temporal role.

I am not a griffin, a woman, in China, a baby, or dead, for different reasons and in different ways. I am not a griffin because
I could not be one; it is a fictitious creature, having no place in
this world, past, present, or future. I am not a woman because
my being a man excludes that status and nature for me,
though it is characteristic of many others. I am not in China;
but though I am now in Washington and therefore could not
now be in China, I could have been there and I might be there
sometime in the future. I am not a baby although I once was
one; at least part of what I was like and what I did then has
some bearing on what I now am and do. I am not dead,
though this I surely will be. All these are at present excluded;
they do not and cannot pertain to me now. They are not simply excluded by my nature; such an exclusion would be
merely formal or logical, making no provision for the fact that
I exist and am a man, that I might have been and could later be
in China, that I had been a baby, and that I will die.

I am now in the process of making determinate some possible characterizations of me—or, alternatively (to avoid, for
the moment, what some suppose to be an undesirable reference to possibilities, and what others take to be a set of determinate eternal objects), I am now in the process of producing
or exhibiting certain features. From either position, the act in
which I now engage is one in which an initial indeterminate,
"being a man," "living in Washington," etc., is distinguished
from a terminal specialization where it is made determinate.
I am now in the process of producing the determinations.
Other determinations might conceivably have been brought
about instead. Whatever ones are produced leave over an
area of indetermination to which I may refer as containing
alternatives to what was in fact realized. When I make myself be one who is now standing somewhat aslant, with one
foot forward, peering at a book, I specialize an indeterminate
man and an indeterminate standing. When I make myself sit
erect with ankles crossed, I specialize the indeterminate man I

had specialized before, as well as an indeterminate sitting. When I say that I might have run instead, I refer to an indeterminate running, and imagine a determination of it, or I set it alongside a standing or sitting—the one when I take the running itself to require determination, the other when I take running, standing, and sitting all to be determinations of a more inclusive indeterminate.

My production of a determination involves the exclusion both of alternative determinations of an indeterminate, as well as what cannot be a determination of it. My being a woman is excluded by the indeterminate man that I make determinate at every moment. My being in China is excluded by the alternative specialization, being in Washington. My being a baby is excluded because it is already determinate, and my being dead is excluded by what is now determinate. The latter two are time-bound. I now exclude my being a baby, since I am now making myself determinate as an adult. My being an adult requires that my being a baby be in the past, since this is the domain of facts, of what has been made completely determinate, incapable of being altered in any particular. I also now exclude my being dead, since I am now alive. My being dead is what I do not now make determinate. But I could make it determinate, and it will surely be made determinate at some future time.

My being a live adult, because it is made determinate now, excludes my being a baby in one way and my being dead in another. Those exclusions are mediated by the live adult which I am now making determinate. They are overlaid and are intensified by other exclusions which a live adult involves. The present impossibility of my making determinate either the already determinate factuality of being a baby and the still indeterminate possible death makes them temporally related to the present in which I provide determinations for my being a live adult. I cannot, of course, reach into the actual past now or now be in the unrealized future. The past is forever gone. I cannot make the slightest difference to it; it is completely determinate, allowing for no addition—which is what my contact with it would involve. The future is not yet; it is inescapably indeterminate. Since I exclude both my now being a baby and my now being dead by means of the determinations that I now provide, it is indifferent whether I say that my being a baby and my being dead are in the past and future of my being a present adult, or that they are excluded by what I now make determinate, particularly since the determinations require not only that my being a baby now and my being dead now be excluded but that these be past and future.

Just as my being a live adult is incompatible with my now being dead, so the others in the present exclude and are excluded by what is in their past and future. Past others are determinates, and future others are indeterminates excluded by what is now determinate or is now being made determinate. The one had and the other might have a supporting they. To speak of "the others who have gone before" is to refer to others who had but now lack a they; to speak of "the others who will come later" is to refer to others who are to be backed by a they. If I do not know whether the others are past, present, or future, I do not know whether or not the others were determinate, are in the process of being made determinate, or might acquire determinations. In any case, those others, who are now being made determinate, make it possible for what is in the determinate past and in the indeterminate future to be set in the past and the future of a they.

Since there are others only relative to something else, the others which are now, it would seem, are just a they approached from the outside. Were this so, one would have to deny that they could be related and be relative to oneself, or that such relating and relativization held of what was there in fact. A similar denial would be in order with reference to what is faced as a you, making the you be irrelevant to another actual man. There would then be no one able to be self-conscious, able to take the position of another and face himself from the other's position.

Since what is relativized has no standing of its own and could not be credited with the power to make the others, or anything else, determinate, it would seem that 'they' would provide just another way of referring to what is referred to by 'the others', the only difference between them apparently being that the first emphasizes what possesses, while the second emphasizes what is being approached from an external position. The difficulty is mainly verbal. Instead of speaking of the others, and of a they which sustains them, one could speak of a sustained they-or-the-others. One would then be able to say that what, from an external position, is a they-or-the-others, is an us for itself.

A new difficulty now arises: There would seem to be no they, any more than there could be a we, which was past or future. Yet it makes sense to say of the Nazis that "They lost the war," and of those in the next century that "They will have to make their own laws." It also makes sense to say "We did it this way last week" and "We will do this tomorrow." Both the 'they' and the 'we' in these cases refer to what has no power to introduce determinations. Like my being a baby or dead now, the they and the we are already determinate, or are to be made determinate. Both refer to what either had governed complexes in the past, or bounds what is precluded from being completely determinate at this time.

5.11. A negating may have a causal role.

A cause and its effect are separated by a negating. That negating has a temporal stretch. Otherwise, the effect would be copresent with the cause, and its effect would be copresent with its effect, and so on and on, with the result that the entire history of the universe would be copresent with any actual or arbitrarily chosen beginning.

The distance between cause and effect requires that when the cause of that effect is present, the produced effect is not, and when the effect of that cause is present, the cause which it replaces is not. Yet cause and effect are necessarily related; 'cause' is correlative with 'effect'. A cause without an effect is no cause; an effect without a cause is no effect. The apparent paradox is overcome, we have seen, with the recognition that a cause necessitates not a real but only a possible effect, and that an effect takes place only after a process of actualization converts a possible into an actual effect. The separation between actual cause and possible effect is vitalized and specified in the process of passing from antecedent cause to consequent effect. That effect occurs at a present moment replacing the moment in which the cause had occurred.

I am a cause. I also am an effect. As the one I am at the origin of dynamic acts by means of which possible effects are turned into actual effects; as the other, I am the outcome of a dynamic causal act. The others are effects too. But, since they are without power, unable to originate any acts, they cannot also be causes, except so far as they are part of a they.

Actual effects are possible effects made determinate. Consequently, when the others have the roles of effects they must have been made determinate by a process of causation which ends at them. Since as just possible effects, the others are not yet available for determination by a they, the process of causation must make those possible effects available for determination by a they at the same time that those effects are being made into determinate outcomes of that causal process.

Though a cause does not have an actual effect except at a subsequent time, and though the effect is the effect of that cause, the cause is not affected. If it were, determination would work backward in time. Still, we attribute to what had been the consequences of some of the activities which begin at them. When I throw a stone I function as a cause. I am fully determinate as just that cause, initiating just that act. If the stone hits another, it does so at a time after I had already become a fully determinate cause of the throw. If the hitting is to be attributed to me, it must be to me as originating it. Does this not require a move into past time? I think not. My accountability here depends on my responsible initiating of the act. That responsibility, if it is to be attributed by moving backward from effect to cause, will require a reference to the originator of the act, and not merely to a point of origin for it. I was responsible when I initiated the act that I intended; the outcome, when traced back to my intending, adds nothing to it. If I outlast the moment, I continue to be responsible, for I am selfsame over time. I accept what is past as having a determinateness which I responsibly produced, acknowledging it not only to be past but to be in *my* past.

5.12. A negating involves an assessment.

I always take myself to have some value. Normally, that value is positive. But it could be negative, setting me well below the level of other men. What I am unable to do is to credit myself with no value whatsoever, positive or negative. In the very act of maintaining myself I negate what is beyond me, and in that negating give myself a value relative to its value. This does not stop me, when I come to judge myself in my full concreteness, from crediting myself with a value which is the value that I in fact have.

When I say "those, not these," I refer to a definite set of men, marked off from others. When, instead, I say, "the others, not these," I leave somewhat indefinite to whom I am referring. That indefiniteness precludes the others from having the exact value that a they can have. The value I assign to the others in the very act of negating, and this without any deliberation or even consciousness, may still be the very value which I assign to the they to which those others belong.

To move from they to the others is to move from definiteness to indefiniteness, depth to surface, from a specific value to a general which can be limited and thereby specified in many different ways, depending on what is allowed to be within its range. Those others may include everything other than myself. Despite their dependent nature, their indefinite range, their inability to have the value of their sustaining they, the others may therefore loom large, even ominously. Throughout my life I face the others as possessing a great positive or negative value compared with my own.

The others are relative to what is beyond them on the one side, and to what sustains them on the other. The results may be quite disparate. The values that the others have in relation to me are not necessarily those that the others have for the they of which the others are the surface. I cannot misconstrue the values that the others have in relation to me, since these are constituted in the very act of my reaching them through a negating. Nor can the they of which the others are a part distort the values that these others have for them, since the values are constituted in the very act by which those others are possessed by the they. Yet I and they can both be charged with misconstruing the values of the others, for the values each constitutes may fail to correspond to the promise for good or ill that can be brought about. For me to take the others to have little value in relation to myself when the others have great value for their they is to fall short of what the others objectively are; for the they to take the others to have little value in relation to that they when the others have great value for me is to fall short of what those others are my world.

5.13 The sustained others are formidable.

The others are sustained by a they. Unlike the they, the others are relative to what is beyond them, are without causal power, and are made determinate by powers beyond their control. Nevertheless, the others loom large, surrounding me by what is at least alien, may well be hostile, surely is insistent, and when beneficial is so on its own terms and in its own way. Instead of starting with an I or a they, or even with a me or a you, an account of what is has warrant, therefore, for starting with the others, and even for explaining all else in terms of them.

One aim of scientific inquiry is to escape from subjectivity and to look even at oneself as though one were just a unit

among others. Everything is to be described and understood
in neutral terms applicable to what exists as it stands away
from the investigator, free from any bearing on him or of him
on them. The others, instead of being measured, or held to be
sustained, or made determinate by something more real, are
to be taken to be the measure, base, and possessors of all else.
This aim can be understood in a number of ways: a) It may be
taken to give an objective account of what is the case. But that
would allow one to concentrate just on a they. Yet a they is
limited in the way in which the others are not, for while
the others may include my body—indeed, everything except
my privacy and its condensations—a they stands in contrast
with my body as well as with my privacy and its divisions.
b) The aim can be taken to require a reference to each existent
item, demanding that it be dealt with as it is. Of course, no
one, not even all of mankind, is able to attend to every item
whatsoever. Nor would it be desirable. We learn a great deal
about the chemistry of copper by studying one piece of copper; nothing is gained by looking at more, even though it may
be worthwhile, as a check, or to avoid overlooking important
variants, to look at more than one or at more than a limited
number of pieces. c) The aim can be taken to require a reference to the others within a common space, time, and dynamism, subject to common conditions and objective laws. This,
I think, is what is usually intended. It does not, though, take
account of the fact that some of the others are parts of wholes
where they maintain themselves and where they are individually subject to common conditions. So far as each is just an
instance or locus for the same conditions, its differences from
other parts are to be dealt with as irrelevant, subjectively
imposed, or as being fully explicable by some complication of
the laws that prevail. Individual insistencies, their reality,
their present existence, as well as their ability to interact with
conditions, will be ignored. Their subjection to the conditions, however, does not mean that any one item can be
substituted for any other, or that it is completely indifferent to
the presence of the rest, nor does it require the denial that

there are dimensions to each which are beyond the reach of a purely objective, universally formulatable account.

They act regardless of what I desire or know. Objectively operating under impersonal, universal conditions, they are not disturbed by my desires, passions, or interests. In their own way, and on their own terms, they satisfy or injure regardless of what I think or wish. More important, they cohere, are interrelated, and function together with insistence and power. Together, they make up a single world of nature, within which whatever could in principle be observed by anyone and could be stated in universally applicable terms is to be found. Nothing is excluded except the purely private, the unintelligible, the merely felt, the false, the muddled, the fictional, the singular, and the personal—what is outside the provenances of implacable, universal laws. It, therefore, includes this as well as every other palpable publicly reachable body.

There are some who hold that the others form a single block, a single extended realm of energy, with a dignity of its own. Some, instead, take it to be made up of small packets, each functioning in considerable independence of the rest, within which there are multiple, independent, irreducible particles acting at random. And some take it to be self-creative, unifying what had been, to make a single unitary whole which immediately gives way to a radical multiplicity of items, and this to another single whole, and so on. Whatever the interpretation, they are acknowledged to be together and thereby to constitute one or a number of wholes within which smaller units occur or can be distinguished. From this position, no account is taken of any I, but only of you's and they's, and then as isolatable within larger wholes, where they are subject to the pressures and influences of the rest.

One holding this view need not claim that there is no I, but only that what this is and does is not relevant to what is being acknowledged. The denial that there is an I entrains the embarrassment that it is made by an I and was offered to other men for private acceptance. So far as the denial could be maintained, what is would no longer be properly referred to by 'they' or 'the others', but only as 'a world', somehow set in contradistinction to oneself.

Did I not have a mind which can formally express the conditions that govern all, I would not be able to know what is true of all. To be able to characterize what is objectively the case and, at the same time, to free it from subjective additions, the structure of my knowledge must answer to the conditions that prevail. Only then will I be able to stand away from the structure and, thereupon, be able to understand it as constituting an objective state of affairs, not relativized or qualified through the introduction of subjective factors.

When I take a stand at myself, I need not position myself at a private center. I can adopt the position of my physical body, my biological body, my human body, or my lived body. The first occupies space; the second is alive, a unit in a species; the third is affected by my emotions, desires, and assessments; the fourth is myself incarnate. Whichever it be, inevitably, apart from all knowledge, what else is present will be faced as relative to that standpoint. Knowledge overrides that relative status by making use of objectively viable, constant conditions.

As relative to my physical or biological body, the other bodies make up an objective set of items which, with that body, are subject to common cosmic or more limited but still quite general conditions. Relative to my human body, with its distinctive kinds of abilities, the other bodies have the double status of making up a single block of items, and of being humanized relative to what my body does and needs. Among them there may be other bodies which are humanized, but as part of a single block of others, they are not separated out. When I do distinguish them, those humanized bodies will make up or be part of a they or, if I join them, a we. The other bodies, together with my humanized body, also make up a depersonalized world which is both distinct from and relative to my lived body, a body which I privately sustain and use in an unduplicable way. Among those others there will be some lived bodies which, as separated out, will make up another they or, if I join them, another we. Finally, the other bodies, together with my lived body, make up an external world having no regard for what I privately am, need, or desire. Among them, there may be some which have similar privacies, but I do not distinguish these unless I am concerned with a you, a they, or another we. In all these cases, the others are sustained apart from, at the same time that they have a status relative to myself. So far as they are sustained, the others are formidable, able to hobble my acts and preclude my continuance.

5.14. My lived body is overwhelmed by all the other bodies.

The thesis that my body is in the cosmos is maintained by materialism, and by physics and chemistry. It is strongly opposed, and even rejected by existentialists and sometimes, too, by ordinary men, perhaps on the mistaken ground that the thesis requires the denial that I do not have a privacy or that I do not affect my body from within. That denial is not required. When I fall from a height, I, while falling in accord with the laws of an impersonal nature, am fearful of being hurt. If what is intended is, instead, simply the denial that a man is merely a body within a cosmos where it is governed with all the rest in common ways, or that when subject to a humanizing or a living, it is no longer just a unit in the cosmos, the opposition is surely justified. A lived body has a private ground as well as a distinctive nature and career and, together with all other bodies, is subject to cosmic and other conditions. It forms close bonds with some; it is united with this or that and with all the rest in many ways, with one dominant at one time and not at another. Its career in a larger world affects what else I can do.

My body, even if mistakenly taken to be just physical or

chemical in nature, is no mere aggregate of ultimate particles or of packets of these. It has its own unity. Even when the ultimate particles or packets act independently of one another, or only in relationship to one another under the governance of common laws, they are together in limited ways within larger compounds. When my body moves, it is limited by what it contains, while what is there is made to go in directions and at a pace which is dictated by that body when it functions as a unit.

My body is attracted and repelled by other bodies in various degrees and ways. Some of these are more congenial, some more threatening, some more alien, some more satisfying, some more familiar than the rest. It coheres more with some than with other bodies, both because of its constitution and because of what it undergoes. Behaviorists rightly, therefore, speak of rewards and punishments and not simply of increases and decreases in magnitude or energy—though there are, as we have seen, distinctive problems implicated in the idea of providing rewards and punishments at the end of an activity, which somehow are to affect how another activity begins or continues.

The connection that my lived body has with other bodies, whether it be the same toward a number or different in every case, and whether it be the same as that which they have to one another or different from this entirely, enables them together to constitute a single set of items which affect that body in a way and to a degree that it cannot affect them. They are connected as congenial, antagonistic, supplementary, or incompatible, in considerable independence of where I am, where each one of them is, or what I or it may need for its continuance or prosperity.

There is no necessary loss in objectivity in the acknowledgment that my lived body is involved with whatever else there is in a way no other body is, for the acknowledgment does not preclude the operation of common conditions on all —an operation which can be differential as well as monotonous. As a full-fledged member of the cosmos together with all the rest, my body is subject to the same conditions that govern other bodies. It is repelled and attracted by them as together to a degree that they are not repelled and attracted by it. Each of the other bodies, of course, is also faced by the formidable presence of all the rest, including my body. Taken in their severalty, each coheres with but at the same time is severely limited by all the rest as constituting one set of items. At the same time every body is within a single cosmos, each is both privately sustained and affected by the overwhelming presence of the rest.

5.15. There is no totality in which my body is a separate unit.

No matter how weak my body is, or how tightly interrelated with the other bodies, it is a distinct unit. The fact does not require the denial of the truth that there are many parts to that body, some of which function in considerable independence of what it is and does. My body is also such a unit when it is together with the others. Were it solely by itself, it would be incomparable, radically alone. While independent of them, it is together with them. Yet they are with one another in a way it is not with them. My body, at the same time that it is with the rest, is challenged by all the other bodies together to a degree it cannot challenge them.

Existentialists tend to exaggerate the degree to which a man lives in an alien world. He, they think, is all vitality, spontaneity, freedom, and concern, while everything else is dead, passive, ruled by implacable laws. They overlook the fact that a man's body is a distinct unit, and that while it is faced with a multiplicity of items that are together with one another in a way that they are not together with it, it is subject to the same universal laws and conditions. There is a world alien to my body, not because this body is mine, human, or lived, but simply because it is a single unit faced by the rest of them together. Starting with that fact, this body could be said to be involved in a cosmos in which it is never fully at home. In this way, though, one not only ignores the truth that nobody, alive or dead, active or inert, useful or useless is ever fully part of the cosmos, but one affirms the opposite of what in fact is the case. My body, though not with the others as they are now together with one another, is with each of them as fully as each is with it or with any other. Just so far as any is a real unit, the remainder have the status of its sustained others, necessarily together with one another in a way it cannot be with them.

The *cosmos* includes all bodies as at once separate and governed by common conditions. To have entities be together in the cosmos, there must be powers governing them all, not constituted by them. A Spinozistic *natura naturata*, a cosmos, requires for its presence and understanding at least one *natura naturans* able to keep items together. Neither is identifiable with an absolute, at once concrete and indivisible.

The *totality* of all bodies abstracts from them as separate units, to have them as just together. By being with one another, the bodies form a single totality. That totality, the same from every position, with all items just together, is where none can be wholly apart. So far as anyone is apart, it faces the rest as together with one another. Could one think of any as entirely separate from all the others, one would have thereby made the totality vanish and, with it, the possibility of having them all together. The reality of separate units necessitates that there be no single state of affairs in which all are just with one another in a single totality.

5.16. The explanation of what a body does lies outside it.

One aim of cosmological science is to find a rationale pervading the universe. The laws of which it speaks today are tentative formulations of a hoped-for ultimate rationale. Taken not as they in fact apply to what occurs but as mathematically expressed structures, the present formulations offer a means for translating every occurrence into every other. Where the ordinary man says that water freezes when it is cold, and where a young student says that it freezes at zero centigrade, a physicist provides a formula which accounts for the freezing at any degree, since it provides for the pressure that is functionally related to this. If the rationale that is being offered be supposed to be confined to the formula, what will be offered will be hypotheses and ways of classifying, not accounts of what occurs in fact. But unless what is said is these are arbitrary and beyond assessment except on the grounds of convenience and elegance, it will present the structure of things, and report the ways in which items are transformable into one another.

My body, as part of a cosmos of bodies, is to be understood in the same neutral terms that are applicable to any other body. Ideally, it should be theoretically possible to transform it into any other, since it presumably differs from the rest only in magnitude, energy, mass, composition, location, and the like. An explanation of what it is, does, and may do will, from that position, take it to be a complex related to other bodies, themselves intelligibly related to it and to one another. No account will so far be given of the distribution of the bodies, and no reference will be made to privacies or to any condition that determines the manner in which they function separately or together.

Since an explanation of all bodies from an absolutely neutral standpoint abstracts from their actual presence in the cosmos, to consider them as making up a totality it should, at the very least, be supplemented by an explanation which is interlocked with the bodies in the form of an organization determining how they are to function together. If those bodies are ultimate particles, all alike, their distribution will help determine what occurs, but the functioning of items more complex than these cannot be understood without taking account of their distinctive powers as well, controlling what is within their confines.

My body, like every other, is a unit within the cosmos. The organization of that cosmos affects the functioning of what is within it. The organization of my body, similarly, affects the functioning of its parts. Those parts are also units within the cosmos. An account of them will be incorrect if it overlooks either the difference that my body makes to them or what they are able to be and do within the cosmos. My heart is to be understood as subject to my body, at the same time that it is to be understood in relation to what is outside that body. And what is true of my heart is true of what it encompasses.

The explanatory value of the conditions governing the cosmos is relevant to all items, whether these be ultimate, irreducible particles, complex organisms, or parts of these. Since the functioning of the parts within the confines of organisms is to be explained in part by the manner in which those parts are related to everything else, an organism can provide only a partial explanation of what takes place within it.

What my body does, depends largely on how the various items within it function as units in the cosmos and on the manner they directly affect one another. The organization provided by my body usually makes comparatively little difference. I also affect it privately, but rarely to a high degree. Vitalism is neither supported nor precluded by this fact—not supported, for what is true of an organic complex body is true of all complexes, since these too provide some explanation for what is within them; and not precluded, for the kind of organization that is provided by a lived or even just a living body has a distinctive quality, origin, and role. If vitalism is to remain within the frame of a scientific naturalism, it must attend to only some bodies, grant that these could provide only a limited explanation for some of the occurrences within them, and concede that a nonvitalistic account may adequately deal with all bodies as in one cosmos.

5.17. The location of a body is mainly determined by other bodies.

My body is here. From its position, all others are there. Each of the others, also, is in its own distinctive here, and from its position this body, as well as every other, is there in relation to it. No matter how feeble or small, each is in a here on its own, and makes every other be there relative to it.

Space is neutral to, indifferent to its occupants. Each body occupies it on its own terms, maintaining itself in opposition to all the others. Each, too, is related to all the others across that space in such a way as to give that space a geometry whose properties are dependent on how bodies occupy it and are thereby related in it. When a body is distinguished among all the bodies in space, it continues to be where it was, continues to be related as it had been, and continues to be bounded off from all the rest. None can occupy the place it does except by suffusing it or filling it out. But a body can be displaced, forced out of its present position by others. Since no single body can withstand all the other bodies, the place it occupies is occupied only on sufferance. Many together can displace it, while it can have little effect on them. The other bodies make up a contoured spatial whole of occupants on which one body can have little effect, while they constitute a perpetual threat to its remaining where it is.

The space this body occupies is persistently and insistently threatened and sometimes challenged by the other bodies. As a consequence, this body's occupation of a particular region of space is precarious. To be sure, so long as it is, it will occupy some place, but it will never be able to make this entirely its own from which it can never be removed. No one of the other bodies, of course, is in a better state. But together they constitute a single occupied contoured space; this, unlike the whole of space in relation to any possible occupant, does not provide an opening for my body. My body's occupied place is symmetrically related to all the other occupied places, but, so far as all the other bodies together constitute a single space, they determine where it will be. Despite the fact that every there is relative to a here, it is the other bodies as there, consequently, that mainly dictate where and how my body can be in a single space together with them. Were all in a single file, any distinguished one would, without losing its place in it, be envisaged as outside the file and simply distanced from the rest. They would be together in a serial order into which, as so distinguished, it did not enter. The situation is not a function of some interest on the part of an observer. Each occupant of a place is separate from all other bodies and, as so separate, faces them as interrelated in a contoured space from which it is excluded.

5.18. The present of a body is distinct from the present of all the other bodies.

The knowledge that physics obtains about distant objects is mediated by light signals. These are understood to move through space at a well-defined pace, arriving at distant places at a later time. The signals are taken to report what had happened earlier and at the point from which their journey was presumably begun. As we have seen, there are many suppositions wrapped up in this view, not the least of which is the unverifiable dogma (as was long ago remarked by Percy Bridgman) that light signals actually travel from place to place, though all that can be observed are discontinuously lighted places. It is also assumed that what is observable at one place is what had occurred earlier at another. These assumptions are perhaps unavoidable at the present stage of scientific theory and inquiry. If they are part of the needed apparatus which is now enabling disciplined inquirers to achieve important theoretical and practical results, criticism of them can be anticipatory at best and obstructionistic at worst, so far as those who are thinking and working within the frame of a common mode of inquiry are concerned. But philosophy owes allegiance to no other discipline. It has neither the need nor the right to accept any other or its assumptions as basic and unquestionable. One of its tasks is to try to get to what is so, regardless of the needs of any other inquiry, and to pursue and accept entailed consequences no matter how dissonant they may be with current views. The failure to remember that fact has trapped distinguished thinkers of earlier eras within the now discarded perspectives of the mathematicians, astronomers, physicists, and biologists of their day.

What is, is in the present. When that moment gives way to the next, whatever continues to be, no matter what its nature, pace, or place, will be present together with whatever else there is. None will lag behind, none will rush ahead; all that continue will be in the next present moment together. Yet this body, though in the same present and in the same succession of presents as any other, will, without losing its temporal conjunction with them, have its own distinguished present moment. It is present here. Where it is, is when it is. It is now here, and here now, with its own stretch, and with its own way of being related to its own past and future.

Together, the other bodies occupy present moment after present moment just as surely as each of them does. What is distinguished from the rest is at a present moment coordinate with theirs. Otherwise, it would not be distinguished within the same cosmos in which they are. If one were to follow Whitehead's lead and suppose that each individual actual occasion is completely in its own present, making use of what the rest of the world makes available in the past, one must, with him, not simply distinguish each occasion from the rest but take it to stand away from them as subject from object, knower from data. What is copresent, on such a view, though not known or knowable, will nevertheless be taken to keep apace with what is completely cut off from it. So far as it could tell, it might be all alone. But one can know that he is not alone in his present, since it is a delimited portion of a larger, common present, encompassing his and others', qualifying and being qualified by them. Only if he had no accidental features due to them, only if he was in an absolutely empty space, only if he encountered no obstacles, could there be any question as to whether or not he was all alone.

My body as lived and I are also in present moments. These are distinct from, but are privately bounded off, from the present of all the bodies together in the cosmos, as well as from the present of biological bodies. Historic events, society, state, and civilization; stories, dances, poems, plays, and musical pieces also have presents of their own. These, too, are bounded off from the present of the items in the cosmos. All introduce distinctions in that common present, incorporating these in distinctive ways to produce their own presents of different lengths and tonalities.

5.19. The causes of this body are others now past.

This body is an effect of what had been, and in turn is a cause of what will be later. Some things have a great effect on it, and it has a great effect on some others. Though following on what occurs in the moment that precedes this, it has many causes at different moments in the past.

Many of the things which will take place at the next moment have remote causes mediated by what now is. The acknowledgment of that fact enables one to join with current physicists in their rejection of the purely mechanistic, deterministic universe of Laplace, but for different reasons. They reject it because it fails to do justice to quanta phenomena. The view they now seem to accept could be taken to allow that all the causes of what is present are in the moment just preceding it. That supposition is avoided with the recognition that causal processes in the cosmos may, like an assassination, stretch over many temporally related occurrences.

Whether or not the causes of this body be taken to be in the preceding moment or at different past moments, this body's present state is the outcome of a great number. These could conceivably have acted with some spontaneity, and they could conceivably originate processes which terminate just at this body, or at it and others. And all could be accompanied by constitutive causes which do not operate in time at all but, instead, unite an interval of time with a number of actualities.

As now together with other bodies, this body is one of a number of effects, all having causes in the past. Those causes are other than it. Otherwise, it might conceivably cause itself and thereby somehow be both earlier and later than itself or, like a self-creating God, make its own existence issue from its own essence. Because it owes its presence and nature to what is in the past and not to any item in the present, it is causally indifferent to, but not necessarily disconnected from, what else is in that present.

Since causation does involve a temporal stretch between past and present, were knowledge a causal product it would now be possible to reinstate the previously rejected view that one knows nothing that is in the present and only of what has already passed away. With better warrant, though, one can also say that since we know some things that are copresent, we therefore know that knowledge is not a causal product. Of course, it has its causes. But some of these are constitutive and not antecedent, and some of those which are antecedent provide only an occasion for a self to function.

This body faces present bodies which are now related to it in noncausal ways. As we have seen, it is also affiliated with them, and they with one another in different degrees. The other bodies are formidable as realities in space and time. But they are not now causally formidable for it, though together they did and will provide a set of causes which determine its course and destiny.

Every body exhibits spontaneities and freedom. The actions of none are entirely predictable. A process of causation is finite and occurs only once; it has a concreteness and development which can be fully known only after it has occurred. Nothing that anyone now does can make the slightest difference to the actions of what was at the beginning of a process of causation that ends at it, or to the action of contemporaries which are at the beginning of processes of causation which will, at some subsequent moment, end at it. But each entity has noncausal connections with its contemporaries and these may make a difference to what sooner or later might be.

Underlying this discussion is an acceptance of three truths about the perceived that seem to be incompatible: 1) What is perceived is in the present, for we are unable to look backward or forward in time. 2) Appearances are not detached from realities; if they were, there would be no passage from the one to the other, and therefore no accounting for the presence of the appearances or our ability to understand realities by means of them. 3) Physical occurrences provide preconditions for perception.

The three can be reconciled by taking a perceived object— the flaming sun for example—to be the origin of light waves which impinge on us, while holding that their travel takes place in their own time and space. The waves are at the sun and the perceiver, but do not move from the former to the latter. They are set in a frame which requires only that the sun be distanced considerably from the perceiver. That distance has its measures, but they are not like what occurs in a society. It is not a distance traversed or traversable; it just separates different items.

5.20. The value of my body is insignificant in comparison with the value of all the other bodies.

There is a good reason and a bad for maintaining that the world of bodies, all subject to the same conditions, is devoid of value. Magnitudes, endurance, energy, and similar aspects of bodies have no apparent bearing on value. But it does not follow from this that the bodies are valueless. In fact, so long as the bodies are unified and complex, they not only have values but have subordinated, ordered, and therefore objectively assessed parts. They also have different positions in the value hierarchies that men forge. Their values there vary considerably from the values that they in fact have, for men order the bodies in terms of their possible benefit or injury to them, or by the degree to which they are like men in appearance, function, and power.

Could any body have more value than all the other bodies together? Two quite different answers are possible:

a) Only as distinguished from this body, do the other bodies have a single summed value. The answer entrains an anomaly: Were this body no longer, the rest would have no value.

b) Unity, like other primary conditions, is all-pervasive. It operates on all, on limited groups, and on single complexes. Everywhere it is a source of value, the degree varying in accord with their consonance with it. The more they are like a comprehensive unity, the greater their value. This body has little value compared with the value of all the other bodies together.

Something like this alternative is tacitly assumed in the teleological argument for the existence of God. Putting aside the questionable and unnecessary assumption that ours is a well-ordered universe, that it shows evidence of a grand design, or that whatever order it has must have been purposively introduced, the teleological argument has the merit of affirming that the cosmos has a single value so great that it cannot be accounted for except by grounding it in a final reality. That conclusion, though, does not justify the supposition that such a final reality is conscious, purposive, or creative. It suffices if it is a unity, able to encompass and order every item in the cosmos.

5.21. A human body contrasts with all other bodies.

A human body is a public, cosmically functioning, unit body —and more. As just a body, it can be understood in terms applicable to other bodies, even inanimate ones. As more, it is beyond the reach of any discipline which treats it as though it were interchangeable or interconvertible with any other kinds of bodies or reducible to some sum of these.

A human body stands in contrast with all other bodies. There is much in the world that it needs for its continuance and prosperity; much there that endangers it; and much more that is indifferent, rigid, or brute, to which it can never wholly adjust. Biologists take it and some other bodies to be part of a single domain with its own characteristic laws and history. This human body, though, is just as sharply distinguished from other kinds of living bodies as all of them are from those that are inanimate: it is part of a milieu into which nothing else can enter except on human terms.

A human body differs from all other bodies in origin, career, tensions, and prospects. It is unique, to be grasped from within and from without on no other terms than those which it makes available. From within it is lived through; from without it is sterile and abstract unless, through sympathy and symbolization, it is used as the beginning of a penetration into it as being lived privately. But, without denying its uniqueness and without penetrating into it, a human body is also capable of being understood in terms which are pertinent to other human bodies. Whether this be done or not, it will not be properly known as it is and functions unless account is also taken of features, traditionally designated as 'accidents'.

For an Aristotelian, snub-nose, Jewish, female, or black are 'accidents', which is to say, features which are outside the provenance of a scientific understanding of a man. Apparently no one, and surely not Aristotle, ever really dismissed such features or took them to be entirely without import to their possessors or to others. Despite his definition of man as a rational animal, distinguished from all other types of animal—a definition evidently applicable to every variety of human— Aristotle held that barbarians were suited to be slaves, and that women had a proper inferior role in the household and, of course, in the state. He did not provide an explanation of why or how this could be. His theory of accidents, his disinterest in history, and the influence of his culture undoubtedly contributed to that fact.

This human body, because of its genetic constitution, has a number of persistent characteristics. Some, like gender and color, may make a difference to the way the body functions and to the way it is dealt with by other men. Though their presence does not break up mankind into unbridgeable kinds or types of men, they often ground different privileges, opportunities, promises, and deserts. Because of common experiences, traditions, and interactions, a body may accrete other features, tendencies, and ways of functioning. Some of these are present for long periods; many of them appear and disappear together. A set of them is usually altered considerably over the course of time.

Each body has accidents, the outcome of the interaction of itself with other bodies. No one of those accidents nor any configuration of them is beyond conceivable alteration or even extinction. But even when blacks and whites, Semites and non-Semites, the strong and the weak, Orientals and Westerners, men and women, the big and small, live in peace, have similar jobs, take on one another's ways, share in the same technologies and education, it will still be a question whether or not every source and effect of their diverse accidents will ever be eliminated. Color and gender seem to polarize humans so readily and deeply as to make it unlikely that all the differences that such accidents make will ever be entirely overcome.

A merely cultural, historical account of the differences among various types of people may enable one to explain the persistence and the possible eventual disappearance or innocuousness of various accidents and their effects, but it does not explain why their possessors and others are affected by their presence. The theory that accidents make a difference to the very substance of individuals, in contrast, while doing more justice to the facts as we now know them, tends to place men in enclaves, despite their equality as persons, and the overriding common human nature that is present in all of them. It also fails to take account of realities and changes in history and culture. One must get in between these extremes, and take seriously the differences that accidents make, while (with the cultural, historical view) remaining alert to the fact that no particular accident need play a significant role always.

Some accidents seem to have persistent, important effects. None, though, divides mankind into fixed kinds. Still, it seems reasonable to say that the attitude and actions of blacks and whites, women and men toward one another will never be entirely and forever eliminated. And if it were, there could still be insuperable differences between them, if only as the result of the way their accidental differences happen to have scarred them or others. It is doubtful that the American blacks will, any more than the Jews do, ever forget that they had been enslaved. They have a common memory, emphasized and preserved in folklore, song, rituals, holidays, familial instruction and practices, and to some extent sustained by differences in appearance and manner. It may even be true that color, gender, and some other accidents will always play effective roles in some individuals, apart from all cultural and historical conditioning. This is quite a different thing to hold, of course, from what is maintained by those who defend a discrimination in rights, jobs, and education for entire classes of men. Nor does it deny the fact that economics and politics produce other accidents of their own which may supplement, add to, subtract from, or replace others now established or effective.

5.22. A human body contrasts with other bodies, affiliated in various degrees and ways.

A human body is unduplicable, and functions in an unduplicable manner. An understanding of publicly knowable men, to be consistent with that fact, will be nominalistic in outlook in the sense that it will understand each man to have a unique body. So far as anyone's is approached from without and spoken of in common ways, of course, it will be known primarily in terms which are applicable to others as well.

There is no reason why we should not attend to other types of living bodies with the same kind of alertness to their distinctive natures and functioning that we exhibit toward the human. It may eventually prove to be the case that we will discover that not much of importance is to be learned about animals' bodies except by studying them in their interaction with one another. What is now evident is that a human body, treated not as something privately lived or as known from within, but just as a body of a distinctive kind, stands in contrast with what else there be, with an import which reflects a distinctive nature, needs, and demands. Man partly converts the nonhuman into possible nourishment, dangers, tools, and opportunities for him to survive, improve, or just to be himself more fully. To say this is in part to revert to an old position which held that the world was there for man, something for him to use. But now, instead of taking all else, as had once been done, to be already designed or prepared for, or to rightly belong to man, it is now being acknowledged that they also have their values, rights, and integrity.

A human body contrasts with others which are together independently of it, congregating, uniting and separating, conflicting with and opposing one another. The other bodies are often threatening, never entirely conquerable, though still able to be intruded upon in theory and in act. The ways they are grouped, attended to, and made available for action affect their status and careers. Daily speech, action, and habit make certain acts more likely than others. To identify something as a gypsy moth is not only to entrain favorable or unfavorable attitudes and acts bearing on gypsies and moths but to associate it with gypsum and butterflies, and thereby open up new avenues for attention and possible moves.

An individual human body, while contrasting with and

standing away from other bodies, affects them. The other bodies contrast with it as surely as it contrasts with them, but most do not attend to it or take account of it in their preparations or actions, even when they use it or adjust to it. Whether attended to or not, each human body is a meeting place of the public and the private. What is made available to that body is never wholly explicable from either side, or even from both together. Already affected by what is external, it is able to achieve some harmony with other bodies; already affected by its privacy, it deals with all else in distinctive terms. As a result, from its position, the world is humanized at the same time that it is faced as resisting and defying the humanization.

While facing the other bodies on its own terms, a human body has to adjust itself and act in new ways if it is able to make contact with and use what exists apart from it. Since the other bodies, independently of it, are variously affiliated, it finds itself frustrated by groups of bodies with careers of their own.

5.23. Other bodies have rights of their own.

A human body contrasts with all other bodies, both human and nonhuman. It is allied both with a limited number of other bodies and with every other human body. The alliances are geographically, historically, genetically, as well as intrinsically determined. It also has its own intrinsic viable rights, rights which need translation, exercise, and public sustaining. The man known to law, politics, technology, medicine, and economics is a human body with a reality and dignity, both by itself and as allied with other human bodies.

Mankind has been slowly inching toward the position where some of the more developed animals are acknowledged to have rights of their own. The movement cannot, without forcing a sharp break in the order of nature, avoid going on to the acknowledgment that living beings of lower

orders, and nonliving beings also, have rights, greatly inferior
though these be to man's.

Rights are claims made by realities. To be real is to have a
right to be, to continue, and to become more complex. So far,
all actualities have the same rights. Within the compass of
those rights, though, are a number of others, answering to the
distinctive claims made by essential dimensions. Each actuality needs different things in order to persist and prosper. This
human body has rights that nonhuman bodies do not. Its appetites, emotions, perceptions, and speech, on behalf of its
dimensions and of itself as a single unduplicable, involve it
with an indefinitely large number of beings which it must
possess, master, and use if it is to be fulfilled. Its claims inevitably come into conflict with those of others: none is able to
achieve a maximum satisfaction of its rights without denying
some satisfaction to theirs. But though this human body, and
all human bodies together, have rights outstripping those of
other bodies, it is questionable whether men's rights may
justly override those possessed by all the rest. In any case, a
man's rights are not acknowledged or sustained by the others.
The rights that this human body has are insisted on against
bodies which function independently of, and usually operate
in some opposition to, the exercise or satisfaction of those
rights.

Though each human body has the same native rights as
every other, the genetic traits of color and gender, and perhaps intelligence, have prompted the insistence on and fix-
ation of clusters of features that are sometimes treated as
though they precluded the presence or exercise of the same
rights that are enjoyed by other humans. Those discriminated
against, then, in addition to facing the obstacles which the rest
of the universe presents to the exercise and satisfaction of
their rights, have to face the obstacles that other men provide. The differences amongst men should provide diverse
ways for achieving the satisfaction of their common rights to
live and prosper in a common civilization where each is

enabled to become as excellent as a human can be. Still, it could be well argued that human bodies must first exhibit a certain level of maturity, efficiency, dexterity, or intelligence before they are to be credited with the same rights, or before their rights can be given the same degree of public satisfaction that others get. Just as the insane, the infantile, and the senile have only some of the viable rights that others have, so one might hold, some groups of men must wait until they have arrived at a certain stage of development before they can have the same rights, or at least have as much hope or warrant for satisfying them that the rest possess, or to which they are entitled. But the case must be made out and not just assumed. One must show that there is a difference amongst these men, that the difference is relevant to real, essential dimensions of them, and that the discriminatory assessments do not merely perpetuate and accentuate advantages enjoyed by the rest, which are just as adventitious as the assumed defects. These considerations make necessary a differentiation between native and acquired rights.

There are rights that men acquire over the course of time, well before the rights are supported by or even acknowledged by a state. So long as women were in a subject role, denied property rights, education, an opportunity to mature, or to exercise political judgment, they were not at the stage where they had a right to vote. The right was theirs when they were qualified to vote, and that was some time before they were given the public right to vote. All the while they had the same native rights that males had, grounded in their unduplicable persons.

So far as law is concerned, native rights could be intrinsic to the human body. But one is then in danger of taking persistent accidents to be essential features, and of denying to some the rights that others already have, not because they have not yet reached the stage where those others are, but solely because they have a different set of accidents. One is protected against that tendency if one remembers that men's native rights are possessed in privacy and are not a function of their bodies.

5.24. A human body has a distinctive rationale.

My human body contrasts with all others. So far, it is set outside the common frame within which all are to be explained and understood. Without losing its place there, it acts as a distinctive kind of body. The intelligibility of that body has various degrees of concreteness. At one limit, it is identifiable with an individual stable structure and with the pattern that activities exhibit over time. At another limit, it is identifiable with the nature of any human body whatsoever. At either, it offers a term for an intelligible relation between itself and the rest of the world. If the term does not instance the meaning incorporated in the relation, it will so far be alien to that relation. As a consequence, from the perspective of the relation, the term will be just a unit terminal point. Conversely, if the relation does not relate the same type of nature that the body incorporates, the relation will be adventitious, externally added to it. And what is true of this body is true of the other bodies with which it is connected. Their natures and their relations will also be alien to one another, if they do not, in their different ways, express the same meaning. The fact has been exploited by idealism. All terms are understood by it to be intelligibles continuous with the intelligible relations connecting them. What it maintains is true from the position of the relation or from the position of the bodies in the guise of mere terms. But in their concreteness, bodies both stand away from the relations and sustain terms for these. This does not preclude the intelligibility of the bodies or their exemplification of some rationale, but it does require that the intelligibility of the bodies be grounded independently of the intelligibility of the relation between those bodies.

5.25. Men humanize space.

The space of a human body is distinctive, voluminous, vivified, contoured, functioning in an incomparable way. It is also near or distant from, and may be contiguous with, the spaces of other bodies. That space specializes as well as delimits a common space. The distances, too, specialize the common space. The bodies are privately enabled to occupy regions of that space.

The space of this individual human body is integral to it, an occupied region whose borders are also borders of the space beyond. Strictly speaking, that body is not able to move, since there is no space into which it could go. Movement, so far as it is concerned, is just a process by which some intervening space is made larger or smaller than it had been before.

This individual human body, without sacrifice to its spatial integrity, can be allied with others in the single humanized space of a community. That space has the status of a self-enclosed region contrasting with others; it is this which interests sociologists, anthropologists, and the naturalists among the biologists. Did it merely delimit a common space, a human community would be just a distinguished part of a single, all-encompassing space, denied the status of a spatialized region, independent of and contrasting with other regions, as well as with that neutral space which intervenes between the community and the nonhuman world.

A supposed neutral space between men is an abstraction obtained by ignoring what is outside the reach of physical instruments. What is near according to some measures may be quite far for the human body; conversely, what is far for such measures may be quite near for the body, i.e., be quite important for it. A commonsense man lives in an amalgam of two kinds of regions. For him there are sharply differentiated ups and downs, rights and lefts, as well as objects distant from and indifferent to the needs of his body.

The extension of humanized space through claim or concept to property, tool, food, and resource, does not affect the occupation by these of their own characteristic regions. Taken as providing challenges to men and their community, they are set in a humanized region. So far, they are in both a nonhumanized and a humanized spatial region. So are we, of course.

5.26. Men humanize time.

Each human body and the groups which they form have their own distinctive rhythms, paces, divisions, and temporal spans. These are not calibrated with the movements of the sun and stars. Within humanized time the story of man is told, but only so far as it is opposed to an all-encompassing time that is pertinent to everything, as well as to the more or less monotonous time of physical things and with the two-generational time of parent and offspring within which most animals live.

Each type of time is independent of the others. Were the world of man merely distinguished within a larger, the fact could be accounted for by taking his different time to be a sub-division of a common time. But so far as men are by them-selves, they exist in separate times. Still, they keep apace with the others, for they also are subject to a time governing all.

Even within the humanized world there are different times. The rhythm, pace, divisions, and temporal span of religious history are different from those characteristic of the history of ideas, art, economics, politics, philosophy, and science. Inde-pendently of all these, human bodies have their own distinc-tive times. The times of those human bodies, of different junctures of them, and of the nonhumanized world beyond, are independent of one another.

The time of a human body both concurs with the times of all the rest, human or not, and functions independently of them. The fact that the distinctive times are all concurrent makes evident that their differences are neither incompatible nor incomprehensible. The units that each actuality distinguishes within the common time are the units in terms of which their careers can be calibrated. But each also has its own distinctive temporal units and career, independently lived through, outside the common time.

5.27. Men humanize causality.

Social life, morality, the legal system, history, economics, and education take account of a causation which is peculiar to men. This operates between accountable sources and relevant outcomes, and not simply between antecedent causes and rationally derivable or likely effects. Perception, inference, discourse, work, preparations, training, discipline cannot be broken up into smaller components without losing a characteristic relevance which relates their beginnings to their endings. The understanding of a human body requires a reference not only to the ways in which its different parts are organically related but to spans in which its unit actions occur.

The order and importance of the steps in an extended activity are dictated by the status that they have within an undivided causal whole. Bodies within the area of a human body or a human community are unavoidably caught up within humanized unit causal processes. The contained and used bodies are property, obstacles, tools, not simply because they have been interpreted to be so, but because they are confined within a humanized area with its own distinctive causality. The fact is exaggerated by those who deny that there can be a knowable or perhaps even a possible world outside the human, and therefore a nonhumanized causality. Such a view has no way of dealing with the recalcitrant, independent functioning of what is known and used. Linguistic philosophy is but one variant of such a theory. Economic determinism, historical determinism, and anthropological relativistic views are others.

What is within the provenance of a human body is caught

within human causal patterns. Each item there also continues to be obstinate, never entirely controlled. Like the human body and the entire set of human bodies, each is limited by what is outside the body and, so far, has a different status and causality from what it has as encompassed by the body.

5.28. An individual human body has its own distinctive value.

A human body has one value. Allied with other human bodies it has another. Standing in contrast with what is not human, its value is maintained independently of the nature and careers of the values that other bodies possess. But it still can be compared with them, since there is a valuational order of them all, under the governance of a common unity.

All values would be a function of man's nature, interests, needs, or prejudice, if whatever else there be were wholly humanized. But what is not human has its own status and its own values. The difference between the human and the nonhuman is not a human product. Men are in the same single universe with them. To remain with that observation, though, is still not to have taken account of what everyone knows—that a man's body is lived in and through, affected by what is not bodily at all. Each man has a body which can- not be understood in bodily terms alone. His is a personally lived, not just a human, body.

5.29. A lived body personalizes what it confronts.

The most persistently maintained view of man holds him to have a body which is possessed, controlled, enriched by, and given distinctive powers by a soul, self, or mind. In modern times, many have come to doubt the existence of a soul. A self, if attended to at all, is taken to be a construct, a conve- nient supposition having no basis in fact, while a mind, many

hope and even more firmly assert, is to be properly and adequately understood by attending to the workings of the brain.
The views have not entirely satisfied, in good part because no
satisfactory accounts are given of man's consciousness, self-
consciousness, intentions, memories, inferences, emotions,
virtues, vices, beliefs, anxieties, native rights, responsibility,
identity, speculations, his I, and his me.

A bolder answer allows for all of these by crediting them to
a privately sustained human body, enriched by the very powers that had previously been thought to have their origin in a
soul, self, or mind. Could such an enriched body be known?
There are at least two good reasons which seem to warrant
answering the question negatively:

a) Knowledge is always abstract and referential. A knowledge of the nature of this body, consequently, will necessarily
keep one remote from it.

b) Whenever we try to attend to our privacies, we find that
there is very little we can get into focus. All we can attend to is
this move, this twinge of pain, this excitement. Each has a
depth, gradually fading away into a more inclusive, impene-
trable density. Yet when we try to represent to ourselves in
memory, imagination, and knowledge what we had attended
to, we find that we have lost this into which they had continued. But—

a) Not all knowledge is formal, verbal, discursive. Some of
it is symbolic. Starting with manifestations of the body, symbolization moves in depth, yielding distinguishable content
well before it is absorbed within a more comprehensive denser reality. Sympathy retraces an expression back toward its
source, beyond any preassignable point.

b) Expressions are differentiated and limited on being produced. We do not walk with our legs alone; our entire body
comes into play. The walking spearheads the whole of the
body in a special way. The rest of the body is then background, overlaid by other specializations and limited forms of
the whole. If we know what it is to walk, we already know

something about a lived body. The knowledge can be expressed in publicly usable forms, though in order for it to be
knowledge of just this body, it must eventually be grounded
there. That grounding assimilates the articulation which
knowing provides. When I know that this man is walking, I
not only know that walking is taking place or that a man is
walking, but that the knowledge I have of the walking is intensified, specialized, unified, and carried out apart from me.

A body, no matter how enriched, cannot know, decide,
remain selfsame, sustain a me, a you, or a we, assume responsibility, hope, imagine, lie, or pray. None of these is secret in
any other sense than that its publicized expressions merge
into a dense controlling privacy. A man expresses himself in
his body in the form of tendencies to act, attitudes assumed,
words readied; he expresses himself at and beyond his body
in a language, activities, changes in direction, use, and emphasis. All are tinged with a private tonality which we can
meet in symbolizing and sympathetic acts.

A man's lived body is continuous with his human body. It
never has the kind of functioning that is possible to a body
operating solely under cosmic conditions. It does not even
have humanized material presented to it for conversion into
personalized items. What it faces is personalized in the very
act of being faced.

Fear, hope, and trust qualify everything the lived body confronts. It does, of course, meet with resistance. What it faces
does not always satisfy it, but when it is satisfied, this is on its
own terms. Just so far as other items resist one, they are toward the less manageable end of a continuum of personalized
items. Since everything maintains itself, everything else is
necessarily faced by a lived body as being toward that end,
even when readily used and fully satisfying.

No matter how much a lived body masters, there is always
something beyond its reach. Together, all the other bodies
make up a powerful, overwhelming world of frustrating, defiant, repelling, but still available and sometimes usable, ob-

jects. This lived body makes contact with them through work and language. They accept it on their own terms, maintaining themselves in radical opposition to it. When the expressions of a number of lived bodies mesh, they make up a humanized world. Nothing that is experienceable or ascertainable about men, separately or together, will then be excluded—except their privacies.

5.30. A lived body terminates at other bodies.

Whatever there be is personalized and thereby oriented toward and sustained by our lived bodies. Even the resistance that others exhibit is given a personalized form, expressing the limit of each lived body's use and control. Since, as personalized, the others are wholly relative to this body, they are not, so far, substantial. They are substantial only as sustained by a they.

If what else there be is only so far as it is the terminus of a lived body, it will act, move, rest, come to be and pass away either because that body makes it do this or because it is credited with these roles. The first of these alternatives makes the lived body so powerful that it will have to be taken to be the source of the known course of nature, the passage of the sun, and the growth of trees. The second alternative, once freed from the supposition that the interpretation is willed or willful, allows for resistances of various types. One object will then approach, another recede, and a third remain fixed in relation to the same lived body in the sense that their usability is increased, decreased, or remains as it had been. When they are, they will be present for it; when they are not, they will be absent for it; when they change they will change in relation to it.

A lived body's limits are the limits of its world. Within those limits there are various distinguishable places which can be marked off as personalized property, possessions, and, ultimately, as the surface at which a penetration in depth can be begun. There is, so far, only a difference in degree of control between what is normally said to be part of a lived body and what is distinguished from this. It is therefore just as correct to say that the lived body is surrounded by a personalized world, as it is to say that there is only a lived body related to what is more or less intimate, more or less controllable, more or less sharply felt. In the first way, though, one risks taking the lived body to be a publicly known body to which private notes have been added, while in the other, one risks having a world just relative to oneself, having no items of its own. The first risk is avoided with the refusal to take a personalized world to be the outcome of additions to what is cosmic. The second is avoided with the recognition that personalizing does not deny an independent sustaining of that in which it terminates.

If account is taken of the fact that the efficacy of a lived body has degrees, both action and motion will be seen to produce changes in the relations it has to others. Through their agency, other bodies will become more or less congenial, more or less intimate, more or less controlled. When they are taken to be fixed, the lived body will be credited with action and motion relative to them. In any case, what is more important for it is nearer than others, even those which are physically close by, if these are comparatively of little interest. The food across the table is nearer to my lived body than the underside of the chair.

5.31. Each lived body has an independent reality.

Sooner or later, other items prove to be beyond a lived body's capacity to control, to use, or to withstand. Nevertheless, others are there for it as more or less controllable, usable, or defied. By another route, we here approximate the position where an individual negates what is beyond himself while holding on to it through the agency of a claim. Now, though, no claim is made. Nothing is negated. Everything else is allowed an independent status and functioning.

5.32. Each lived body makes possible an explanation of all other bodies.

The achievements of physics, chemistry, and biology in understanding even highly complex living entities are astounding. Nor does there seem to be a limit that anyone can antecedently set to scientific discoveries and clarifications about what occurs in this world. It makes good sense to try to account for man's presence, nature, and functionings in terms of what one has learned about animals and eventually things, or about machines which can be constructed and perhaps even only imagined. Since an explanation is made from a position beyond what is explained, one must then either move to some nonempirical realm or explain man in terms of what else there is in the world. If the categories applicable to what is nonhuman were applicable to man, then were there dimensions to him which remain untouched, they would ground an explanation for other bodies—unless he were outside the knowable world in which they also are. One should therefore be able to explain them in terms of what we know about men. Such explanations are not yet within the reach of the exact sciences. But they could conceivably make provision for them by adding to the concepts, pertinent to inanimate things or the subhuman, others which are pertinent to man alone.

5.33. Each lived body has and exists in a vitalized space.

A lived body is voluminous, and is in a voluminous space. In both there is a right and left, an up and down, a back and front, each with a vital import, affecting what is there. The right is also the correct, the desirable. Left is sinister, wrong, corrupt, adverse. Up is where and how one ought to be. Down points toward failure and dirt. Front is forward, onward, toward what is desirable. Back is what is and should be left behind. Each direction continues a distinctive, felt emphasis of the lived body, an emphasis which remains even when one speaks of and deals with that body and what is present in impersonal terms. The space pertinent to a lived body continues indefinitely beyond that lived body, where it provides places for all other bodies.

5.34. Each lived body is in time.

The time of a lived body is its own, divided, paced by it. It is that body's "inner sense" as Kant would say, though bodily pervasive, variable in its divisions, rhythms, and stretch. It is all present, distinguished from past and future. It cannot be subdivided; it allows for a distinction between a before and after, and not between an earlier and later. To be sure, a lived body does this first and then that. But from the position of that body, the distinguished items do not replace one another in successive moments. They remain within its undivided present, held on to in different ways.

Within the compass of a single, extended, lived, present moment a multiplicity of nuances occur, each of which emphasizes what the others keep subordinate. Were one to try to freeze a present moment at a position where one nuance is to the fore, one would find the others blurred with it. No portion of the present time of a lived body can be isolated, set earlier than another, except retrospectively, as already fully determinate, factualized, no longer part of a single ongoing moment.

A present can stretch from the beginning to the end of a physical pulsation, a theatrical performance, a political career, or from birth to death. One might withdraw from such a conclusion on behalf of a desire to take account of the contemporaneity of cosmological occurrences. But then one would abandon the position of a lived body to take up another, perhaps that of a God or some other common conditioning temporal power. And, unless one were also to deny that the lived body can observe what is external to it, the present time which characterizes that body will also have to embrace what is spatially distant.

A lived body has a memory and expectations. The one is oriented toward some particular occurrence which is before, the other is oriented toward some occurrence which is after what is focused on. Such memory and expectations are quite different from a remembering and an awaiting. A remembering *refers* to what is past, an awaiting *refers* to what is future. Lived time is a tensional time, retrospective, prospective, and focused all at once.

5.35. No lived body has antecedent causes or later effects.

For a lived body, only what is relevant to it could exist in a preceding or succeeding time. For it, there therefore is nothing which acted and nothing which it could produce. And, since when together with other lived bodies it is copresent with them, neither it nor they could be causes or effects for one another. Nor could there be such causes or effects connecting the lived body with anything else, since everything else is caught within its present. These conclusions are more radical but also more consistent than those which follow on a Humean account of causality with its supposition that there are temporally distinct occurrences that men habitually associate as causes and effects, for there are no past or future items available to a lived body which it could use for such a purpose.

Within the all-inclusive present of a lived body, there is a determinate content and an undetermined one. These have different roles in a continuum of stresses. The lived body is a process of causation, for which the determinate content is an antecedent, and the terminus of the body's determining is a consequent. What is, or is made determinate is not thereby brought within the private recesses of the lived body. It may be remote in space, not altogether controlled.

The causation that a lived body exhibits in its act of determination reaches to the limits of that body's world. But though the causation is due to it, it is inseparable from the items that it is making determinate relative to itself. But surely the lived body came into existence? Surely it had causes exterior to it, is now the effect of some of them, and is engaged in acts for whose effects it is accountable? Yes, but only from the position of some other lived body, or from a position overarching them all. When one takes a stand at a lived body, one allows no room for causes and effects. There are lived causes and effects, not because everything is confined within a single punctuate moment, or because every item is part of the inward being of a lived body, but because the lived body is in a time and space in which all limited causal ongoings take place.

5.36. The values possessed by what is encompassed by a lived body are relative to its value.

For a lived body, some items are more satisfying and controlled than others. All, though, are centered by it. All, too, have values proportionate to the degree that they can be included within it without alteration. Ideally, everything would be equally and fully part of it, to make it an all-encompassing whole, equally dense everywhere. But as it now is, it distinguishes what is at its dense center from what is not, giving these a value less than they could conceivably have. So far, none of them has intrinsic value, since none of them has a genuine independent reality. It alone is real; it alone has intrinsic value; all others are real and have values only relative to it. Of course, once it is granted that there are items which exist independently of man, and that he and they are together within a single cosmos, there is no need to deny a value to anyone of them, measured in terms of their ability to be harmoniously together. A simple relativity of values is the undesirable product of a refusal to adopt any other position but that of a particular lived body which casts its shadow over everything whatsoever, to yield, not a value-free world, but a man-constituted world of values.

Values relative to man are either not objective or are produced by him. On the first alternative, no true judgment can be made about the value of anything. On the second, no error is ever made in assigning a value. There is a sense in which both consequences can and should be maintained, and at the same time. Men never state precisely the nature of the values things objectively have, nor do they misconstrue what their human interest in fact constitutes. But if there is also to be provision for both truth and error, these alternatives must be supplemented by another which recognizes that values are intrinsic to whatever there be, but can be dealt with from special angles.

To take one's stand solely with a lived body and to acknowledge only what it permits will get in the way of the admission that there is more than one type of lived body, as well as of the admission that there is a cosmos in which men's bodies are but tiny, ineffective, rather unimportant, parts.

5.37. A mature man has a distinct person and self.

A lived body is single and undivided, a source of multiple expressions. A man withdraws beyond this to deal with what his body cannot reach, moving back into his person or self. All his expressions, whether originating from his body or issuing directly from him as beyond all differentiations, are sustained by or grounded in these epitomizing condensations of his privacy. These cannot be reached from the outside, whether the attempt be made by oneself or another. No one can get further than to a me or a you, as sustained from a depth which is adumbrated beyond the point at which judgment and claim come to a halt.

A human being has a limited privacy, partly expressed in

and through a distinctive kind of body. As he matures, he achieves a person and a self. The person and the self have their own distinctive epitomizing condensations, each with its own expressions. To be at his best, he must attain the stage where all the condensations of his self and person are exercised independently and conjointly. To be a fulfilled man, he must also express himself compatibly with others in a humanized world and in the cosmos.

Recapitulation: The Topical Headings

Index

Recapitulation: The Topical Headings

CHAPTER 1
You, Public and Sustained

1.1.   You are confrontable.
1.2.   You have a dense depth.
1.3.   What is confronted neither speaks nor acts.
1.4.   Discourse transforms language.
1.5.   Knower and known are both private and public.
1.6.   'You' is a semantic vector.
1.7.   A discourse is an interchange of complementary and supplementary expressions.
1.8.   'You' has different roles in discourse and communication.
1.9.   'You' in language is without a referential role.
1.10. 'You' in fiction is a component in a single created term.
1.11. A representative of a public domain provides model references.
1.12. The grammatical subject, 'you', is a relative pronoun.
1.13. 'You' and you have distinct careers.
1.14. You are accountable.
1.15. You are responsible for what you do.
1.16. The attribution of accountability is a responsible act.
1.17. You have both a public and a private status.
1.18. You are objective and unrelativized.
1.19. Common constraining conditions enable men to be present to one another.
1.20. Men are affiliated.

1.21. An intermediary 'you' presupposes related men.
1.22. Men are intelligibly together.
1.23. A scientific knowledge of individuals is possible.
1.24. A public you occupies space.
1.25. You are perceivable.
1.26. You persist.
1.27. What you will be is now indeterminate.
1.28. You have a temporal span.
1.29. You are a free causal agent.
1.30. Causation is an observable necessitation.
1.31. You exist.
1.32. You have value.
1.33. Your value is absolutized.
1.34. A value is implicated in the use of 'you'.
1.35. 'You' may have a fixated referent.
1.36. 'You' can be anticipatorily ascribed.
1.37. 'You' has a collective and a distributive use.
1.38. You have a predominantly bodily role.

CHAPTER 2
You and me

2.1. A me is partly coincident with a you for another.
2.2. A me faces in two directions.
2.3. 'Me' inescapably addresses me.
2.4. The referent of 'me' is a sustained me.
2.5. There are three ways to determine accountability.
2.6. I make myself into a moral being.
2.7. 'Me' addresses my-me.
2.8. Me and you are publicly together.
2.9. Another can have knowledge of me.
2.10. I can know me.
2.11. The perceived is grounded beyond the perceiving.
2.12. Perceptual conditions constrain.
2.13. My me is multiply differentiated.

2.14. Some things are mine by right; others are mine only through possession.

2.15. Thoughts and feelings are knowable.

2.16. Me is a person publicized.

2.17. I know that my me is like another's me.

2.18. I know that another can know himself as a me.

2.19. Each me is irreducible.

2.20. Men are affiliated.

2.21. My me thinks.

2.22. The being of me is part of my total being.

2.23. Each me has rights.

2.24. My being continues into the being of my person.

2.25. Me has a general meaning and a singular role.

2.26. I locate me with certainty.

2.27. The conditions for meaning can be meaningfully expressed.

2.28. 'Me' carries an intent as well as a meaning.

2.29. Both me and 'me' unite meaning and intent.

2.30. I know me intropathically.

2.31. Any me can be dislocated.

2.32. Each me is in an indivisible present.

2.33. You and me are contemporaries.

2.34. The past and future are operative in me.

2.35. Each me is now partly detemporalized.

2.36. Each me is both free and necessitated.

2.37. Neither you nor me originates acts.

2.38. Each me has some liberty.

2.39. This is me, therefore I am.

2.40. Each me has a value.

2.41. 'Me' entrains relativized and absolute assessments.

CHAPTER 3
The Self and I

3.1. A self encompasses an I and other distinguishable sources of privately initiated acts.

3.2. A self-reference can be self-conscious.

3.3. I can speak intelligibly about myself.

3.4. I am known to others.

3.5. Self-reference has three distinguishable termini.

3.6. I privately know what is publicly reachable.

3.7. I intrude and am intruded on.

3.8. I attend to myself from many different positions.

3.9. I seek to be self-complete.

3.10. I presuppose a self.

3.11. I possess a self.

3.12. I feel.

3.13. I can become coordinate with other private foci.

3.14. A self and its epitomizing condensations are sources of meaning.

3.15. I can be located.

3.16. A self and its epitomizations are in the present.

3.17. I am both free and necessitated.

3.18. I exist.

3.19. I am both undivided and diversified.

3.20. I am both primary and derivative.

3.21. I am both principal and instrument.

3.22. I am both central and peripheral.

3.23. I have a relative and an absolute import.

3.24. I am a spatial source, terminus, and unit.

3.25. I am present in many presents.

3.26. I am subject to a universal necessitation.

3.27. I act freely.

3.28. I am an evaluated base of evaluations.

3.29. I am an individual.

3.30. I am a being and have a being.

3.31. I am eventually overwhelmed even by what is most congenial.

3.32. I am meaningfully related to other independent realities.

3.33. I occupy a position in space.

3.34. I occupy a position in time.

3.35. I freely make use of necessity.

3.36. I am a reality evaluationally ordered in relation to others.

3.37. I am a person.

3.38. I have a mind.
3.39. I am intelligible.
3.40. I exist.
3.41. I am a truth-condition.
3.42. I and others are within a common space.
3.43. I and others are within a common time.
3.44. I and others are within a common causality.
3.45. I am a natural existent.
3.46. I am a unity.
3.47. An I is the measured measure of all things.
3.48. An I is a one for a many.
3.49. A fictional I has a created individuality.

CHAPTER 4
We

4.1. 'I' and 'we' have different referents.
4.2. A we is simple, factual, or complex.
4.3. A simple we provides a condition which, with interrelated men, constitutes a complex we.
4.4. A complex affiliative we is conditioned by a simple social we.
4.5. An equitable single we is an equalizing condition.
4.6. An organizational we prescribes positions for interrelated individuals.
4.7. A distributive we distinguishes locations.
4.8. There are three types of temporally distributive we's.
4.9. A synchronizing we ranges over copresents.
4.10. A sequential we orders men temporally.
4.11. A processive we has a twofold spread.
4.12. A transactional we sets the limits of a causal situation.
4.13. An assessive we ranks what it governs.
4.14. A simple we may be both governed and related.
4.15. A simple we is a partial analogue of an I.
4.16. Us is a partial analogue of me.
4.17. There are conditions which apply to every we.

CHAPTER 5
They and the Others

5.1.   They sustain the others.
5.2.   The others terminate negations.
5.3.   There are two types of others: the distributive and collective.
5.4.   A they is the others as anonymous and oppositional.
5.5.   What is beyond the others can be known.
5.6.   A negating may have a contrastive terminus.
5.7.   A negating may have an attributed terminus.
5.8.   What is negated may be completive.
5.9.   A negating may terminate at a distance.
5.10. A negating may have a temporal role.
5.11. A negating may have a causal role.
5.12. A negating involves an assessment.
5.13. The sustained others are formidable.
5.14. My lived body is overwhelmed by all the other bodies.
5.15. There is no totality in which my body is a separate unit.
5.16. The explanation of what a body does lies outside it.
5.17. The location of a body is mainly determined by other bodies.
5.18. The present of a body is distinct from the present of all the other bodies.
5.19. The causes of this body are others now past.
5.20. The value of my body is insignificant in comparison with the value of all the other bodies.
5.21. A human body contrasts with all other bodies.
5.22. A human body contrasts with other bodies, affiliated in various degrees and ways.
5.23. Other bodies have rights of their own.
5.24. A human body has a distinctive rationale.
5.25. Men humanize space.
5.26. Men humanize time.
5.27. Men humanize causality.
5.28. An individual human body has its own distinctive value.
5.29. A lived body personalizes what it confronts.
5.30. A lived body terminates at other bodies.
5.31. Each lived body has an independent reality.

5.32. Each lived body makes possible an explanation of all other bodies.

5.33. Each lived body has and exists in a vitalized space.

5.34. Each lived body is in time.

5.35. No lived body has antecedent causes or later effects.

5.36. The values possessed by what is encompassed by a lived body are relative to its value.

5.37. A mature man has a distinct person and self.

Index